MW00329081

'*Facing Patriarchy* is a highly acces[sible] problem of men's violence to wom[en] and making strong contributions to stopping it.'
— Jeff Hearn, author of *Men of the World* and editor of *Unsustainable Institutions of Men*

'In the struggle for sex/gender justice, Bob Pease's title is on target – the key is *Facing Patriarchy*. His radical analysis demonstrates over and over that we will not make serious progress against men's violence and a host of other problems without a deep critique of patriarchy. In a cultural moment where academic jargon and political euphemisms are designed to derail radical feminism, Pease's book is a welcome addition to our toolkit for challenging men to be fully human.'
— Robert Jensen, University of Texas at Austin, author of *The End of Patriarchy: Radical Feminism for Men*

'In this current era of populism, a rabid anti-feminist backlash, and a rising right, this is a much needed book. Pease's ground-breaking offering reminds us of the importance of emphasizing a rich gendered understanding of men's violence against women. Indeed, as he correctly points out, we cannot understand and eliminate woman abuse without recognizing that a substantial number of male actions, values and beliefs are micro-social expressions of broader patriarchal forces. *Facing Patriarchy* is destined to become a classic piece of feminist scholarship, one that every man must read.'
— Walter S. DeKeseredy, West Virginia University

FACING PATRIARCHY

ABOUT THE AUTHOR

Bob Pease is currently Adjunct Professor in the Institute for the Study of Social Change at the University of Tasmania and Honorary Professor in the School of Humanities and Social Sciences at Deakin University. He was formerly Chair of Social Work at Deakin University and Professor of Social Work at the University of Tasmania. He has been involved in profeminist politics with men for many years, was a founding member of Men Against Sexual Assault in Melbourne, and continues to be involved in community education and campaigns against men's violence against women. He has published extensively on masculinity politics and critical social work practice. His books include: *Recreating Men: Postmodern Masculinity Politics* (2000), *A Man's World? Changing Men's Practices in a Globalized World* (edited with Keith Pringle, 2001), *Men and Gender Relations* (2002), *Migrant Men: Critical Studies of Masculinities and the Migration Experience* (edited with Mike Donaldson, Ray Higgins and Richard Howson, 2009), *Undoing Privilege: Unearned Advantage in a Divided World* (2010), *Men and Masculinities around the World* (edited with Elizabetta Ruspini, Jeff Hearn and Keith Pringle, 2011), *Men, Masculinities and Methodologies* (edited with Barbara Pini, 2013), *Men, Masculinities and Disaster* (edited with Elaine Enarson, 2016), *Radicals in Australian Social Work: Stories of Lifelong Activism* (edited with Carolyn Noble and Jim Ife, 2017), and *Critical Ethics of Care in Social Work* (edited with Anthea Vreugdenhil and Sonya Stanford, 2018).

FACING PATRIARCHY

FROM A VIOLENT GENDER ORDER
TO A CULTURE OF PEACE

Bob Pease

ZED

Facing Patriarchy: From a Violent Gender Order to a Culture of Peace was first published in 2019 by Zed Books Ltd, The Foundry, 17 Oval Way, London SE11 5RR, UK.

www.zedbooks.net

Copyright © Bob Pease 2019

The right of Bob Pease to be identified as the author of this work has been asserted by him in accordance with the Copyright, Designs and Patents Act, 1988

Typeset in Plantin and Kievit by Swales & Willis Ltd, Exeter, Devon
Index by ed.emery@thefreeuniversity.net
Cover design by Steve Marsden
Cover photo © Mads Nissen, Panos Pictures

Printed and bound by CPI Group (UK) Ltd, Croydon, CR0 4YY

A catalogue record for this book is available from the British Library

ISBN 978-1-78699-288-8 hb
ISBN 978-1-78699-287-1 pb
ISBN 978-1-78699-289-5 pdf
ISBN 978-1-78699-290-1 epub
ISBN 978-1-78699-291-8 mobi

MIX
Paper from
responsible sources
FSC® C013604

Not everything that is faced can be changed,
but nothing can be changed until it is faced.
James Baldwin

CONTENTS

ACKNOWLEDGEMENTS

I want to first acknowledge the feminist women in the violence prevention movements, which span over 40 years, who have challenged, educated and supported me in my activist and intellectual work over the course of those decades. Almost everything I've learnt about men's violence I've learnt from feminist women, and the men I have learnt from have themselves largely also learnt from women. I want to particularly mention Wendy Weeks (who died on 31 July 2004), who encouraged and supported my engagement with profeminist men's writing, teaching and activism. I often find myself in political situations and intellectual discussions when I wonder, 'What would Wendy think?' Invariably, I wonder what she would think of this book.

As I extended my thinking about men's violence against women, this book took me into intellectual spaces that were outside of my comfort zone. However, I have been fortunate to have been surrounded by some wonderful feminist and profeminist activist scholars. As I completed each draft chapter, I wondered, 'Who will take me to task and challenge me to extend my thinking on this topic?' Hence, I am immensely grateful to the following people who commented on specific draft chapters: Christine Beasley, David Duriesmith, Sarah Epstein, Stephen Fisher, Gillian Fletcher, Michael Flood, Ron Frey, Jeff Hearn, Louise Johnson, Chris Laming, Janine Little, Sherilyn MacGregor, Pavla Miller, Carolyn Noble, Deb Parkinson, Ben Swanton and Ben Wadham. I am indebted to them all for giving critical feedback, sharing their views (not always in agreement with my own), suggesting additional reading and offering their encouragement. Of course, it goes without saying that I am solely responsible for any weaknesses or misinterpretations in the argument that follows, and none of my 'critical friends' have had the opportunity to read the manuscript as a whole.

I would like to thank Andrew Singleton and Mathew Clarke from Deakin University, who supported my appointment as Honorary Professor in the School of Humanities and Social Sciences. This provided a good intellectual and practical 'home' for the writing of the book, given the school's expansion of gender and sexuality studies. I am grateful for the conversations with social science colleagues about some of the ideas in this book and the opportunities to present aspects of the argument of the book at various symposiums and seminars at Deakin. I have also presented some parts of the work-in-progress of the book at local, national and international conferences over the last two years, and I have benefited from feedback received at those events.

Living a profeminist life as a man, as an academic and as an activist is not an easy 'road to walk' and it is not a journey one can take alone. During most of the last 40 years, I have got by 'with a little help from my friends'. When you get involved in profeminist politics, you realise how often men's friendships are at the expense of women. Many men bond with each other by putting down women, and it is often hard to find male friendships that explore other ways of relating as men. I have had the privilege of such non-collusive male friendships, but sadly two of my close male friends, Ian Bell and Bob Fuller, died during the time I was writing this book. I miss their warmth, their holding me to account and their physical presence in my life.

I would like to thank my partner of 30 years, Silvia Starc, and my daughter Cassie for their love and support during the writing of the book. Living with someone writing a book is not always easy, and fitting the book in with all the other demands on the family takes a toll. I hope that I was able to keep it in perspective and to remind myself at the key moments that there were more important things in life than 'the book'. I would also like to express my appreciation for Silvia, who read the full manuscript and assisted me to get rid of over 1,000 superfluous words that were cluttering the text.

This book contains some material that was adapted from earlier publications. An earlier version of the autobiographical sketch in the Introduction was published as 'Why Don't We Talk About Patriarchy Anymore?', in C. Noble, B. Pease and J. Ife (eds), *Radicals in Australian Social Work* (Connor Court, 2017). Parts of Chapter 1 were published in 'Theorising Men's Violence Prevention Policies: Limitations and Possibilities of Interventions in a Patriarchal State', in N. Henry and A. Powell (eds), *Preventing Sexual Violence: Interdisciplinary Approaches to Challenging a Rape Culture* (Palgrave Macmillan, 2014). An earlier version of the section on mateship in Chapter 5 was published as 'Mateship', in A. Ledeneva with A. Bailet, S. Barron, C. Curro and E. Teague (eds), *The Global Encyclopaedia of Informality: Towards Understanding of Social and Cultural Complexity. Vol. 1* (UCL Press, 2018). A portion of Chapter 11 is modified from 'Interrogating Privilege and Complicity in the Oppression of Others', in B. Pease, S. Goldingay, N. Hosken and S. Nipperss (eds),

Doing Critical Social Work: Transformative Practices for Social Justice (Allen & Unwin, 2016). Some parts of Chapter 12 are developed from 'Do Men Care? From Uncaring Masculinities to Men's Caring Practices in Social Work', in B. Pease, A. Vreugdenhil and S. Stanford (eds), *Critical Ethics of Care in Social Work: Transforming the Politics and Practices of Caring* (Routledge, 2018).

INTRODUCTION

Facing patriarchy

Although most of this book was written over the course of two years, many of the ideas and experiences that have informed the book are located in my involvement in critical masculinities scholarship and activist gender politics over a period of 40-plus years.

I first engaged with feminism in the 1970s in response to being challenged by women about my privilege as a man. My then partner would come home from women's consciousness-raising meetings and challenge my limited participation in housework and my overcommitment to study, activism and paid work at the expense of our relationship. I had to determine what these challenges would mean not only for my personal relationship, but also for my chosen career of social work and my political activism on issues of social justice.

As an activist who was involved in progressive community politics, I found it relatively easy at the intellectual level to see the validity of feminist claims and my own complicity in the oppression of women. I understood theoretically how as a man I was implicated in patriarchy and how I had not escaped the socialisation into patriarchal expectations about women. However, at the emotional level, I was deeply threatened by feminism. Listening to the experiences of my then partner, and women more generally, brought complex reactions, from sorrow to outrage to confusion, about how to respond.

To begin to address these issues, I co-founded an anti-sexist men's consciousness-raising group in Hobart in Tasmania in 1977. Many of the men were partners of feminist women. None of us at that time had a clearly defined theoretical perspective on gender issues for men. Many of us had some level of commitment to feminism; however, as we were to discover, we all meant different things by that. Our meetings were focused around set topics each night. We discussed housework, homosexuality, sexual experiences, pornography, rape, violence, masculinity, work, love and many other topics.

As the group evolved, a tension developed inside the group. Some men wanted to focus primarily on ways in which they felt stunted as men. They did not want to hear about the privileges we held as men or the social power we exercised over women. Other men concluded that we were hopeless oppressors and that very little could be done about that personally or politically. A third group, of which I was a part, thought that there had to be another alternative, although we didn't know what that was at the time. The larger group disbanded as men went off in one of three directions.

Four of us decided to get a better grasp about what women were saying about men, so we set up a reading group on feminist theory. We started with Mary Wollstonecraft and then read key feminist authors chronologically. We shared our emotional and intellectual responses to these books and endeavoured to locate our experience as men in the context of women's experiences and feminist theory.

After I moved to Melbourne in 1983, I joined with five other men to establish Men Against Sexism. We organised monthly forums on issues such as pornography, domestic violence, rape and sexuality. We produced booklets on men's responsibility for contraception, what men can do to challenge rape culture and ways in which men can explore loving and joyful expressions of sexuality. We gave talks in schools to boys about masculinity, bullying and sexism. We facilitated training workshops for health, law enforcement and welfare workers on the causes of men's violence and what to do to challenge it.

However, it was not until 1989, when I co-founded Men Against Sexual Assault (MASA) in Melbourne, that I moved into public activism against men's violence against women. The purpose of MASA was to encourage men to take responsibility for action against sexual violence through community education, social action, public media work and anti-sexist workshops. In September 1990, we organised the first men's march against sexual assault, in which over 300 men marched through the streets of Melbourne. There had been Reclaim the Night marches by women for many years, but men were conspicuously absent in public demonstrations against men's violence. While the march was generally welcomed by feminist women, some feminist activists were critical of the march because for them it undermined the radical feminist view that all men were potential rapists. There was an understandable mistrust of men's motivations, and I was starting to learn that profeminist politics by men was fraught and politically controversial.

In 1992, we organised the first White Ribbon Campaign against men's violence in Australia. The campaign was inspired by the Canadian campaign founded by Michael Kaufman in response to the massacre in Montreal on 6 December 1989, when 14 women were killed by a gunman at the University of Montreal. Thousands of men across Canada wore white ribbons to show their opposition to men's violence against women. The aim of the campaign was to provide a means for men to make a public statement about men's violence and to encourage men's responsibility for action against it.

In those early days of the campaign, there was no government funding and there were no paid staff. We purchased reams of white ribbon, cut them up, ironed them into a V shape and inserted safety pins in them. We then distributed them to supportive venues and encouraged men to wear them through media releases and radio interviews. Now White Ribbon Australia is a publicly funded foundation with 31 paid staff, over 3,000 White Ribbon ambassadors in Australia and over 700 events organised Australia-wide in the last year. However, as White Ribbon has grown exponentially, as a campaign, it has also become corporatised, as social marketing strategies and public health promotion models take over from social movement politics.

Over the years, I have sought strategies to educate men in the wider community about sexism and men's violence against women. There are very few sites where men can explore gender issues outside of university gender studies courses and, ironically, men's behaviour change programs, where men have used violence against their female partners. To address this gap, in 1994, I co-designed a two-day Patriarchy Awareness Workshop based on anti-racism workshops that I had experienced. The aim of the workshop is to address the problem of patriarchy and its impact on the lives of women, children and men. The workshop uses small group discussions, simulation exercises and videos to explore issues such as men's personal journeys in relation to gender issues, analyses of patriarchal culture, men's experiences of power and domination, alternatives to patriarchal power, the impact of men's domination on women, social and personal blocks to men's ability to listen to women, and visions, obstacles and potential for men to change. The workshops provide an opportunity for men to identify ways of moving profeminist politics beyond the arena of personal change to incorporate collectivist and public political action.

Since the 1990s, I have facilitated hundreds of these workshops as part of violence prevention and gender equality training within workplaces (including local councils, church-based organisations, schools, universities and the corporate sector) and as interventions in community-based and social movement organisations and political parties. The workshops aim to disrupt men's emotional investments in privilege. If men are to be engaged in challenging men's violence and promoting gender equality, they need to recognise the role that emotions play in sustaining their privilege and address the barriers that inhibit them from experiencing compassion, empathy and sadness in response to the suffering of others (see Chapter 12).

In 1985, I developed and taught an elective subject on men and masculinities at RMIT University in Melbourne. Although the elective course was originally intended primarily for male social work students, it became popular with female students who wanted strategies to deal with men in their personal and professional lives. The course provided an opportunity for me to bring a feminist-informed scholarship on men and masculinities into the social work curriculum.

Activist work on men's violence against women and educational work on men and masculinities took me into research with men about the pathways by which some men become profeminist and how to analyse men's power and resistance to change. My PhD research undertaken between 1990 and 1996 focused on profeminist men's involvement with feminism and the dilemmas they confront in their personal relationships, their professional lives and their politics. I invited self-defining profeminist men to participate in a collaborative inquiry group to examine how men who were supportive of feminism were responding to feminist challenges through an exploration of their experiences and dilemmas of attempting to live out their profeminist commitment.

Over the years, I have maintained a commitment to political activism in relation to men's sexism and violence against women. I continue to be involved in campaigns against men's violence and in facilitating workshops engaging men in violence prevention. I also try to make a difference through my writing and publications. I regard writing as a form of activism and political practice. I am interested in writing as a form of resistance, where I can express my political commitments. I have always been concerned that my writing reaches audiences beyond academia. Hence, I have tried to balance the pressure within universities to publish in prestigious high-ranked journals with publishing in activist newsletters, professional journals and books, and writing opinion editorials in newspapers.

This brief biographical sketch provides the backdrop to the experiences that inform this book. A significant moment occurred in 2015 when I was waiting to speak on a panel at a Violence Against Women conference in Sydney on the topic of 'Rethinking Violence Against Women Prevention Policies'. As I listened to other papers presented at the conference during the previous day and a half, I was frustrated by the level of analysis and the conduct of the discussion at the conference. I suspect that my frustration had something to do with the fact that it was 40 years since I went to my first conference on violence against women, and what I had been hearing over the course of the previous two days left me feeling that it was almost as if the last 40 years had not happened. I was left wondering what we had learnt since the 1970s. What impact have we had on the problem of men's violence against women? Why is the language we use so depoliticised after 40 years of second-wave feminism?

In articulating the problem of men's violence against women to the wider community, feminist activists and researchers have faced problems about the language they use to name the issue. At times, they have had to locate themselves in the dominant discourse to enable them to gain some traction on women's victimisation. This means that they have been forced to soften their analysis or omit some aspects of their understanding of the problem.

In the context of a backlash against feminism, liberal feminist ideas have gained dominance. Social movement politics against men's violence informed by radical, socialist and multiracial feminisms have been supplanted by liberal feminist, public health and professionalised approaches to violence prevention. Consequently, we have witnessed a deradicalisation of feminism and gender analyses, strategies for engaging men that overemphasise reconstructing masculinity rather than challenging patriarchy, a 'not all men' refrain from so-called 'good men', and a greater acceptance of anti-feminist backlash politics within the mainstream.

The impetus to write the book has come out of a series of concerns with these developments, which have not only occurred within government, but have also influenced community-based responses to violence against women. It seems to me that new and conservative orthodoxies are being established. When we allow one paradigm to dominate the discourse about violence against women, a regime of truth is established, and other theoretical approaches are marginalised and excluded to the point of ignoring their existence.

One of the main arguments in *Facing Patriarchy* is that gender analyses of violence against women have been depoliticised and accommodated to neoliberal government policy discourses. While the concept of gender is sometimes used in policies of government, many of the references to gender in relation to violence against women refer to sex differences and individualised conceptions of gender roles. This book locates men's violence against women within the structures and processes of patriarchy. The book also explores links between men's violence against women and other forms of violence by men, in relation to boys and other men and men's involvement in military conflict, wars and terrorism, as well as environmental violence and 'man-made' global warming.

I argue that we cannot understand men's violence against women outside an understanding of patriarchy, and consequently that we need to bring back the language of patriarchy as the basis for a nuanced conceptual framework for addressing men's violence against women. A nuanced conceptualisation of patriarchy accounts for men's structural power over women and the intersections of gender power and other forms of structural inequality, patriarchal ideologies, men's patriarchal peer relations, the exercise of coercive control in family life and the patriarchal subjectivities of individual men. These different levels, or what I call the 'pillars of patriarchy', provide the basis for a feminist conceptual framework to understand and address men's violence against women.

The analysis of patriarchy and the links to men's violence against women in this book are most relevant to contemporary Western societies. Although the analysis may well apply to countries in the Global South, I make no assumptions about the transferability of the theorising. Patriarchy takes on different forms in different social and political contexts, and I do not address the nuances and variations in other male-dominated societies outside the West. Although I use the language of patriarchy in the singular, it will be evident that I do not frame it as a monolithic, fixed, ahistorical and universal structure, but rather to refer to historically and culturally specific structures in the plural, with changing dynamics and intersections with transnational processes and other structures of inequality (see Chapter 3).

While the analysis of this book may inform women's practices in opposing patriarchy, the main focus is on how men can understand and resist patriarchy from their own structural location within it. I am thus primarily writing for a male audience, although women may well find the book useful in understanding men's capacity for, and resistance to, change. In addressing the dynamics of patriarchy primarily through the experiences of men, I do not suggest that I bring any specifically unique knowledge as a man to this project. In fact, the analysis I develop has drawn extensively upon feminist writers, as well as critical masculinity theorists. However, the strategies to understand patriarchy and to overcome it are from the standpoint of my position within it. This may well create some blind spots, and no doubt there will be some scepticism about a class-privileged white man writing about challenging patriarchy from within.

Of course, there is also a danger that I am again foregrounding a male voice and centring men's experiences at the expense of women. As men, we must be aware of our privileged speaking and writing positions. What does it mean when profeminist men who challenge patriarchy and men's violence are listened to more than feminist women who are involved in the same work? It has been argued that this is a way of using privilege to challenge privilege. Men are perceived by some men as more credible, and thus they will be listened to more. However, such men can carve out an area of expertise for their advantage and this can reinforce barriers that prevent women from having their own voices heard. I am aware of these dangers; however, I hope that my insider positioning as a man has something to offer in challenging patriarchy from within.

My work on men and masculinity has been informed by my engagement with a number of feminisms, including various versions of radical feminism, especially those that acknowledge the importance of class, race and other forms of intersectionality. In taking up some feminist positions instead of others, I am not suggesting some feminists are not doing feminism 'the right way'. Some will argue that men should not express particular views at all about particular feminist perspectives, as it could be read as them having input into what feminists should be prioritising. I do not claim any special moral authority in advocating particular positions, and I am aware of the importance of doing justice to those feminist perspectives that I do not agree with.

Much of the writing about patriarchy seems to be premised upon biologically distinct men and women who constitute a gender binary. We now know that this distinction does not work for many people. What does current work on dismantling the binary and acknowledging transgender and intersexualities mean for the analysis developed here? As will be evident in Chapter 12, I favour ultimately moving away from the gender binary, but my focus in the meantime is on cisgendered men and their practices in patriarchy because they are the perpetrators and perpetuators of most of the violence. I acknowledge the vulnerability of transgender people to the violences of these men, but I do not address the politics of transgender issues or questions about how such politics sits in relation to the analysis and strategies advocated.

Invariably, the question will arise, 'What about women's violence?' It will be clear to the reader that I do not believe the minority of violence perpetrated by women should be avoided, and throughout the book I make reference to women's violence in the home, women's involvement in the military and terrorist organisations, and women's broader complicity with patriarchal gender relations. I do not believe that an acknowledgement of this violence is inconsistent with a feminist analysis. In fact, there is a strong case for a feminist theory of women's violence (Enander 2011; Carrington 2015; Lynch 2015; Abrams 2016). While I do not undertake that analysis fully here, the implications of the move away from a purely structuralist account of patriarchy opens up ways of understanding women's use and abuse of power within patriarchal gender orders.

Architecture of the book

Although there is a logic to the structure of the book and the chapters are written to be read in sequential order, at various points I make reference to ideas in other chapters. Readers may thus sometimes want to 'jump' to another chapter to see how particular ideas are developed.

Facing Patriarchy is divided into four parts. Part One engages critically with the dominant conceptual models for understanding violence against women and the neoliberal state policy context within which violence prevention policies are enacted.

In Chapter 1, I critically interrogate the public health framing of violence against women and the social-ecological model of violence prevention embedded within it. I outline how the public health-informed ecological model has assumed primacy as the main conceptual framework for understanding violence against women in the West. I argue that the social-ecological approach lacks a coherent theoretical framework, and that consequently it is unable to make meaningful connections between the various levels of analysis of violence against women.

Chapter 2 notes that the promotion of gender equality has been espoused as an important part of the prevention of violence against women. The expectation has been that as gender equality increases, violence against women will decrease. However, the language of gender equality is often couched in terms of treating men and women equally within a patriarchal framework, as it is often measured in terms of policies that grant women equal access to privileges available to men. In this context, there is contradictory evidence about the relationship between gender equality and levels of violence against women. I note the backlash response by some men as societies move towards greater formal equality, whereby men endeavour to keep women subordinated through violence, and I interrogate the apparent paradox where countries can be gender-equal and patriarchal simultaneously.

Part Two locates men's violence against women within five pillars of patriarchy: men's structural power over women and the intersections of gender power and other forms of structural inequality, patriarchal ideologies, men's patriarchal peer relations, the exercise of coercive control in family life, and the patriarchal subjectivities of individual men.

In Chapter 3, I examine critiques of the concept of patriarchy from both within and outside of feminism, and argue the case for a nuanced conceptualisation of patriarchy that accounts for a variety of patriarchal structures within a transnational world. I also explore how patriarchy is linked with other systems of inequality and must be theorised in relation to other forms of hierarchy such as class, race, ethnicity, age, sexuality and geopolitical location. It advances a view of patriarchy as operating on multiple levels, including the macro levels of structures of government, law and the market, the micro level of family and intimate relations, and the intra-psychic level internalised within individual men.

Following on from this framework, in Chapter 4 I differentiate between the structural dimensions of inequality involving women's access to institutional positions of power and authority and ideological beliefs about the status of women. I argue that structural changes towards gender equality may not necessarily lead to a lessening of patriarchal ideologies among men. While changing structural relations will modify patriarchal beliefs about gender and gender inequality, the core structure of hegemonic beliefs may remain intact even in the context of increasing gender equality at the structural level. Numerous empirical studies indicate a link between sexist attitudes by men and the likelihood of engaging in violence against women. What is less acknowledged in the community attitudes literature is the relationship between sexist attitudes and patriarchal ideology that sustains men's cultural domination of women.

In Chapter 5, I demonstrate that dominant forms of masculinity linked with men's violence against women are generated through men's relations with other men. This is evident through studies of homosocial bonding, fratriarchy, mateship and male peer support. I explain how men's abusive practice with women is both a way of affirming a particular form of masculinity and a means of bonding with other men at the expense of women. I explore how competitive team sports becomes one of the key sites for developing and affirming dominant masculinity and is also an institution that rewards violence by men against women. I analyse male peer group cultures to demonstrate how men's complicity with some forms of homosocial bonding reproduces a culture that allows men's violence against women to flourish.

Chapter 6 explores the limitations in framing violence against women in the family as a series of violent incidents versus locating violence in the context of a range of abusive and exploitative practices by men. It also examines how the concept of coercive control, as a particular form of injustice against women, is not captured by the language of violence. The chapter explains how coercive control may be more common in countries where patriarchal, legal, religious and cultural customs have been challenged and greater levels of equality for women have been achieved. It locates coercive control in the context of men's privilege in the family and links the interpersonal dimensions of power and control to the wider institutional and cultural supports for men's violence against women.

In Chapter 7, I argue that to address men's violence against women, we need a theoretical framework that enables us to understand how men subjectively experience patriarchy. Patriarchy is embedded in men's psyches and it involves intra-psychic processes that give meaning to men. This means that the psychological dimension of patriarchy must be challenged alongside the material, discursive, homosocial and interpersonal levels. Men will need to construct their sense of self outside of the framework of patriarchal masculinities. It is thus necessary for men to understand patriarchy and its influence on their lives if they are to find a way of challenging it.

Part Three of the book links men's violence against women to other forms of patriarchal violence: men's violence against other men, men's violence in the context of militarism, war and terrorism, and men's environmental violence and contribution to global warming.

In Chapter 8, I note that patriarchy has a generational dimension, whereby older men oppress younger men and boys. I also observe that hegemonic masculinity dominates men who are marginalised and subordinated by class, ethnicity, culture and sexuality. Thus, I argue that inequality between men is part of patriarchy. This means that men's domination of other men is a central element of men's oppression of women. While men's violence is constructed as gendered when it is targeted at women and girls, it is rarely seen as gendered when it is directed towards men and boys. I argue that 'men-to-men' violence is also one of the ways in which some men affirm their manhood. Engaging with men's violence towards men and boys as a gendered phenomenon provides opportunities to explore links between men's violence against women and violence among men.

Chapter 9 demonstrates the ways in which war produces and is constitutive of hegemonic forms of masculinity. I consider the links between men's violence against women and militarism and men's violence in wars between nation states. I note that the less patriarchal a society is, the less likelihood there is of advancing state interests through force and violence. When militarised masculinity is widespread in a society, it is likely that violence will be viewed as an acceptable means of imposing domination, and consequently that there will be greater levels of men's violence against women. I also discuss how issues of national security are interwoven with ideas about masculinity. I argue that anti-state terrorism can be understood in part as a response to a masculinity that has been damaged by the West, and that state responses can be seen as needing to demonstrate masculine strength and fortitude in response to aggression.

Chapter 10 notes that the impact of global warming is differentially felt in terms of geographical location in the world and also in terms of social locations of gender, class and race within particular geopolitical spaces. While the research on the impact of global warming on vulnerable populations is widely recognised, I argue that little attention has been given to addressing gendered power and patriarchal discourses in the construction of 'man-made' disasters. Hegemonic forms of masculinity promote an expectation that men enact control over themselves, and other men, over women and over the environment. In the context of framing global warming as a crime and as a form of environmental violence, this chapter explores the links between the forms of masculinity involved in men's ecologically destructive practices and men's violence against women and other men.

Part Four, the final part of the book, outlines strategies for men to overcome a violent gender order. These chapters differ from most writing on engaging men in violence prevention in that they focus on the requisite knowledge men need and the personal transformation necessary for them to become effective aspiring allies in solidarity with women.

The argument of Chapter 11 is that to engage men in violence prevention, we have to disengage them from the structures and processes of patriarchy. This approach challenges the dominant model for engaging men, which is to position non-violent men as the 'good men' who will protect women from the 'bad men'. I note that most men who are not violent are ignorant of the role they play in reproducing and perpetuating a culture of violence. This chapter argues that while men vary in their relationship to violence, all men are enmeshed in relations of power and dominance over women. If men refuse to examine their complicity in reproducing a violence-prone culture, the changes required to bring about an end to men's violence against women will be slower to develop. The chapter articulates a social connection model of responsibility, where it is argued that men have a responsibility to get involved in challenging men's violence and patriarchy because they are causally embedded in processes that produce such violence and unequal social divisions.

Chapter 12, the final chapter of the book, demonstrates that men who are engaged in caring roles are less likely to commit violence against their partners and their children. Because men are discouraged from expressing their emotions, they are often unable to provide the emotional labour required in relationships and are largely absent from caring roles. Dominant definitions of masculinity do not include caregiving as a component of men's lives. Ascribing caring and emotional work to women reproduces patriarchal discourses and male privilege. Thus, fostering caregiving subjectivities and practices among men is an essential part of facing patriarchy. I argue that developing a feminist ethic of care in men provides a grounding for valuing non-violence over violence in families and in political conflict. Through being more involved in caring roles and responsibilities, men are able to construct forms of subjectivity based on nurturing, empathy, vulnerability and political solidarity with women.

I am doubtful that the analysis of patriarchy and men's violence against women advanced in this book will be translated into policies and programs within the neoliberal state. Feminist 'think tanks' and activist networks outside state-sponsored academic conferences and state-based policy forums are needed to provide opportunities for civil society organising unencumbered by state policy discourses. In this context, I hope this intellectual 'work in progress' might provide some useful conceptual tools for a radical political analysis of the violences of men. The pace of change in gender relations in the last forty years has been too slow. It is time to return to the problem of patriarchy and devise strategies to overcome it.

PART ONE

RETHINKING FRAMEWORKS AND POLICIES ADDRESSING MEN'S VIOLENCE AGAINST WOMEN

1 | THE LIMITS OF PUBLIC HEALTH APPROACHES TO VIOLENCE AGAINST WOMEN PREVENTION

Introduction

Public health approaches to violence prevention have now become the dominant paradigm in the prevention of violence against women in the West. State-based anti-violence policies and programs are now largely framed by a wider public health promotion agenda (Messner et al. 2015; Flood 2018). While the public health frame has allowed violence against women prevention to reach larger audiences, it has also limited and depoliticised anti-violence work.

Of course, public health is not a homogenous discipline. There are critical public health perspectives (Bunton and Willis 2004; Ratelo et al. 2010; Legge 2018; Mykhalovskiy et al. 2018) that emphasise the political and economic implications of structural inequality for health. There are also feminist engagements with public health that bring a gendered lens and a gender inequality framework to the health issues facing women (Hammarstrom 1999; Rogers 2006; Stewart et al. 2010; Our Watch 2015). However, as Mykhalovskiy et al. (2018) note, critical and feminist approaches *within* public health are subjected to institutional pressures and 'trade-offs' that subordinate their critical social science insights to public health epistemologies and frameworks.

The public health model of prevention is grounded in prevention science, which is primarily concerned with the control and prevention of disease. Primary prevention aims to prevent a disease before it occurs, secondary prevention aims to reduce the impact of a disease, and tertiary prevention aims to help people manage health problems and illness (Institute for Work and Health 2015). While historically public health prevention models have focused on the prevention of infectious diseases, more recently they have been concerned with promoting health, and within that wider public health framework they have started to address violence against women.

The premise of the public health approach is that primary prevention approaches in other health-related fields such as HIV transmission and smoking can be applied to violence prevention (Casey and Lindhorst 2009). The primary prevention model may be appropriate for preventing infectious diseases because it aims to address a virus as a single agent of transmission of the disease (Woody 2006). However, violence is not an illness or a disease, but a behaviour and a social phenomenon. It is not something that goes into remission or something that someone has. When primary prevention is applied to violence against women, it removes reference to disease, although the language often remains, for example, in 'the epidemic of violence against women'.

Many public health approaches have moved beyond the biomedical model and public health promotion in relation to smoking and HIV transmission, for example, and embrace a social determinants of health approach. This approach acknowledges gender and income inequality, but as 'social gradients' in relation to social status. The constitution of the 'social' in the social determinants approach relies more upon epidemiology and the quantification of risk factors than it does on critical sociological theory (Schofield 2007). Furthermore, men's violence against women is not comparable to these other public health problems, and consequently primary prevention models in addressing these public health issues are not transferable to tackling the underlying structural and discursive causes of men's violence against women.

The prevailing violence prevention approaches within public health argue that a Western science-based model is the most effective strategy to address violence against women (Storer et al. 2016). The concept of prevention provides reassurance to the public that a particular problem can be resolved. It is premised upon the notion of being able to understand cause and effect and prediction through science. It is an empiricist project at heart that involves social engineering and scientific expertise, and is usually concerned with cost-efficiency in the context of limited resources and neoliberal restructuring of social services.

Within this perspective, social problems are assessed, diagnosed and predicted by the application of scientific knowledge (Stepney 2014). The public health approach of gathering data, identifying groups to target, developing intervention methods and measuring effectiveness is consistent with managerial policymaking and has significantly shaped how violence against women is understood by government.

Primary prevention strategies within public health have historically primarily focused on behaviour change interventions. More recently, they have become concerned with 'unlearning' violent behaviours and challenging the norms that legitimate violence. The focus is on eliminating the culture of violence. When structural gender relations are mentioned, they are framed primarily as rigid gender roles, gender norms and unequal access to resources and support systems (VicHealth 2007; Our Watch 2015).

Change the Story, Australia's primary prevention of violence against women framework, is informed by the 'evidence base' and techniques of public health and the social-ecological model of individual behaviour (Our Watch 2015). Primary prevention focuses on settings such as workplaces, universities, sports, religious institutions, media and community services. However, as Castelino (2010) identifies, a focus on changing attitudes and behaviour in settings does not address the structural causes of violence against women.

The failure of the primary prevention approach to violence against women is due in part to the institutional forces and ideologically based power of interest groups that are threatened by the prevention initiatives. There appears to be no political will to challenge these vested interests. Often the scope of prevention is limited to social policies that ignore the broader political and economic context in which the problem (in this case, men's violence against women) is situated. The ideologies of governments and government instrumentalities shape the parameters of how prevention is understood and what strategies can be enacted (Gough 2013).

Interrogating the ecological model of violence prevention

Since 1998, primary prevention in public health has been conceptualised within an ecological model focused upon risk factors associated with multiple layers of an individual's social environment. Twelve years ago, the Victorian Health Promotion Foundation in Australia claimed that the ecological model of violence 'reflects the consensus of international opinion around the world' (VicHealth 2007: 29).

The ecological approach has historically been the dominant approach to the prevention of disease and health promotion in public health. It focuses on environmental and individual determinants of behaviour, drawing upon Bronfenbrenner's (1977) ecological framework of human development. Utilising a systems metaphor, it emphasises micro, meso, exo and macro system influences (Richard et al. 2011).

The ecological metaphor is adapted from the discipline of biological ecology and explores the relationship of individuals to the social environment (Richard et al. 2011). As it utilises a systems approach, it focuses on the principles of adaptation and interdependence (Richard et al. 2011). Within the context of biology, ecology refers to the dependence of living creatures on their environment.

The premise of the ecological model is that the relationship between individuals and their societal context can be understood by reference to the principles informing biological ecology. Bronfenbrenner's (1977) ecology of human development purports to be a scientific study of the relationship between a human organism and the environment in which it survives. In Bronfenbrenner's (1977) view, '[e]nvironmental structures and the processes taking place within and between them must be viewed as interdependent and must be analysed in systems terms' (p. 518).

Stanger (2011) defines an ecosystem of being 'composed of the scientific observation of interactions, organisms and environments' (p. 168). He notes that ecosystem is used as a metaphor in various public discourses to describe interrelationships between humans and their cultural and political context. However, this is problematical because the ecosystem concepts of equilibrium, diversity and resilience fail to capture the dynamics between men and women under patriarchy. Stanger argues that political and economic discourses are not comparable to ecosystems in terms of their complexity. Similarly, Stojanovic et al. (2016) argue that society cannot be adequately conceptualised as a form of social-ecological systems because it is unable to address power and privilege. They depoliticise the social and accept existing social relations as 'natural'.

Even biological scientists and ecologists have become critical of using the ecosystem concept for studying the ecological environment. Some are concerned that the ecosystem concept is a machine analogy derived from systems analysis within engineering. The analogy is challenged because it is at odds with the fact that ecological systems do not always achieve equilibrium as is the case with mechanical systems. The ecosystem is not an objective scientific observation about nature. Rather, it is a paradigm for developing a particular perspective on nature. While it focuses on some properties of nature, it ignores others (O'Neill 2001).

Heise (1998) suggests that it is possible to incorporate feminist and social science insights about family violence into the ecological model.

She argues that many feminists are reluctant to acknowledge causes other than patriarchy for explaining men's violence against women, and attributes this in part to the resistance to feminist analysis within mainstream discourses of violence. However, she also believes that the feminist emphasis on male dominance and patriarchy is unable to explain why many men are not violent towards women, even though they are subject to the same cultural messages that socialise men into male superiority and privilege. While she acknowledges that patriarchy is important to theorise men's violence against women, in her view it does not fully explain why particular men become violent towards women.

Heise (2006) argues that violence against women results from the interaction of a multitude of factors at different levels of the social ecology. It is seen to be the result of an interplay between personal, situational and sociocultural factors. Individual micro-level factors include having an absent or rejecting father, alcohol abuse, witnessing family violence as a child or being abused as a child. Exo-system factors include unemployment, low socio-economic status and delinquent peer groups. Macro-system factors include masculinity, rigid gender roles, male entitlement and cultural condoning of violence.

Sliwka and Macdonald (2005), who are less feminist-sympathetic than Heise, also argue that the feminist approach to violence against women does not explore multiple layers of explanation, and they frame 'the feminist theory' (as if there is only one feminist theory) as being a linear-type model that excludes class and race, for example. For them, the ecological model is able to encompass a wider and more diverse range of factors and acknowledge the complexity of the causes of violence against women.

The ecological framework is referred to as a 'multi-level theoretical formulation'. In arguing that no single factor can adequately explain violence, the World Health Organization (2009) report extrapolates that no single theoretical framework can analyse the multiple causal factors at different levels that impact on violence against women. Wall (2014) also argues that an ecological model enables one to consider theoretically the diversity of influences on violence against women.

The implication of these views is that the ecological model is not a theory, but a neutral framework that can be used to relate different theories to empirical data. The premise is that the ecological model is an unbiased framework that is able to accommodate a diversity of theoretical perspectives (Ratelo et al. 2010). The claimed scientific neutrality that underpins the ecological model fails to recognise how critical theoretical frames are marginalised.

Quadara and Wall (2012) maintain that the ecological model enables conceptualising the interactive nature of the multiple causal factors in relation to violence against women. However, risk factors are static representations of determinants of violence without any analysis of how they intersect. Furthermore, when Quadara and Wall (2012) list factors at the individual level (including alcohol and drug use, anti-social tendencies, childhood history of sexual abuse and witnessing family violence), the interpersonal level (including workplaces, schools and neighbourhoods) and the societal level (including government policies and laws and societal norms and cultural belief systems), they do not ground these in the context of overall theoretical understanding. Without an overarching theoretical framework, it is not possible to make coherent connections between the various levels.

An eclectic so-called integrated framework that draws upon approaches from many different disciplines and theoretical approaches is problematic because it attempts to integrate constructs from discourses of knowledge that are incommensurable with other discourses. This means that because it is not possible to construct an integrated intervention plan, some discourses are likely to be prioritised over others. This is often most evident when structural issues that are difficult to address are marginalised in intervention programs where more attention is focused on behavioural and attitudinal change interventions, which can be more easily measured and addressed.

While radical feminist approaches emphasise the political and social structures that reproduce gender inequality and men's violence against women, they are still concerned with other levels of explanation (see Part Two). However, gender-neutral theories that emphasise personality disorders, psychopathology, attachment disorders, substance abuse, depression, child abuse and history of witnessing violent behaviour are in tension, if not in contradiction, with a comprehensive feminist analysis. It is not that these issues are necessarily irrelevant; rather, their theorising needs to be gendered and framed with a nuanced understanding of patriarchy.

As I have argued elsewhere (Pease 2014a), the premises underpinning feminist analyses at the societal level in the ecological model are at odds with the premises underpinning gender-neutral psychological approaches to personality factors at the individual level. A feminist analysis has relevance at all levels in terms of explaining patriarchal structural forces, patriarchal ideologies, men's peer support for patriarchy, men's sexist practices with women and men's internalised dominance. However, non-feminist psychological and systems approaches that are gender-neutral suggest alternative interventions to address violence against women. This means that the ecological model does not construct a theoretically integrated conceptual framework.

While adherents of the ecological model talk about the complexity of the causes of violence against women, they rarely identify the main causes. Instead, they talk about determinants of violence and risk factors. While gender inequality is sometimes presented as a social determinant of violence, when it comes to prevention approaches they tend to focus on the individual level of intervention (Our Watch 2015). For example, Quadara and Wall (2012) state that primary prevention is predominantly concerned with changing behaviour.

Some writers refer to what they call a 'feminist ecological model' (Meyer and Post 2006; Flood 2008a; Powell 2014a). Flood (2008a) argues that feminist and ecological models are compatible because the ecological framework is able to address determinants of violence against women at multiple levels. Powell (2014a) similarly makes the case for what she calls an integrated feminist ecological framework. However, one of the limitations of the ecological approach is that men's dominance is regarded as only a contributing variable in relation to violence against women, rather than as the central organising framework. It is the difference between regarding gender as one variable in a model versus developing a critical gender-centred theoretical framework that elucidates how violence against women is played out in a gendered social context with other social divisions such as class, race, sexuality, age, nationality and religion (Hunnicutt 2009).

Combining conflicting theoretical explanations under one model is incoherent. As noted earlier, some of the theoretical explanations drawn upon in the ecological framework are at odds with a feminist analysis rather than complementing it. If it is recognised that the multiple dimensions of patriarchy are the primary cause of men's violence against women, then not all theories are compatible with this analysis, and consequently not all theories can be integrated into a feminist framework. It is important to incorporate interpersonal and psychic dimensions alongside structural analyses (see Chapters 6 and 7).

However, these different emphases need to be integrated into a theoretically coherent framework. When gender or gender dominance is just a variable or a risk factor amidst many others, it is likely to become sidelined.

Contemporary feminist analyses recognise the importance of interrogating the intersections between gender and other social divisions. While early feminist approaches understandably foregrounded gender in their analysis of violence against women, increasingly there has been a widespread recognition of the value of gender's intersection with other sources of oppression such as class, race, national origin, sexuality and disability. This intersectionality framework is substantially different from considering gender as just one among many risk factors.

An intersectional feminist approach differs from the ecological approach advocated by Heise (1998), the World Health Organization (Kruger et al. 2002), VicHealth (2007) and Our Watch (2015) because the feminist approach is the lens through which other theories are held together, rather than simply being one component as in the ecological model. Consequently, feminist analysis is enriched by other perspectives rather than marginalised and deradicalised, as happens in the ecological framework. Intersectional feminism should be the basis for deciding on the inclusion or otherwise of different theories. In this way, other perspectives are utilised when they complement and enrich a feminist understanding. Not all theoretical approaches are consistent with a feminist analysis, and ungendered factors need to be reconsidered through a gendered lens.

I acknowledge that it may be possible to do feminist work within an ecological framework and that such a framework may allow discussion of patriarchy and male dominance in ways that may be more acceptable to government. However, there is nothing specifically feminist about the model per se, and it has lent itself equally to anti-feminist commentators and researchers (e.g. see Dutton 1994; Dutton and Nichols 2005; Sliwka and Macdonald 2005). Also, as argued previously, at the level of epistemology, ecological systems models are at odds with structural, discursive and interactional feminist understandings.

It is concerning that Heise (1998), who espouses a feminist approach, and Dutton (1994, 2006), who is anti-feminist, make the same argument that the ecological model is able to move beyond the limitations of feminist theories of patriarchy because they allegedly cannot explain why only some men commit violence against women (for a feminist explanation of why only some men use physical violence against women, see Chapter 6). Such arguments do not do justice to nuanced and complex theories of patriarchy that acknowledge multiple and intersecting structures and discursive and interactional dimensions of men's domination. There are, of course, multiple feminisms, and many feminisms acknowledge the intersections of gender with other social divisions. In the context of a backlash against feminism, any association of feminism with linear and monocausal analysis is likely to further marginalise feminist theories.

Heise (1998) acknowledges that the ecological framework is a heuristic tool. The ecological model is a paradigm for organising ideas, and it is premised upon various assumptions about the social world that limit our thinking and our analysis. Ecological frameworks do not identify the links between psychological and sociological dimensions across the various levels. They simply provide a model for specifying a large range of factors that are seen to influence violence towards women. Theoretical and conceptual frameworks are necessary to understand how the various levels intersect and what is needed to address these levels.

The ecological framework is also presented in the form of a logic model. Logic models involve diagrams that purport to explain causal relationships that are represented in the form of a flow chart. They are premised upon the idea that one can analyse how certain factors influence other factors. However, they are unable to grasp the complexity of causal relationships in the material world and they restrict thinking about solutions (Lee 2017).

Epidemiology and risk factors

While public health models of violence prevention sometimes identify social determinants of violence (Our Watch 2015), in practice most prevention programs address individual risk factors (Broom 2016). The framing of multiple dimensions across the individual, family, community and societal levels in an ecological framework is the integration of multiple risk and protective factors (Fulu and Heise 2015). While 'macrosocial processes' are sometimes mentioned as risk factors, these risk factors are decontextualised from the wider social relations in which they are embedded.

The systematic evidence review that Fulu and Heise (2015) conducted using the ecological model emphasised quantitative research and measurable dimensions of violence in assessing the various risk factors influencing violence against women. Such risk factors included in the review were genetic endowment, personality profile, developmental history, communication style and the dynamics of relationships. Genetic and biological factors sit alongside social categories of analysis such as class, gender and race. The focus on psychological and biological factors obscures the political, economic and social causes of inequality. Broader social formations such as capitalism, neoliberalism or patriarchy do not appear in this analysis.

Within public health, violence against women in general, and sexual violence against women in particular, are conceptualised as a matter of risk of future perpetration or future victimisation of violence (Carmody 2009). Chung et al. (2006) note that there has been a lot of attention devoted to the development of risk assessment procedures for measuring the risk of sexual violence recidivism. There has been an increase in the language of risk and 'the risk society' since the 1990s. Cowburn (2010) identifies an enormous amount of psychological literature that deals with risk management and risk assessment of sex offenders.

Risk assessment frameworks profess to be able to predict the level of risk of either being a victim or perpetrator of violence. In this view, violence against women is framed as a consequence of various risk factors at multiple levels of the society, from the community to the individual. Men are framed in this discourse not only as gendered, but also as an amalgamation of risk factors stemming from childhood experiences. Considerable attention is given to the influence of childhood experiences in shaping attitudes towards women (Boyd 2009). In this view, men's violence is understood as arising from the personal history of the perpetrator rather than from the wider context of gender inequality. Gender privilege and hegemonic masculinity disappear and individual men's experiences of victimisation come to the fore. Furthermore, with the increased focus on risk assessment of convicted offenders, the larger unconvicted population of men are not addressed at all. Risk models do not address why men as a group commit violence on women as a group (Bacchi 1999).

Carmody (2009) has appropriately asked whether a risk focus is the most effective way of addressing violence against women. Notwithstanding the claims of evidence-based policy and practice, there is no 'evidence' that risk factor frameworks are effective when applied to violence prevention. Webb (2006) argues that the notion of risk is used to legitimate neoliberal policies of governance. There are links between risk-based models of violence and neoliberal agendas of individual responsibility for crime prevention (Hoyle 2008). Interventions addressing violence against women are increasingly framed within a neoliberal policy framework (see Chapter 2). Neoliberalism constructs discourses of risk for its own purposes. Policy interventions are aimed at lessening risk rather than meeting needs (Culpitt 1999).

Understanding causes is more than understanding correlation between risk factors and violence. To understand the causes of violence to women, we need to develop theoretical explanations of how so-called risk and protective factors shape outcomes (Hawkins 2006). The ecological model does not address how various risk factors occur. How is it that political, economic and social forces reproduce the environment in which risk factors are manifested? Models of multiple causation in the web of numerous and interconnected risk and protective factors fail to identify the theoretical underpinnings of these models.

Gender as a social determinant or risk factor

One problem with a social determinants approach to public health is that the economic, political and social processes that shape the social determinants are not identified (Hankivosky and Christofferson 2008). The social determinants of health model has been critiqued for failing to explicate how various forms of power are reproduced within political institutions (Schofield 2007; Navarro 2009).

The social determinants of health approach is not informed by a critical sociological analysis of how the 'social' creates social and health inequalities. Rather, drawing upon epidemiology as a supposedly scientific approach, the focus is on statistical correlations between social factors and health outcomes. What is not understood is how inequalities of resources and power produce social inequalities (Schofield 2015) or how power and privilege embedded in social structures are reinforced.

In mainstream public health, gender is treated as a variable in statistical analysis rather than as an explanatory theory (Fulu and Heise 2015). This decontextualises and depoliticises gender, which is often conflated with sex as a social determinant or risk factor (Inhorn and Whittle 2001; Thurston and Vissandjee 2014). The use of gender in public health approaches to violence prevention is primarily to do with the gendered differences between men and women. Power disparities between men and women are often acknowledged as a macrosocial factor. However, there is no recognition of the wider form of male dominance and male supremacy within which these gender inequalities are situated.

The public health approach to gender sits within what Connell (2012) refers to as 'categoricalism', a view of gender as dichotomous categories of male and female and man and woman. This categorical approach to gender in public health framings is unable to understand gender as a process of enactment, and consequently cannot conceptualise how gender inequalities are created and sustained. Numerous commentators have observed that public health frameworks do not have sufficiently nuanced understanding of sex and gender to connect the macro level of social structure to the micro level of individual practices (Hankivosky and Christoffersen 2008; Austerberry 2011). The key theoretical developments in feminist theory and critical masculinity studies have generally not been adopted in public health approaches to violence against women.

Science and the evidence base

Evidence-based approaches to health issues are now central in public health. There is an increasing emphasis in public health promotion on building the evidence base, whereby the aim is to develop a scientific foundation for prevention (Broom 2016).

Consequently, the evidence base is an important part of public health framings of violence against women. This is premised upon an empiricist approach to knowledge that emphasises experimental knowledge and randomised controlled trials. In the UK, this approach is evident in the 'What Works to Prevent Violence' program, which assumes that violence can be prevented through the technical application of scientific knowledge. Fulu et al. (2014), for example, state that evidence demonstrates that violence is caused by the interaction of multiple factors at different levels of the 'social ecology', as if the social ecology was an actual social formation that can be scientifically observed rather than a socially constructed metaphor, as discussed earlier. After reviewing a multitude of 'risk factors', including those that focus on genetic endowment, personality profile and developmental history of individual perpetrators, readers are told the quality of the evidence gathered is best if there is at least one randomised controlled trial.

In this frame, violence against women is understood as a phenomenon that is stable and able to be objectively measured. As noted earlier, however, violence is not a disease or a virus that can be measured. Putting aside critiques of evidence-based medicine (Gupta 2003; Griffiths 2005) from which evidence-based policy and practices is derived, what may work in relation to physical diseases will not necessarily work in relation to social phenomena such as violence against women.

Population health is located within epidemiology and so-called objective cause and effect relations (Raphael and Bryant 2002). With a focus on management and actuarial measurement, risk assessment policies rely upon rational models of policy development that purport to be able to objectively define and measure the level of risk among a given population (Webb 2006). Risk is portrayed as an objective entity that can be measured and calculated to determine probability (Cowburn 2010). Hall (2004) frames this as the belief that 'information will save you' (p. 5). If only we have enough information, then we can eliminate the problem. Beck (2007) argues that the prediction of risk cannot be subject to scientific assessment. As I have argued elsewhere (Pease 2009), evidence-based policy frameworks do not provide the best basis to produce knowledge that is concerned with social justice and social change.

Some feminists have endeavoured to develop a feminist epidemiology that has embraced a form of feminist empiricism, which Harding (1986) noted over 30 years ago was an attempt to acknowledge gender within a positivist paradigm without challenging the epistemological basis of that paradigm. So, while public health approaches may well be integrated with some forms of feminism, they are at odds with forms of feminism that challenge the epistemology of positivism.

The dominant perspective on public health approaches to violence prevention is that science is a neutral, non-ideological mechanism for investigating social phenomena. Can positivist research paradigms, within which most public health promotion models are situated, address the complexity of the phenomena of violence against women? Evidence-based practice relies heavily upon experimental forms of knowledge that are located within a positivist scientific paradigm that emphasises experimental research designs. It gives less attention to interactive and local knowledge derived from lived experience and

critical knowledge that is concerned with the influence of social structures and power relations (Raphael and Bryant 2002).

Concepts of evidence and objectivity can be used for emancipatory projects and to demonstrate the prevalence of a social problem.
However, the 'what works' mantra is premised upon a particular set of
assumptions about the nature of knowledge. Such a project assumes
the superiority of experimental knowledge above that of interactive
knowledge from professionals and critical knowledge derived from
sociopolitical analysis (Clegg 2005). Furthermore, when there is a
'strong evidence base' for a particular intervention, it is neglected if it
contradicts dominant ideas and challenges vested interests.

Systematic reviews are a tool of evidence-based practice. The
process of systematic reviews privileges a narrow form of empiricist evidence and excludes or marginalises other forms of knowledge (Clegg
2005). They are premised upon the assumption that knowledge can be
extracted outside of context or social relations. They are a product of
the 'audit culture' that is located within scientific positivism (MacLure
2004). Systematic reviews offer no analysis or interpretation of the
'evidence' and they ignore other forms of knowledge (MacLure 2004).
Cornish (2015) demonstrates that systematic literature reviews decon-
textualise empirical reports. Such reviews restrict the definition of what
constitutes evidence, ignore context and complexity, and aspire to scientific objectivity. Thus, the mantra of 'what works' fails to consider
the social relations and political context of the local site on which the
study was developed.

Conclusion

The public health approach to violence prevention, and the social-
ecological model that underpins it, have enabled implicit feminist
perspectives to be enacted in government and community agendas
and have widened the opportunities for the involvement of men in
anti-violence work. However, the dominance of this framework to the
exclusion of other theoretical perspectives has limited, and in some
cases subverted, progressive analyses and feminist activist work on violence prevention.

A clearer conceptual understanding of violence against women
outside of the public health framing is required. Any conceptual framework that aims to address men's violence against women needs to move

beyond the limitations of the ecological model. Such a framework must emphasise the centrality of gender as relational, enacted, institutionalised and intersected with other social divisions; be theoretically integrated and internally coherent at multiple levels of intervention; specify the main causes of men's violence against women; and emphasise the primacy of structural factors alongside patriarchal ideology, men's peer support for violence against women, the exercise of coercive control in family life and the patriarchal psyche of individual men (see Part Two).

2 | THE LIMITS OF GENDER EQUALITY POLICIES FOR VIOLENCE AGAINST WOMEN PREVENTION

Introduction

The promotion of gender equality has been espoused as an important part of the prevention of violence against women for many years (VicHealth 2007; World Health Organization 2009; Wall 2014; Our Watch 2015; Gracia and Merlo 2016). The expectation has been that as gender inequality (measured by inequalities in employment, salaries and political participation) decreases, violence against women will also decrease. While gender equality is regarded as a key objective of violence against women prevention, it is unclear which aspects of gender equality are most important and also how gender inequality relates to class and race inequality (Wall 2014), as well as status power differentials, cultural practices and misogyny. Understanding the link between gender inequality and men's violence against women will require a multidimensional analysis of what constitutes gender equality.

Interrogating the concept of gender equality

There are different understandings of what gender equality means. The concept of gender equality is complex, and furthermore the links between gender inequality and violence add another level of complexity. While it is generally agreed among feminists that gender inequality is a major source of women's oppression, there is considerable disagreement about the causes of gender inequality (Nooraddini 2012).

Wall (2014) defines gender equality as 'equal rights, opportunities, responsibilities and access to resources' (p. 3). She notes that gender equity is often used interchangeably with gender equality, but in her view the former concept primarily is a pathway towards gender equality. The World Health Organization (2009) defines gender equality as 'Equal treatment of women and men in laws and policies and equal access to resources and services within families, communities and society at large' (p. 3).

Many forms of gender equality are based upon liberal notions of power where it is framed as formal equality before the law. In these instances, gender equality is understood as equality of opportunity, where men and women are seen to have equal rights. This means that gender equality is formulated in gender-neutral terms as non-discrimination. Such an approach is based upon challenging prejudice of individuals rather than addressing social structures that privilege men (Nousiainne et al. 2013). This frame of liberal reform feminism is restricted to realising women's potential within the current structurally unequal gender order (Hearn and Husu 2016).

Treating men and women equally in laws and policies developed by men does not address the subordinate position of women or the privileged position of men. McLellan (2012) argues that anti-discrimination and equal opportunity policies ignore structural inequality between men and women. Where men and women are treated as the same, the wider inequalities built into the system are ignored. For example, domestic violence is seen to take place between equals within a family.

Formal approaches to gender equality in the public sphere do not address gendered inequalities and power in the private realm of the family (Nousiainne et al. 2013). When gender equality is understood in terms of liberal economic and political categories, it limits the framing and ignores the perpetuation of gender inequalities in the private sphere, where much of men's violence against women occurs.

The language of gender equality is often couched in terms of treating men and women equally within a patriarchal framework of gender relations (Dragiewicz 2011). Gelb and Palley (1996) differentiate between 'role equity' and 'role change' policies in their analysis of gender equality policies in the United States. They found that gender equity policies that granted women equal access to privileges available to men were easier to accomplish than those policies that aimed to transform the structural roles of women, because the latter changes required an acknowledgement of patriarchy.

State-based backlash strategies against gender equality have shifted from discriminatory laws to the appropriation of the language of equality. The promotion of formal equality in state policymaking often ignores structural inequalities between men and women (Ferber 2007). Dragiewicz (2008) observes that fathers' rights groups use the language of formal equality to argue that policies should be gender-neutral.

Anti-feminist men's rights groups use the language of 'equal rights' to advance a patriarchal men's agenda (Dragiewicz 2011). Many men's rights advocates proclaim their support for what they call 'equality feminism', which they set up against radical and other feminisms that are seen as women-focused and anti-male (McLellan 2012). If men's rights advocates proclaim their support for equality, the concept may have been corrupted. Concepts of gender and equality can thus be used in support of patriarchal interests.

Hence, it is recognised that the measurement of inequality is contentious and complex. There are conflicts in the definitions and operationalisation of inequality as a concept. Wall (2014) makes the point that we need to be clearer about which dimensions of gender inequality are most important in relation to violence against women. Hunnicutt (2009) suggests that the variability of results in measuring the relationship between gender inequality and violence against women may be due in part to the different ways of measuring gender equality and the limited theorising about patriarchy.

Gender equality tends to be measured primarily by socio-economic indicators. For example, gender inequality is operationalised by Whaley (2001) on the basis of income levels between men and women, levels of labour force participation, gender ratios of executives and managers, and levels of educational attainment. Titterington (2006) draws upon the Gender Equality Index developed by Baron and Strauss (1987), where three dimensions of gender inequality are measured: socio-economic, political and legislative forms of inequality. Gubin (2004) also uses three major dimensions of inequality: inequalities in educational attainment, inequalities in workforce participation and unemployment, and inequalities in political participation, including representation in parliaments.

Bradley and Khor (1993) conceptualise women's inequality as comprising three dimensions: political, economic and social. In their view, all three dimensions are critical in analysing women's status. Furthermore, in this view, all three dimensions have both private and public domains. Htun and Weldon (2010) argue that gender equality requires the transformation of the sexual division of labour where housework and childcare are delegated to primarily to women and where men are expected to assume public responsibilities. Similarly, Hearn and Husu (2016) argue that gender equality should be envisioned beyond political representation and economic participation to include freedom from violence.

The implications of the interrogation of the concept of gender equality for policy is that the structural dimensions of unequal gender relations in both the public and private domains need to be clearly explained when formulating interventions. Otherwise, the equal treatment of men and women, so often referred to in policy documents, will not address the systemic inequalities in the structure of gender relations.

Gender mainstreaming

The major strategy for achieving gender equality has been that of gender mainstreaming (Charlesworth 2000; Flood 2005a; Walby 2005; Squires 2007; Burrell 2014). Gender mainstreaming aims to represent the interests of women through the policymaking machinery of the state (Squires 2007).

Gender mainstreaming arose as a result of a concern that gender was considered only as a problem for women. Rather than focusing on policies relating specifically to women, gender mainstreaming proposed a strategy that would examine gender issues in all policy arenas (Walby 2004). The argument was that if we regard gender to be essentially about women, then we are unable to recognise the relational dimension of gender and the way that institutionally based unequal power relations are reproduced. Men's gender identities are also left unexamined, and are thus seen as natural.

Since gender mainstreaming was adopted by the European Union as the foundation for its gender policies, it has become clear that its impact varies considerably across the different policy domains and between different countries (Walby 2005). As a result of this variance, there is considerable debate about whether gender mainstreaming has furthered the project of gender equality on an international scale (Bacchi 2004).

A number of male writers have also raised the issue of whether gender mainstreaming adequately takes men and masculinities into account, and they advocated the importance of mainstreaming men to ensure that men and masculinities are integrated into gender mainstreaming (Ruxton 2004; Flood 2005a). What does taking men and masculinities into account mean? If gender mainstreaming is to be successful, it means that men's behaviour needs to change. One of the progressive implications of gender mainstreaming is that the project of promoting gender equality becomes the responsibility of men as well as women (Coles 2001). However, there is a concern that the focus on men may shift the debates away from women's interests and a danger that men and women will be treated as facing similar obstacles. Various feminist commentators have argued that there is a gap between the espoused aims of mainstreaming and the reality of its achievements (Charlesworth 2000; Walby 2005; Squires 2007; Repo 2016). In their view, gender equality has been framed in terms of neoliberal economic objectives in relation to market transactions and competition where the focus is more on sex differences between men and women than gendered processes that reproduce patriarchy.

Gender mainstreaming also does not seem to have come to terms with intersectionality. Kantola and Dahl (2005) have suggested that white middle-class working mothers are the women who appear to have benefited most from gender equality policies, resulting in many women being left out. A number of writers have argued that gender equality and gender mainstreaming should not be seen in isolation from other social divisions and that we need to avoid essentialising and homogenising men and women (Walby 2005). Women and men are not homogeneous, and the constitution of gender is shaped by race, class and other forms of inequality.

In Australia, the concept of gender mainstreaming is viewed critically by many women's organisations because it has legitimated the closing down of women's policy units and women-specific services. The rationale was that if gender was mainstreamed, then specific policy units and services concerned with women's interests were no longer needed (Bacchi 2004). We have to locate this development in the context of the election of a conservative Liberal Government in Australia in the 1990s. When then Prime Minister John Howard came to power, he downgraded the existing women's policy machinery (Sawyer 2003) and relocated the Canberra-based Office of the Status of Women from the Prime Minister's Department to the Department of Family and Community Services.

Mainstreaming was not only used to cut women's services; it also legitimated the funding of men's services. In 1999, the then Minister responsible for the Status of Women portfolio allocated $100,000 to the Lone Fathers' Association to set up a refuge for men who were allegedly assaulted by their female partners (Sawyer 2003). In Australia, gender mainstreaming was also used to support the claims of men's rights activists that Australian men were victimised by the Federal Government's Child Support Scheme. It led to a major review of the Child Custody Legislation and resulted in men having equal access to children after separation and divorce even when there was suspicion of violence and abuse. So, in Australia, gender mainstreaming fuelled the men's rights discourse about men as victims and led to a retreat by the Australian government away from gender equality.

The Australian case is worth studying to learn about what not to do. Charlesworth (2000) argues that 'gender mainstreaming [in Australia] has deployed the idea of gender in a very limited way and has allowed the mainstream to tame and deradicalise claims to equality' (p. 2). In her view, gender mainstreaming has constructed a bland and insipid concept of gender that has little potential for social change. She observed in 2000 that there had been little progress towards gender equality after 10 years of gender mainstreaming practice. At the time of writing (2018), this is still the case.

Gender inequality and violence against women

Numerous studies provide empirical support for the feminist thesis that women will experience lower levels of violence in the context of being more equal to men in employment, education and income (Whaley and Messner 2002; Gubin 2004; Yodanis 2004; Titterington 2006). This is known as the ameliorative feminist thesis. Whaley and Messner (2002) also note that greater gender equality reduces the motivation of men to enact all violence, not just violence directed towards women.

In contrast to the ameliorative feminist thesis, a number of feminist writers also posit a backlash thesis in relation to moves towards gender equality (Whaley 2001; Martin et al. 2006; Whaley et al. 2013), where men endeavour to keep women subordinated through violence. There is also empirical support for the backlash thesis (Martin et al. 2006). Moves towards greater gender equality do appear to generate a backlash of violence by men in particular circumstances.

Yodanis (2004) notes differences between women's overall status in society and violence against women and the levels of gender equality at the micro level of intimate relationships. In the latter, there is more evidence of men feeling threatened by their female partner's success and sometimes using physical violence against them to maintain their subordination. Furthermore, sexual violence against women can be a way in which men express their hostility towards women who step outside of traditional female roles (Whaley 2001). In these instances, violence against women results from men's threatened egos (see Chapters 6 and 7).

Many men are likely to perceive a move towards greater gender equality as a threat to their interests and their sense of masculinity, which is founded on gender inequality. As a result, they may enact violence against women as a way of sustaining or doing a form of hegemonic masculinity. Men may resist the loss of their privileges through the expression of hyper-masculinity and the use of violence (Pease 2010).

The empirical research thus demonstrates both positive and negative consequences for women's safety of greater gender equality. The question is: Under what circumstances will greater gender equality *lessen* men's violence against women, and under what circumstances will it lead to *increases* in men's violence against women?

The backlash is seen by some as being a temporary unintended consequence of greater equality for women. Greater levels of gender inequality may lead to increased violence against women as men who are threatened by women's empowerment may use violence to reassert their dominance and control over women. Whaley (2001) argues that backlash violence may occur initially when gender equality measures are achieved but this will reverse as time passes.

There is a paradoxical relationship between gender inequality and violence against women. While discussing rape and sexual violence, Whaley (2001) notes that higher levels of violence against women may have resulted initially from the gains made by women's demands for legal equality. Thus, in the short term at least, greater gender equality is said to lead to higher levels of sexual violence. In positing this link, of course, it should not be interpreted as lessening the demands for gender equality. Rather, it suggests that interventions need to be targeted at men who feel their masculinity is under threat by women's empowerment.

Men's decreased earnings and/or unemployment create hostility for those men who hold traditional gendered attitudes about male dominance (McCloskey 1996). For lower-class men, their frustration and oppression within the class hierarchy may lead to violence against women (Walby 1990). If men lose power over women as a result of reduced power in the public realm, they may resort to physical violence to reassert their dominance.

The backlash hypothesis operates at the micro level of individual families, as well as the wider societal level of increased status of women. If individual men earn less than their female partners, it is hypothesised that they will be more likely to use violence in their relationships than when men have equal or greater income and status compared with their partners (Resko 2014).

Whaley (2001) proposes a refined feminist theory of the links between gender inequality and violence against women that posits a short-term backlash effect and a longer-term ameliorative effect. The refined feminist theory developed by Whaley (2001) and Whaley et al. (2013) demonstrates that these two apparently contradictory consequences can be framed as complementary and form part of an integrated feminist theory of the links between gender inequality and violence against women.

It should be noted that men can use violence against women in the context of high gender inequality with little concern about punitive consequences (Whaley et al. 2013). In this context, men do not need to use physical violence to control women. Legislative discrimination against women, patriarchal gender ideologies, institutionalised male privilege and structural barriers to women's full participation in society provide adequate forms of social control. This is why we need to locate men's violence against women as only one of the myriad ways in which men oppress women (see Chapter 6).

The Nordic ideal and men's violence against women

The Nordic countries (Sweden, Denmark, Norway, Finland and Iceland) are renowned for their espoused state policies of gender equality. Within these countries, women have key leadership roles and senior positions within the state. Over 30 years ago, Hernes (1987) regarded the Scandinavian welfare state as 'women-friendly' to differentiate it from patriarchal states. It was believed that women had attained sufficient political and social power through their involvement with the state that it was now a vehicle to serve women's interests (Kantola and Dahl 2005). However, the concept of 'women-friendly' states in Scandinavia, and the Nordic countries more widely, is not without criticism (Borchorst and Slim 2002; O'Connor 2015).

What can we learn about the links between gender inequality and men's violence against women from the Nordic countries, where gender equality policies are seen as international role models (Lindvert 2002; Eriksson and Pringle 2005; Pringle et al. 2010; Holter 2011)? We cannot, of course, regard all Nordic countries as the same. They all have different histories, different forms of welfare state provisions, different forms of civil society organising and different forms of feminist engagement with the state.

Holter (2011) points out in relation to Norway that while almost 90 per cent of men and women agree that there should be equality between men and women in relation to the division of domestic labour, workforce participation, and income and decision-making in the home, less than 30 per cent share equal responsibility in practice. Similarly, in Sweden, Eriksson and Pringle (2011) note that Sweden is not as uniformly positive for women as we are led to believe, while in the relatively gender-equal society of Finland, Hearn and Niemi (2011) identify that patriarchal practices by men to further their gendered interests prevail in spite of the ideology of gender equality. Clarke (2010) notes that violence against women in Finland is notably higher than in other Nordic countries. In contrast with Sweden, where there is a strong link between domestic violence and gendered practices (Government Offices of Sweden 2016), in Finland domestic violence prevention policies are framed as gender-neutral and are linked to family dynamics and mental health problems (Virkki 2017).

Pringle et al. (2010) note that, notwithstanding the level of legislative gender equality in Nordic countries, men's physical and sexual violence against women remains an endemic problem. Eriksson and Pringle (2005) also observe that in spite of strong ideologies and legislative achievements of gender equality and high levels of women's involvement in the public sphere, men's violence against women and children in Nordic countries remains a major problem that is equal to or greater than other Western countries. In a study carried out among European Union countries, the Nordic countries reported higher levels of violence against women than other member countries (OECD 2017). Nguyen (2014) suggests that one possible reason for these results is that women may feel freer to report such violence because there is less stigma. She also says that increased workforce participation of women may result in higher levels of sexual harassment. However, the high rates of violence against women in Nordic countries alongside high levels of gender equality is often framed as a 'paradox' (Gracia and Merlo 2016).

Lindvert (2002) notes that the focus of gender equality policies in the Nordic countries was on discrimination in public life, and violence against women was neglected as a focus of attention. She observes that the focus of gender equality policies in Sweden, for example, are related to the politics of distribution (of material goods and economic power) as distinct from the politics of recognition (involving cultural domination). Eriksson (2015) also says that the focus of gender equality policies in Nordic countries focuses mainly on women as citizens and workers, with attention given to political participation, labour force involvement, equal pay and shared unpaid work in the home. Less attention is given to women's bodily integrity, and violence against women has not been explicitly addressed until recently.

Kelly (2005), in commenting on the Nordic experience, says that violence against women has relative independence from other dimensions of gender inequality, and therefore must be addressed separately as part of the project of promoting gender equality. Kelly (2005) makes the point that violence against women 'is both a cause and an outcome of women's inequality' (p. 11). The former notion that violence against women is a causal factor and/or a practice in the inequality of women is not as readily acknowledged in the violence prevention literature. In this view, gender equality cannot be attained while men's violence against women still remains. This raises the question about the level of achievement of gender equality in Nordic countries, where violence against women is still prevalent in spite of more traditional equality measures being in place.

It appears as if various forms of gender inequality continue to flourish in the context of espoused gender equality at the governmental level. The notion of gender equality in Finland supports the framing of family violence as a gender-neutral phenomenon (Hearn and McKie 2006). In this context, the idea of a 'women-friendly' welfare state, through the mechanisms of gender neutrality, obscures the role the state plays in perpetuating gender inequalities and violence against women. In Finland, there is little evidence of feminist approaches to men's violence against women at either the policy or professional practice levels. In fact, family violence is framed as being gender-neutral (Kantola 2004; Burrell 2014).

The continuing levels of men's violence against women in the Nordic countries undermines the espoused claims to gender equality. If men's violence against women is flourishing in these so-called 'gender-equal' societies, then it raises questions about the limitations of definitions of what constitutes gender equality. Eriksson and Pringle (2005) point out that patriarchal power persists in the context of progressive gender equality policies. Eriksson (2015) suggests that part of the problem is that these countries are both gender-equal and patriarchal simultaneously. While liberal state-based reforms have implemented legislative gender equality policies in relation to some forms of political and economic equality, men's cultural dominance and control in the private sphere remains.

The Nordic experience indicates the importance of locating men's violence against women and gender inequality in the wider context of patriarchy. It also means that it is important to recognise in violence prevention policies and practice that socio-economic indicators of equality in the public sphere are a necessary but insufficient precondition for the elimination of violence against women.

Engaging with the state

Gender equality and prevention of violence against women are both now widely supported by many governments. This is understood as resulting in part from greater engagement of feminist activism within the state. There is an ongoing debate within feminism about the extent of feminist achievements from their involvement with the state. A number of feminist commentators have argued that feminism has become complicit with neoliberalism as a consequence of its greater engagement with the state (Squires 2007; Bumiller 2008; Fraser 2013; Elomaki 2015). Conceptualising gender equality as equality of opportunity rather than as equality of outcome is an example of this turn to neoliberalism (Hearn and McKie 2010), although it can also be seen as consistent with classical liberalism.

Gender equality has been transformed into a technology of power, in that the emancipatory ends of gender equality initiatives are undermined through forms of neoliberal governmentality (Repo 2016). The language of gender equality has been translated into the notion of rigid gender roles, where the aim is not to eliminate gender roles because they were oppressive to women, but to relax them to allow men and women to perform a wider range of behaviours within them that are consistent with neoliberal policy reforms.

In the 1990s, Pringle and Watson (1990) identified a shift in men's domination from 'private patriarchy' towards 'public patriarchy', which includes the state. It is clear that to address men's violence against women, feminists will need to develop some form of alliance with the state. Such an alliance, labelled by Rankin and Vickers (2001) as 'state feminism', involves 'activities of state structures that are formally charged with furthering women's status and rights' (p. 6).

There are a number of arguments in favour of state feminism. First, feminist policy analysis can highlight how gender relations have become normative and institutionalised within the state. Second, they can deconstruct the ways in which women are represented within state policymaking. Third, they can promote alternative epistemological approaches to challenge objective knowledge claims (Phillips 1996).

All social justice movements face the danger of having their approaches co-opted by the state. To what extent does the feminist project within the state accommodate existing gender regimes and to what extent does it transform traditional gender relations? We must become aware of limitations as well as the potential of using the state to meet women's interests (Bumiller 2008). When women's issues are advanced within institutions of government and government-funded organisations, they are usually framed within already established discourses and frameworks. Thus, we need to critically interrogate the discourses within which feminist policymaking takes place to ensure that they do not accommodate feminist-inspired policy reforms to neo-liberal government priorities.

This question of how the state influenced feminist politics was a key issue in the 1980s and 1990s in Australia, with feminists gaining senior positions within selected policy sites (Franzway et al. 1989; Watson 1990). Questions were asked about the extent to which feminists were forced to compromise and whether their demands had been deradicalised.

It was during this time that the question was raised about whether feminism needed a theory of the state (Allen 1990). So many feminist demands in relation to domestic violence, rape, pornography, abortion, childcare, affirmative action and sexual harassment required policy and legal reforms, and it seems that an explicitly feminist theory of the state was required. In the 1990s, there were various attempts to consider the implications of different theories of the state for feminist practice. Debates were conducted between Marxist feminists who emphasised the class nature of the state and its link to capitalist social relations, radical feminists who framed the state as patriarchal, and liberal feminists who argued that the state was a neutral arbiter between competing interests (Franzway et al. 1989; Watson 1990).

The liberal feminist view that saw the state as a vehicle to advance women's interests and bring about significant changes in gender relations dominated much of the discussion at this time. Other feminist critics argued that this conception of the state led to co-option of feminist demands (Watson 1990). It comes as no surprise that feminists working within government bureaucracies were more likely to support the optimistic view of the state as a neutral arbiter as it legitimated their presence and their practices (Allen 1990).

Equal opportunity and affirmative action reforms within the state have been much criticised by feminists for their relativity problems, posing the question of 'Equality with whom or what?' (Noble and Moore 2006). Is the goal to become equal to the normative male individual? Franzway et al. (1989) argued 30 years ago that the equal opportunity strategy informed by liberal feminism has limited the agenda of the wider women's movement. They also argued that the response of the state to sexual violence has largely been to diffuse more significant demands challenging patriarchal relations. They maintained at that time that the state was unable to deliver gender equality without a transformation of both the state and the wider gender order.

To what extent can the state advance the interests of women? Thirty years ago, it was argued that the state was masculine (Franzway et al. 1989) and that male interests were institutionalised within the state (Witz 1992). The state itself is gendered in that gender is an aspect of the social processes that constitute the state. In this way, the state can *do* gender, just as men do gender. Almost all states of the world are controlled by men. It is thus argued that the state acts on behalf of men and predominantly serves men's interests.

In Walby's (1990) view, the state is one of the structures of patriarchy. While she does not regard the state as monolithic, as it is a site of political struggle, it is biased towards men's interests. Patriarchal assumptions are embedded within state policies and practices. Consequently, it is more likely to maintain the patriarchal gender order than address the structural changes necessary to eliminate men's violence against women. Walker (1990) draws upon Dorothy Smith's institutional ethnography to interrogate the state as a form of relations of ruling. She identifies the ways in which the practices of ruling enable the state to sanction some forms of violence within the military and the police, while espousing policies against other forms of violence.

Although there was ongoing engagement with the state from the 1970s to the 1990s, there has been very little theorising of the state since then. Has anything substantially changed? More recently, Costello (2009), through a detailed analysis of the Australia Says No anti-violence campaign, demonstrated how the then Howard Coalition Government co-opted feminist ideas and practices and converted them into vehicles of domination. Although the state appeared to be responsive to feminist concerns, it did so in a way that undermined the key feminist principles and theories. Government reports consistently used ungendered language and focused on 'family' violence to the exclusion of other forms of violence against women. Violence against women was constructed primarily as a problem of dysfunctional families and pathological individual men. Similarly, in Canada, non-threatening language describing violence as gender-neutral was used by state policy makers to achieve short-term gains at the expense of a gendered analysis (Collier 2012).

One of the ways in which the state influences the problematisation of violence against women is through the transformation of men's violence into a legal, medical and social problem involving the creation of professional languages to intervene in rape and domestic violence. Such professional language rationalises violence against women as a problem that can be measured and treated rather than as a socio-political problem that is at the heart of patriarchy. The effects of men's violence are transformed into treatable symptoms that can be managed by human service professionals (Bumiller 2008). Women's services have become more professionalised and moved away from grassroots organising and consciousness-raising. State funding of non-governmental organisations has placed these services within the 'terrain of the state' (Reinelt 1995).

Bumiller (2008) questions about how much we can trust the state to address men's violence when state-sponsored violence is escalating. She believes that the growth of neoliberalism has increased concerns about whether the state can advance the interests of women, arguing that the contemporary feminist alliance with the state has taken place within the neoliberal project of social control. Fraser (2009) also argues that neoliberalism has incorporated feminism into the state by being complicit in the neoliberal project. The neoliberal state promoted liberalism within feminism by promising women increased autonomy, greater choice and meritocratic advancement.

Kantola and Squires (2012) note that there has been a shift from state feminism to market feminism, where public policies are shaped increasingly more by the neoliberal economic market. This has meant that gender equality has become reframed by forms of rational empiricism, evidence-based practice and a categorical understanding of gender as sex category differences between men and women.

Conclusion

Women's policy work within the state reflects the priorities of the government of the day, which is focused more on technical expertise within existing policy frames than on the interests of women. Such policy work seems to be more accountable to government bureaucracy than to women's movements in civil society (Squires 2007). There is an ongoing tension between 'feminism from above', where state-based gender equality reforms are implemented by welfare state professionals, and 'feminism from below', where grassroots activist women are mobilised through social movements to make demands on the state (Borchorst and Siim 2008).

Kivel (2007) notes that even with good intentions, it is all too easy to be co-opted by the agenda of dominant groups. The process of co-option can be so smooth and subtle that we do not recognise how our allegiances have shifted. Individual actions from within can be important, in that we can accept or reject the agenda of the state. However, how do we know when we have been co-opted? Ultimately, we cannot trust our own perceptions of whether our practice is serving the gender interests of women, and consequently we must ensure that we build in processes of accountability to women's groups that are external to the state to ensure that we are held accountable.

When Htun and Weldon (2012) undertook a comparative analysis of policies addressing violence against women across 10 countries, they found that autonomous women's movements were more important than women in government in advancing the interests of women. Thus, if policy change towards gender equality is to be effective, it must be located within the context of strong, autonomous women's movements that are applying ongoing pressure on the state. This analysis provides support for the view that autonomous women's movements are the main drivers of policy change because they generate ideas that are outside the discourses of a neoliberal state.

While radical feminist analyses of men's violence that emphasise the necessity of dismantling patriarchy and achieving equality between men and women can be criticised for not developing practical interventions in the immediate term (Gavey 2005), it is important to maintain political discourses about men's violence against women outside of the state framework to ensure that community education programs and law reforms do not individualise and decontexualise what is a systemic problem rooted in patriarchy (Gotell 2010). While we have to make political compromises to achieve practical outcomes, we must continue to be reflexive about the political implications of the reforms and practices we advocate.

PART TWO

LOCATING MEN'S VIOLENCE AGAINST WOMEN WITHIN THE PILLARS OF PATRIARCHY

3 | TRANSNATIONAL AND INTERSECTIONAL STRUCTURES OF PATRIARCHY

Introduction

One of the objectives of this book is to bring the concept of patriarchy back into our lexicon for addressing men's violence against women. We cannot understand men's violence against women outside an understanding of patriarchy. While the focus of this chapter is on patriarchy as a structural formation, it also has ideological and discursive dimensions (see Chapter 4). The theoretical framework advocated in this book is that patriarchy is manifested at structural/material and cultural/discursive levels of social organisation. Materialist analyses of patriarchy are often presented as antagonistic to post-structural analyses because they underplay the role of language, culture and discourse in reproducing men's dominance. I agree with Hearn (2014a) that post-structural critical theories can enhance materialism rather than negate it. Culture and discourse reproduce and constitute patriarchal structural arrangements.

Patriarchy also functions at the levels of homosocial bonding among men, in interpersonal relationships between men and women, and in the identities and subjectivities of individual men and women (see Chapters 5, 6 and 7). The ideological level of patriarchy naturalises male supremacy and shapes the ways in which men internalise gender domination in their psyches. Macro and micro patriarchal systems are symbiotically connected. Consequently, we cannot understand interpersonal gender dynamics outside the macro-level gender order (Hunnicutt 2009). Patriarchy and male dominance are best understood through the levels of the material world, discourse, homosociality, interactional dynamics and the psyche.

Bringing patriarchy back into the frame

The literal meaning of the word 'patriarchy' is rule of the father, and it was originally used to describe a specific type of male-dominated family form (Sultana 2010/2011). However, the term has been expanded to encompass men's dominance in the public as well as the private sphere, and is generally used to refer to unequal social relations between men and women. The concept of patriarchy has been used as an 'umbrella' term for describing men's systemic dominance of women.

Millett (1972) was one of the first feminists to use the term to describe the unequal relations of power between men and women. Her focus was on ideology and psychic structures, which she believed provided the bedrock of patriarchal social relations. Walby (1990) describes patriarchy as 'a system of social structures and practices through which men dominate, oppress and exploit women' (p. 20), and Ramazanoglu (1989) similarly calls it 'a concept used to attempt to grasp the mechanisms by which men manage to dominate women in general' (p. 34).

For Marxist feminists, patriarchy is a reflection of the structures governing economic production. Family and gender relations are seen as sites where the relations of production are produced and reproduced. Marxist feminists focus on the ways in which male dominance benefits capitalism as 'the material base upon which patriarchy rests lies most fundamentally in men's control over women's labour' (Hartmann 1981a: 15).

Radical feminists, in contrast, point out that Marxists ignore the centrality of male power in the oppression of women. Rather than seeing gender dominance as arising from economically unequal relations, it is considered to be the primary source of oppression and men's power over women and is regarded as the most basic and important organising principle of social life (Firestone 1971).

There are also historical debates about the extent to which capitalism and patriarchy are two interacting systems. In dual systems theory, they are regarded as parallel and autonomous systems of social relations that sometimes meet and intersect. In patriarchal capitalism (Hartmann 1981a) or capitalist patriarchy (Eisenstein 1979), they form a unity.

Contesting the concept of patriarchy

The concept of patriarchy is heavily contested. Hunnicutt (2009) identifies five major criticisms: that it oversimplifies power relations; that it implies a false universalism between women and men; that it ignores differences among men; that it cannot account for violence by men against men; and that it cannot account for women's violence. I now interrogate these critiques.

Patriarchy was seen by some writers to imply a timeless and universal structure that reduces gender relations into only one form. It is presented as being too simple to explain a complex world (Bryson 1999). Barrett (1980) criticised it for being fixed and unchanging, suggesting a transhistorical and universal oppression. Thus, it is said to neglect cultural specificity and multiple oppressions related to class, race and ethnicity (Acker 1989).

The concept of patriarchy has thus been widely criticised for presenting an overly simplistic view of male domination, as being universal and insufficiently aware of cultural differences and diversity within genders. Further, it is claimed that its universalistic claims are based on the experiences of white middle-class Western women (Bryson 1999).

Some feminist writers have critiqued patriarchy for being ahistorical. Rowbotham (1981), for example, rejected it because of its biological connotations and the suggestion that male dominance was unitary and unchanging. Whitehead (2007) similarly expresses reservations about the concept because he says that it implies a static and fixed state of women's oppression rather than recognising the extent to which male dominance is fluid and changing. He believes that patriarchy does not acknowledge feminist achievements and advances towards gender equality and does not capture the complexity of men's dominance over women.

Implicit in some theories of patriarchy was the notion that male dominance and masculinity were reflections of each other, where all men are seen as a generic gender class with the same vested interests in controlling women. Such analyses *are* biologically and structurally determinist and the political prognosis is pessimistic. If all men are the enemy, then it would be difficult to envisage the possibility of men and women working together against patriarchy (Edley and Wetherell 1995).

It is claimed by some critics that the concept of patriarchy only focuses on the macrostructural level and ignores human agency and women's resistance (Pollert 1996). Employing the concept of patriarchy does not mean to imply that women lack agency or that all women are subject to men's power in the same way, as some critics argue (de Boise 2013). While the structures and discourses of patriarchy are deeply embedded, they are amenable to change (Edstrom et al. 2014).

Many feminists acknowledge that patriarchy is not monolithic and that it contains contradictions (Rahman 2007). Patriarchy is not fixed, as its form changes and different aspects of it have greater or lesser significance in different contexts (Walby 1990). Patriarchy is best understood as a historical structure with changing dynamics, and it needs to be seen as involving the intersection of numerous factors and multiple levels of experience.

Understanding men's violence in the context of patriarchy

Historically, feminists have argued that violence against women is a reflection of patriarchal structures that subordinate and oppress women. Dobash and Dobash (1979) published a landmark book on men's violence against women in the context of patriarchy in the late 1970s. They argued that to eliminate men's violence against women, we must first understand it and then encourage men to own it and address it. To do so requires us to understand the society in which it occurs and how certain cultural patterns and institutional practices reproduce it. For them, this means that we have to mount a struggle against patriarchy and the ideologies, subjectivities and practices that support it. To reduce men's violence against women, we must address women's subordination to men and transform the gendered inequalities in both personal and public life.

O'Toole and Schiffman (1997) understand violence against women as 'a logical output of the imbalance of power between men and women' (p. viii). Hayward (1999) argues that 'the major cause of violence against women and girls is the unequal role and relationships between men and women' (p. 2), where men actively assert their superiority against women in both the public and private spheres. Itzin (2000) identifies the most significant contribution of feminism to the domestic violence field has been to 'conceptualise this as a problem of men's violence in the context of social power relations gendered in terms of male dominance and female subordination' (p. 360).

Collier (1995) says that this means we must address 'the legal structures of women's dependent position in the household and the ways in which male authority within the family continues to be constituted through naturalised discourse of masculinity' (p. 251). Patriarchy is also manifested in the public realms of paid work, politics, the media and other sites where these social dynamics are enacted. This clearly implies the need for fundamental structural change. To effectively address the problem of men's violence, and coercive control and sexism more generally, we need to bring about change in the patriarchal arrangements of society that reinforce the violence and abuse. Feminist analyses thus emphasise the importance of changes in the social relations of dominance and subordination 'as necessary preconditions for any change in the incidences of wife abuse' (Warters 1992: 9).

Pushing back against naming patriarchy as a cause of men's violence

Those who are antagonistic to feminist analyses argue that the concept of patriarchy does not explain men's violence against women (Dutton 1994; Cunningham et al. 1998; Goldner 1999; Watson 2001; Dutton 2006). Goldner (1999) argues that feminist theories cannot account for why such a small percentage of men are physically violent towards their female partners. Similarly, Russell and Jory (1997) maintain 'that attributing men's abuse of women to the patriarchal structure of society fails to account for why only some men batter their partners' (p. 126). Of course, as noted in Chapter 6, these critiques fail to acknowledge how most, if not all, men engage in various forms of everyday sexism and control, and that all men benefit from patriarchal gender relations. Not all men need to be violent for patriarchal power to be enacted.

Lenton (1995) says that 'any theory based entirely on gender inequality is nevertheless bound to be inadequate because it is not able to deal effectively with several observations of family violence research' (p. 11), which focuses on interactional dynamics between men and women. Goldner (1999) similarly argues to focus solely 'on power and inequality misses crucial elements of the relational bond' (p. 1), which in the view of family violence researchers has its origins in attachment theory.

Dutton (1994) dismisses patriarchy as a single-factor explanation for men's violence against women. He argues that if patriarchy is the cause of men's violence, then individual men cannot be held responsible for being violent. He further argues that the concept of patriarchy is unable to explain women's violence or why individual men commit violence against women. Dutton does not understand the multiple dimensions of patriarchy noted earlier, and how they are enacted through interactional dynamics between men and women and situated within individual men's subjectivities (see Chapters 6 and 7).

Heise (1998), although feminist-supportive, similarly argues that feminism proposes a single-factor explanation and is unable to explain why only a minority of men are violent towards women. Tracy (2007) also uses the statistic of only a minority of men using physical violence against women as a form of evidence against the feminist analysis that violence against women is a result of patriarchy. In Tracy's view, the feminist analysis of patriarchy only applies to non-Western cultures, which he accepts may be patriarchal. He argues that because women in the Western world have more power than before, there must be other explanations for men's violence that have nothing to do with patriarchy.

In many of the representations of feminist theory among these critics, patriarchy is presented as though it was a monolithic and static institution, whereby all men oppress all women. For example, Cunningham et al. (1998) criticise feminist explanations of men's violence resulting from patriarchy as being 'unidimensional' and 'fixed'. However, such representations do not acknowledge the contested nature of the concept of patriarchy within feminist theory and the more complex dynamic theories of male dominance.

Many of the critics of feminist views of patriarchy being the main cause of men's violence against women only understand patriarchy at either a macrostructural level or at an attitudinal level (Dutton 1994; Heise 1998; Watson 2001; Dutton 2006; Corvo and Johnson 2010). Also, contemporary feminist theories of patriarchy do not suggest that all men who are violent towards women necessarily do so consciously to maintain male privilege (McKee 2014). Furthermore, most men do not have to resort to physical violence to maintain their power and control over women. Also, many men who are violent to their intimate partners do so because they *lack* power in the wider society. Thus, their violence is not a way of *maintaining* power and control over their partner, but as a way of *gaining* a sense of power and control (Websdale 2010).

As mentioned earlier, patriarchy operates on multiple levels and exists structurally, ideologically, homosocially, interpersonally and individually. Thus, patriarchy is implicated in globalisation, imperialism, unemployment and class deprivation, social norms and community attitudes, male peer support, and intimate relationships between men and women. These multiple influences on men's violence against women do not disprove the causal explanation of patriarchy, but are rather manifestations of it.

Differentiating multiple structures of patriarchy

Walby (1990) identified six structures of patriarchy for analysing different forms of gender inequality: households (where women's household labour is exploited by husbands and male partners); paid work (where women are excluded from high-status jobs, receive less pay and are often employed in segregated sections of the labour force); the state (where there is a systematic bias in favour of men's interests); male violence (which is legitimated by the state); sexuality (where compulsory heterosexuality and sexual double standards reign); and cultural institutions (which represent women in negative ways in the media, religion and education). In Walby's (1990) account of multiple structures of patriarchy, the elimination of any one structure will not lead to the end of patriarchy as a social formation. Furthermore, she argues that men's violence against women will persist as long as society is framed by gender inequality in each of these structures.

Walby (1990) refers to forms of control beyond the family as public patriarchy and an individual man controlling a woman in the private realm of the family as private patriarchy. Similarly, DeKeseredy and Schwartz (2013) differentiate between social patriarchy involving men's domination at the societal level and familial patriarchy, which refers to men's control of women in domestic settings. Ogle and Batton (2009) also differentiate between two components of patriarchy: institutionalised male domination, where male power is embedded in social structures, and interpersonal male domination, whereby men exercise power over women individually and collectively.

These two levels of patriarchy are interconnected, and the interpersonal dynamics of men and women need to be considered in the macro-level gender order. Much interrogation of gender power at the family level focuses on the interpersonal dynamics of men in relation to women outside of the patriarchal power structures in the wider society within which men and women are embedded. Thus, while patriarchy operates at the structural level of government, law and bureaucracy, it also focuses on the interpersonal level of interactions between men and women (Hunnicutt 2009). Furthermore, it is reproduced by the practices of individual men (Ogle and Batton 2009).

Johnson (1997) describes three dimensions of patriarchy: male-dominated, male-identified and male-centred. Male-dominated refers to men's authority and control over the major social, political and economic, religious, legal, and military institutions. Male-identified refers to the cultural ideals about good, normal and desirable forms of masculinity and the various ways in which women are devalued in society. Male-centred refers to the way in which men's experiences come to represent human experience more generally.

Greig (2012) identifies four levels of gender power under patriarchy: internal, interpersonal, ideological and institutional. As noted earlier, I add a fifth level to that framework, the homosocial bonding between men. There is considerable evidence that men's male friends provide peer support for men's violence (see Chapter 5). Research evidence demonstrates that there is strong peer support for men using violence to control women. This includes both family and friendship networks as well as the wider community and cultural context in which violence is practiced. While anti-violence advocates promote a prescriptive message of the unacceptability of men's violence against women, these messages compete with imperatives among men to maintain male supremacy and male entitlement, which support men's violence against women (Dragiewicz 2011).

Hunnicutt (2009) advances a nuanced conceptualisation of patriarchy that accounts for a variety of patriarchal structures, understands how men are also situated in hierarchies with other men, acknowledges that patriarchal ideologies may continue even when greater gender equality has been achieved, and recognises other forms of hierarchy. She identifies patriarchy as operating at multiple levels, including the macro level of structures of government, law and the market, the micro level of family and intimate relations, and the intra-psychic level of being embedded within individual men. These multiple levels are in symbiotic relation to each other. Dragiewicz (2011) similarly identifies the cultural level where patriarchal ideologies define dominant gender norms, the community level reflected in discriminatory laws, the interpersonal level of family and the division of labour in the home, and friendship relations between men where there is often peer support for men's violence against women.

Intersectionalising patriarchy

Early formulations of patriarchy did not give sufficient attention to inequalities between men in relation to class, race, sexuality and other social divisions. These theories often assumed a generalised view of men as all being white, heterosexual and middle to upper class (de Boise 2013). Any analysis of patriarchy must include an understanding of the intersections of gender with other social divisions.

While some privileged white women may have failed to grasp the experiences of oppression of women based on class and race, this is not necessarily a limitation of patriarchy, but rather the way in which patriarchy has been selectively employed by some women (Bryson 1999). Many feminists have embraced intersectionality and multiracial perspectives on women's oppression, noting that men and women experience patriarchy in different ways depending upon their class location and racial positioning.

Patriarchy can elucidate a multiplicity of variations in gender relations within a diversity of patriarchal systems. It can encompass an analysis of cross-cutting intersections of class, race, age and so on. Patriarchy is part of what Collins (2000) calls the 'matrix of domination', where it intersects with class, race and other social divisions. Thus, more nuanced conceptions of patriarchy have been developed that acknowledge the multiple sites of domination and oppression within patriarchy (Hearn 2009).

Hunnicutt (2009) also notes that patriarchy is linked with other systems of inequality and must be theorised in relation to other social hierarchies such as race, ethnicity, class, age, sexuality and geopolitical location. Even back in Walby's (1990) account over 25 years ago, the importance of understanding the different forms of gender inequality across different ethnic and class groups was emphasised. Hence, any theory of patriarchy must recognise the specific forms that are defined by different cultures and different historical times. This also entails understanding how racist, heterosexist and classist ideologies and practices perpetuate men's social dominance and their violence against women.

Hearn (2012a) talks about intersectional gender structures as a way of noting the links between gender and other social divisions. Acker (2009) uses the notion of inequality regimes to describe the intersectional gender barriers that produce patterns of inequality. For her, inequality regimes capture the intersections of gender, class and race that inhibit women's advancement towards gender equality. The concept of inequality regimes analyses the ways in which class, race and ethnicity intersect with gender to create inequalities at the level of institutions and organisations. If we focus only on gender imbalance in upper-level positions or gender-based pay inequalities, we will not address the class-based inequalities and other social divisions that impact on many women.

To address women's disadvantage and discrimination, it requires not only policies addressing women's position relative to men, but also the differences and inequalities among women (Htun and Weldon 2010).

Vieratis and Williams (2002) note that most gender equality research assumes that women are a homogeneous group, and consequently it ignores the intersection of gender and race. Their empirical research in the United States demonstrates different consequences for white women of greater gender equality when compared to the experiences of black women.

Legislative equality may be less significant for women with limited financial resources (Titterington 2006). Class and other forms of marginalisation are important to consider because low-income or no-income women have less opportunity to leave a violent relationship (Hunnicutt 2009). It is clear that the causes and impact of violence on women will vary depending upon their class, race, religion, age, ability/disability and other forms of social difference. Women are located in multiple systems of inequality.

The implications for violence prevention policy and practice are that the intersections between gender and other social divisions need to be clearly explicated so that gender is understood as being filtered through men's and women's other social locations.

Globalising patriarchy

Some of the earlier work on patriarchy ignored geographically specific forms of gendered power and the relationship between territorial boundaries within transnational and global processes (Mohanty 1984). As a number of writers have identified, patriarchy is now a global phenomenon (Eisenstein 1998; Hearn 2009; Patil 2013; Ortner 2014; Connell 2016).

To understand patriarchy, we need to locate the global dimensions of men's gendered power. Connell (2016) identifies four powerful groups of men who replicate patriarchy on the world scale: owners and managers of transnational corporations such as the World Bank; oligarchs who possess extreme levels of wealth; military and political dictators of authoritarian countries; and elites within neoliberal governments in the Global North. This means that to address the global dimensions of patriarchy, we need to explore the links between patriarchy, the capitalist world order, and nation, class and race.

Eisenstein (1998) identifies how transnational globalism creates new forms of patriarchal privilege. She uses the language of 'transnational capitalist patriarchy' to describe forms of global patriarchy.

Hearn (2009) uses the concept of trans-patriarchy to move our analysis beyond the boundaries of a particular culture or country and to incorporate transnationalisation and intersectionalities into our analysis. The concept of trans-patriarchy enables us to identify the global dimensions of men's dominance that constitute a world gender order (Hearn 2015).

It is more useful to refer to patriarchies in the plural to acknowledge the culturally specific forms that arise from different regions of the world and in relation to different forms of oppression (Hearn 1992). Talking about patriarchies in the plural enables us to identify the importance of locating patriarchy transnationally and to move the analysis beyond national and cultural contexts. Hearn (2009) also argues that patriarchy takes on multiple forms within transnational patriarchies and advocates the use of intersectionality analyses to interrogate the different levels of power within gendered hierarchies.

It is important to acknowledge that this book is located in the hegemonic North, and consequently it is positioned within one of the most powerful regions in the world. The interrogation of patriarchy and the violences of men in this book is mainly focused on Western societies. As patriarchy takes different forms in non-Western societies, the forms of men's dominance may differ. A more global analysis of these various forms of gender inequality has yet to be undertaken.

Whither patriarchy?

We do not talk much about patriarchy any more. Many men experience the language of patriarchy as being offensive. However, McCaffrey (2012) makes the point that terms that are less offensive to men are unlikely to challenge men's privilege. While the language of patriarchy may make many men uncomfortable, men's responses should, of course, not be a key determinant of the utility of such terms.

Many men experience any discussion of patriarchy as a form of 'male-bashing' or blaming all men for the violence of a few. However, the argument of this book is that all men are implicated in patriarchy, whether they consciously defend and support it or not (see Chapter 11). This is not to suggest that all men gain equally from what Connell (2005) calls the patriarchal dividend. Many marginalised and subordinated men may receive little of the privileges associated with patriarchy. Furthermore, as many feminists acknowledge, women may also collude with patriarchy through their conscious support of it and through their child-raising practices with their daughters and sons (Bennett 2006). Women are not passive victims of patriarchy. They often negotiate what Kandiyoti (1988) calls 'patriarchal bargains' as they strategise to resist and accommodate to their oppression.

Lerner (1986) has usefully undertaken a historical analysis of patriarchal systems that are socially constructed by both men and women. In her view, patriarchies can only survive through the compliance of women, whether this be through indoctrination, misinformation or coercion and violence. Thus, women's subordination under patriarchy is reproduced by their accommodation to men's domination.

Because the concept of patriarchy has been derailed by criticism from within and outside of feminism, men's domination and women's subordination have had to be presented in disguised language (Hunnicutt 2009). The concept of patriarchy has been replaced by terms such as gender, gender relations, sexism, gender regimes, gender inequality and so on. Even Walby (2011), who has done so much to advance contemporary theorising about patriarchy, now prefers to use the language of gender regimes to describe the macro-level gender institutions and micro-level gender relations that constitute the social structure of gender. She notes that gender regimes mean the same as patriarchy, but she no longer uses that term because it is too often misinterpreted as essentialist, ahistorical and reductionist. However, these alternative terms fail to explicitly convey the notion that men are the dominant and privileged group. Also, this disguised language does not enable us to understand the links between various levels of patriarchy and men's violence against women.

Notwithstanding the criticisms, I argue that the concept of patriarchy is still useful to describe men's systemic dominance over women across a wide range of social institutions and gendered sites. The benefit in continuing to use the term 'patriarchy' is that it focuses attention on the systemic and global nature of women's subordination, and it provides a framework for identifying the privileges and advantages accruing to men as a result of their dominance.

Further, it is important to resurrect the concept of patriarchy to address co-optation of gender and gender analysis under neoliberalism. Campbell (2014) argues that the government focus on gender equality through new laws on equal pay, marital status, sexuality and reproduction constitutes a form of neoliberal patriarchy, as the sexual division of labour in the home and men's violence against women have continued in spite of any other gains for women that have been achieved. Even Acker (1989), one of the feminist critics of the concept of patriarchy in the 1980s, expressed concern about abandoning the concept of patriarchy for gender, as the political and critical sharpness that it conferred may be lost and feminist theoretical analyses may be co-opted and assimilated into mainstream theories and politics. I believe this is now the case.

Conclusion

The concept of patriarchy continues to be a useful way of analysing the various forms of men's power and dominance over women. It is necessary if we are to understand the multiple dimensions of men's dominance across various levels of gender hierarchy. Patriarchy is still a valuable way of describing the oppression of women by men, in both interpersonal relations and through the discriminatory practices and policies of public institutions. Patriarchy continues to be useful to interrogate the various structural forms of men's gendered power (Hearn 2009). The concept of patriarchy also enables us to maintain a focus on understanding how individual violent men are influenced by wider social structures. The term can also help us to avoid the danger of 'phallic drift', where gender issues revert back to the traditional male viewpoint (Sandroff 1994).

This analysis can take into account a diversity of patriarchal structures, differentiate between structure and ideology, and acknowledge other forms of domination and oppression. We need frameworks that enable us to link the wider structural and cultural dimensions of patriarchy to the experiences and practices of individual men. This is in part what this book sets out to achieve.

Concepts matter; they enable us to understand the world and our place within it. Concepts provide us with analytical tools to galvanise us to take action against sources of injustice (Enloe 2017). Miller (2017) argues that patriarchy is a lens through which to understand and frame various forms of gendered inequality. I argue that patriarchy has value both as an analytical concept and as a description of particular unequal gender orders and the social relations within them.

If the problem of women's oppression has no name, it can easily be colonised by traditional categories of political thought. When feminist ideas do not flourish, patriarchy is less likely to be acknowledged.

Thus, if feminist ideas are discredited, patriarchy is more likely to be invisible (Enloe 2017). However, if we promote the view that patriarchy does not exist, we reproduce it.

Consequently, any struggle for gender equality and the elimination of men's violence against women must also involve the undoing of patriarchy. Rather than jettisoning the concept, we should explore its usefulness in increasing awareness of men's power and privilege within structurally based and individually experienced gender relations. Because patriarchy is a historical construction, it can be transformed. With the links between patriarchy and militarism and ecological destruction (see Chapters 9 and 10), the survival of the planet may well be at stake if we cannot break free of patriarchal world views. Any effective interventions against the violences of men will need to transform patriarchal gender relations and abolish patriarchal privileges.

4 | PATRIARCHAL IDEOLOGY AND HEGEMONIC GENDER BELIEFS

Introduction

The concept of patriarchal ideology was first framed by Kate Millett (1972), who understood it as a justification of men's domination. She and others noted that changes in the structural relations of patriarchy may not necessarily lead to changes in the ideological dimensions of patriarchy. At the same time, in arguing that psychic structures constitute the basis of patriarchy, Millett can be accused of foregrounding ideological phenomena to the exclusion of social structures.

Juliet Mitchell (1974) also argued that patriarchy has an ideological dimension, and emphasised the importance of understanding women's oppression as psychological and cultural terms as well as in material terms. Mitchell, however, also regarded the ideological mode of patriarchy as autonomous and separated from the economic mode of capitalist society. She did not see a connection between the ideological dimensions of patriarchy and the material conditions of women's and men's lives.

In more contemporary feminist writing, Yodanis (2004) differentiates between the structural dimensions of inequality involving women's access to institutional positions of power and authority and ideological beliefs about the status of women. Thus, it may be more useful to refer to traditional gender role attitudes as 'hegemonic beliefs' (Ridgeway and Correll 2004). Such beliefs are not only held by individuals, but are also institutionalised in the structures and ideologies of public institutions. That is, they are embedded in organisations, laws and practices, and thus reproduce gender inequality and men's dominance. As Johnson (1997) notes, patriarchal societies are not only structurally dominated by men; they are also male-centred and male-identified.

Hunnicutt (2009) similarly discusses the differences between the structural conditions of patriarchy and patriarchal ideologies, which she says can often continue after gender equality has been achieved. Drawing upon the work of socialist feminists, she argues that the matrix of domination is such that structural changes towards gender equality may not necessarily lead to a lessening of patriarchal ideologies among men. Structural inequality is thus only one feature of patriarchy, and attention must be directed at patriarchal ideologies as well. This means that social change movements must address both structural and ideological dimensions of patriarchy simultaneously. While changing structural relations will modify patriarchal beliefs about gender and gender inequality, the core structure of beliefs may remain intact even in the context of increasing gender equality at the structural level (Ridgeway and Correll 2004).

McKee (2014) differentiates between institutional and individual levels of patriarchal ideology. Individual-level patriarchal ideology refers to values, attitudes and beliefs that are embedded within individuals. Such a notion overlaps with the concept of hegemonic masculinity and sex and gender role ideologies. Hegemonic masculinity is one of the ways in which patriarchal ideology is sustained. The concept of hegemonic masculinity acknowledges that patriarchal domination is not only structural. Patriarchal ideologies reproduce patriarchal structures and social relations. Furthermore, the discourse of hegemonic masculinity values all forms of masculinity over femininity and legitimates men's gender dominance. Hence, the internalisation of traditional masculinity plays a significant role in promoting men's violence against women. Men adapt to the gendered expectations through their engagement with a patriarchal culture (see Chapter 7).

Misframing patriarchal ideology and hegemonic beliefs as social attitudes

In the mainstream violence prevention literature, the construct of 'attitudes' is used to explain the ways that cultural support for gender inequality and violence against women is manifested. Numerous empirical studies indicate a link between sexist attitudes by men and the likelihood of engaging in violence against women (Pease and Flood 2008; Flood and Pease 2009; York 2011; Diemer 2014; Harris et al. 2015). Consequently, various attempts have been made to measure community attitudes about violence towards women through opinion polls and attitude scales such as the gender equality scale (Singh et al. 2018).

In most community attitudes research, people are categorised into two groups: patriarchal individuals who support men's domination of women, and egalitarians or feminist-supportive individuals (Herzog 2007). However, such classifications fail to capture negative attitudes towards women that are expressed in more socially acceptable forms. Herzog argues that openly hostile and negative attitudes towards women have become stigmatised. Rather than being replaced with egalitarian attitudes, sexism remains in the form of benevolent attitudes that still view women as inferior to men. Such attitudes, Herzog argues, support patriarchy in the same way that hostile attitudes towards women do.

Glick and Fiske (2001) also argue that traditional gender role attitudes are both hostile and benevolent in relation to women. While hostile sexism involves an antipathy towards women, benevolent sexism involves chivalry and protection of women who adopt traditional female roles. Benevolent sexism is also a form of prejudice, and as such legitimates gender inequality and men's privilege. Barreto and Ellemers (2005) suggest that benevolent forms of sexism must be addressed in the project of promoting gender equality. However, they also note that such sexist prejudice is likely to be more difficult to change.

Benevolent attitudes by men about women may involve protective elements that may inhibit violence towards women. Allen et al. (2009) found that men who held benevolent sexist attitudes were less likely to perpetrate violence against women than men with less benevolent attitudes. Furthermore, women who conform to men's sexist expectations of them were less likely to experience violence than those women who challenge traditional gender roles, which evoke hostile responses by men. Women who accept a subordinate status placate men.

There is a risk that such research can be seen as encouraging women's greater acceptance of traditional gender roles to avoid men's violence. Within the wider patriarchal ideology, women who challenge men's sexism can be blamed by sexist men for their partner's violence. However, what this research illustrates is the importance of targeting patriarchal attitudes about women that are internalised by men.

In an earlier publication (Pease and Flood 2008), Flood and I interrogated the concept of attitudes. We noted that the construct of attitude is located in the disciplinary field of social psychology in which a purportedly scientific study of attitudes involves an investigation of the factors influencing how they are formed and changed, and how they are translated into motivation and behaviour. We noted also that attitude theory is premised upon understandings of the intra-psychic world, as emphasised in cognitive psychology, where attitudes are seen as underlying mental constructs.

Unlike the concept of ideology, which has moral connotations and suggests an imperative towards social change, the language of social attitudes and norms has a morally neutral tone. Also, while ideology is a sociopolitical framework that focuses on individuals' membership of social groups, societal attitudes are regarded as individual attributes. From a psychological perspective, attitudes are only social because they are seen as individual responses to social stimuli. Thus, social phenomena such as collective values are reduced to the behaviour of individuals, whereas an understanding of ideology is more concerned with how individual character is shaped by material conditions and social consciousness (Pease and Flood 2008).

From social attitudes to social norms

Social norms are seen to both perpetuate gender inequalities and promote violence against women (Paluck and Ball 2010; Jewkes et al. 2015a). In Mackie et al.'s (2015) view, social norms are one of the major causes of violence against women. Ozaki and Otis (2017) demonstrate how cultural contexts with high levels of patriarchal values contribute significantly to men's violence against women. They argue that patriarchy and men's violence against women are sustained through the ongoing presence of patriarchal social norms.

But what exactly are social norms? Mackie et al. (2015) define social norms as 'what people in a group believe to be typical and appropriate action in that group' (p. 10). The World Health Organization (2009) defines oppressive gender norms as involving beliefs about masculinity, violence and the acceptability of violence within intimate relationships. Connell and Pearse (2014) talk about norms as involving attitudes, laws, values, rules, conventions, ideologies, culture, customs, traditions and assumptions. When applied more specifically to gender, as in gender norms, they refer to beliefs and rules about the appropriate behaviour of women and men within given institutions and communities. They are usually assumed to be what is held in common in communities rather than what is preferred.

Gender norms are seen as representing the consensus within a society about appropriate gender roles for men and women. Boys and girls internalise the norms about gender through parents, schools, peer groups and mass media. However, as Connell and Pearse (2014) identify, there are a number of flaws in this model: the assumed consensus about values and roles does not bear out in practice; there is an assumed passivity by those who are socialised; there is a significant gender difference between men and women in terms of their support for patriarchal values; and there is a one-dimensional view of the transmission of gender-based values.

Changing social attitudes and social norms

An important strategy in tackling men's violence against women involves campaigns for changing gender norms through education (Paluck and Ball 2010; Connell and Pearse 2014; Alexander-Scott et al. 2016; Haylock et al. 2016). Haylock et al. (2016) draw upon social learning theory to inform the use of role models to change individual attitudes and social norms. Many strategies aimed at norm change involve the engagement of men who are not violent towards women to challenge the sexism, aggression and violence of other men (Jewkes et al. 2015a). This involves encouraging men to change the ways they understand themselves as men.

The social norms approach to engaging men is premised upon the idea that men underestimate the extent to which other men do not support sexist behaviour towards women. That is, many men maintain that while they do not themselves endorse patriarchal values, they wrongly believe that most other men do (Fabiano et al. 2003). Thus, if it can be demonstrated to men that other men do not support patriarchal social norms, they will be more willing to change their own behaviour.

Rachlinski (2000) talks about the limits of social norms because they are often premised upon rational choice theory, which is not useful for theorising the links between norms and behaviour. Much educational work with men focused on changing norms fails to understand how deeply embedded patriarchal ideas are in men's psyches and subjectivities. Also, attempts to change patriarchal gender norms are deeply resisted by anti-feminist men's movements, churches and the corporate sector (Connell and Pearse 2014).

While attitudes and values that are a part of norms are seen to reside within individuals, ideologies, customs, rules and laws are embedded within social institutions (Connell and Pearse 2014). Gender norms are thus sustained and reproduced within social institutions as well as being deeply embedded within the subjectivities of individuals.

Discussing norm creation in the context of global governance, True (2010) is critical of the constructivist approach to norms for ignoring the power dynamics. While feminists are interested in changing patriarchal norms, especially those that legitimate men's violence against women and gender inequality, True is concerned that the creation of new norms, even those that promote gender equality, may obscure other forms of violence and oppression. She believes that norms are not power-neutral and that internalising new gender norms may not necessarily bring about normative change.

The language of social norms obscures the ways in which patriarchal values are promoted through expectations about the roles of men and women. Social norms are a euphemism for patriarchal ideology. However, sex and gender role attitudes and social norms do not reflect the complexity of patriarchal ideology. Thus, what is insufficiently acknowledged in the community attitudes literature is the relationship between sexist attitudes and patriarchal ideology, which sustains men's domination of women. Violence against women is justified not by free-floating attitudes of individuals clustered together as 'community attitudes' or 'social norms', but by patriarchal ideologies adhered to by men to support their dominant and privileged position.

So-called social norms are often enforced by members of dominant groups because they serve the interests of those groups. Thereby, social norms become oppressive to subordinated groups. Notwithstanding this, members of oppressed groups may also endorse and enforce oppressive social norms that harm them (Mackie et al. 2015). However, while women may contribute to patriarchal ideology as well, men have greater responsibility to recognise the ways in which their ideas and practices reproduce the patriarchal gender norms that shape men's violence against women. The argument advanced here is that all men are particularly implicated in the reproduction of patriarchal ideology (see Chapter 11).

Challenging rape culture

Fletcher (2010) regards rape culture as encompassing attitudes, customs and beliefs that normalise anti-women values and reproduce oppressive social practices. Buchwald et al. (2005) define rape culture as 'a complex of beliefs that encourage male sexual aggression and supports violence against women and girls' (p. xi). Such a framing conceptualises sexual violence along a continuum that ranges from sexual remarks through to rape.

Powell and Henry (2014) define rape culture as 'the social, cultural and structural discourses and practices in which sexual violence is tolerated, accepted, eroticised, minimalised and trivialised' (p. 2). For them, to challenge rape culture involves engaging men to rethink their attitudes and beliefs about gender, sexuality, masculinity and violence. They also frame the educational task as promoting alternative cultures and practices of masculinity.

The concept of rape culture is a contentious one. Many commentators regard rape as involving the conscious decisions of a small group of men to commit sexual violence, and they argue that such decisions are not influenced by cultural factors. Some critics argue that the concept of a rape culture takes away personal responsibility on the part of the rapist. However, while rape culture does not specifically direct men to commit acts of sexual violence, it blurs the boundaries between what constitutes consensual sex and non-consensual rape (Jensen 2017).

Fletcher (2010) suggests that women are also complicit in reproducing rape culture in that they too transmit misogynistic values because such values are embedded in the wider patriarchal culture. However, women's complicity should not in any way equalise the responsibility for maintaining patriarchy. The primary focus for challenging rape culture must remain on the roles that men play in perpetuating it. Fletcher suggests that the task is to develop a different kind of masculinity and manhood that is not premised upon male superiority and the denigration of women. However, what if all conceptions of manhood and masculinity involve men differentiating themselves from women (see Chapter 12)?

The role of language in framing violence against women

Patriarchal ideology shapes the ways in which men's violence against women is perceived and represented. The language of 'domestic violence' to describe the problem, for example, either ignores the gendered dimensions of the problem or focuses on the behaviour of atypical men (Hearn and McKie 2010). Language plays a key role in framing how men's violence against women is understood and responded to (Burrell 2014). Gender-neutral framings of men's violence against women distract attention away from men as perpetrators. Berns (2001) refers to anti-feminist responses to gendered analyses as 'patriarchal resistance' because they resist feminist endeavours to situate men's violence against women in the context of patriarchy.

As Walker (1990) notes, concepts are not neutral descriptions of phenomena; they shape the ways in which knowledge is constructed. When we take up certain conceptual ways of describing a problem, we become embedded within the limits of particular discourses. Such discourses are, according to Walker, a fundamental part of the practices of ruling. Social problems, including the problem of men's violence against women, are framed and actively constructed through language (Klein 2013).

Shepherd (2008) has pointed out that the language we use to speak about gender and violence not only describes these phenomena, but is also constitutive of it. Even within feminism, different conceptions of feminist theory are embedded in different ways of framing men's violence. She links the language of 'violence against women' with radical feminism, while the language of 'gender violence' is seen to reflect liberal feminism. She contrasts both approaches with a post-structural framing of the 'violent reproduction of gender'. The latter approach focuses on how gender is performed through the practices of violence.

Patriarchal ideology then can function as a form of symbolic violence. Bimbi (2014) defines symbolic violence as a form of invisible violence that is embedded in oppressive social practices. To the extent that oppressive social practices are normalised and hidden, they function as a form of gender-based violence. The concept of symbolic violence is similar to the notion of 'cultural violence' developed by Galtung (1990) to describe aspects of culture such as ideology, language and religion that are used to legitimate structural and direct forms of violence. Cultural violence renders other forms of violence as being acceptable and legitimate in society.

Irrespective of whether one accepts the post-structural framing of violence advocated by Shepherd (2008), her work alerts us to the ways in which specific discourses produce particular understandings of violence and gender. Flowing from such discourses, specific epistemological and methodological approaches determine the courses of action taken to address violence against women and gender inequality.

Robinson (2003), for example, argues that masculinity scholars rarely acknowledge the debates within feminism when discussing violence against women and tend to draw upon those feminists who are sympathetic to men's issues. Hence, reconstructing masculinity has become a focus of much anti-violence activism. By focusing on masculinity as the cause of men's violence, there is a shift away from the men who perpetrate violence. A critique of men and men's practices in the context of patriarchy is replaced by a critique of dominant forms of masculinity (see Chapter 12).

McLellan (2012) similarly argues that framing men's violence against women in terms of 'gender-based violence' depoliticises the power relations involved in men's violence against women. 'Gender-based' violence, she argues, is another way of refusing to talk about men's violence against women. She believes nothing will change unless the perpetrators of violence against women are explicitly named. The representation of men's violence against women promoted here is one that situates such violence in the context of men's practices within patriarchy.

Analysing patriarchal culture through discourse analysis

Discourse analysis provides one approach to understanding how patriarchal culture is created and maintained. Foucault (1980) defined discourses as 'historically variable ways of specifying knowledge and truth – what is possible to speak at a given moment' (p. 93). Discourse analysis examines the assumptions, language and myths that underpin particular positions in order to show that discursive practices are ordered according to underlying codes that govern what may be thought at any time (Tilley 1990). Often the prevailing view is only able to prevail because people are not aware of other views.

Foucault's (1991) concept of governmentality is useful in understanding the ways in which operationalising of power in everyday practices can also reveal ways in which populations are governed. It provides a valuable way of connecting micro levels of power analysis to analysis of overall structures of domination (Macleod and Durrheim 2002).

Patriarchal ideology can be understood as a hegemonic discourse, which, in Foucauldian terms, can be resisted through subverting or resisting the dominant discourse. This involves challenging phallocentrism, whereby the phallus, as the representation of the penis, comes to embody patriarchal authority and hegemonic masculinity. Phallocentrism operates at the discursive or symbolic level of male privilege and is generally used to refer to the assumed dominance of masculinity and male-centredness across multiple sites of cultural and social relations (Davison 2007).

Adams et al. (1995) identify the ways in which men use language to reinforce their assumptions about male dominance. Men construct what Adams et al. call a 'discourse of entitlement' that reinforces the belief that they are designed to dominate women. Hatty (2000) argues that such discourses legitimate violence against women. From a discursive perspective, one challenges phallocentric discourse by replacing the phallus with alternative forms of symbolic power.

Changing cultures or transforming structures?

Salter (2016) notes that in high-income countries, primary prevention of men's violence against women focuses on changing gender norms and community attitudes rather than changing the material conditions of women's lives. The aim to change attitudes towards violence against women through education frames the problem of men's violence primarily as a cultural problem. When violence against women is defined primarily as a cultural problem, the focus of prevention tends to be on challenging men's sexist beliefs about women. Such sexist views about gender inequality are seen to be synonymous with structural gender inequality.

In many anti-violence campaigns, transforming masculinity is disconnected from the economic, social and political processes of society. In such campaigns, structural gender inequality is subsumed under gender norms about gender inequality. Aiming to change gender norms is seen to be more achievable than transforming structural gender inequalities. The focus of educational campaigns targeted at the attitudes of men and boys is on changing men's conception of masculinity towards alternative notions of what it means to be 'a real man' (Salter 2016). The question is whether alternative conceptions of strong masculinity undermine the aims of violence prevention.

One of the contributing factors shaping this shift of focus is seen to be 'the cultural turn' within feminist theory that involves greater attention to the discursive and symbolic dimensions of women's oppression than the structural relations of gender inequality. Fraser (2005) documents a shift away from the gender injustices within the political economy towards status hierarchies within the culture. While she acknowledges the importance of cultural transformation, her critique is focused on the decoupling of cultural change from political and economic transformation. This is seen as a move from the politics of redistribution to the politics of recognition, whereby cultural struggles replace materialist struggles.

This tension between recognition and redistribution is sometimes framed dichotomously as the affirmation of and revaluation of aspects of subordinated groups that are marginalised versus the transformation of structural relations of power that marginalise them (Pallotta-Chiarolli and Pease 2014). Fraser (2001) highlights that progressive politics has been divided for some time between political struggles focused on redistribution of resources and political struggles focused on respect for difference and affirmation of culturally dominant identities. Social justice requires both recognition and redistribution, and consequently feminist struggles against men's violence against women must acknowledge both material and discursive dimensions of patriarchy and male domination.

Weissman (2007) explores the impact that global economic conditions have on the levels of men's violence against women. Exploitative workplace conditions that weaken men's sense of being in control in the public sphere overflows into the domestic sphere. While Weissman contrasts the influence of the global political economy with the influence of patriarchy, they are not mutually exclusive as gender relations are impacted by global economics. Men who adhere to patriarchal notions of men as economic providers and head of the household experience a threat to their masculinity under conditions of economic uncertainty and unemployment. In such situations, men may use violence against their female partners to re-establish their authority and power.

Conclusion

Salter et al. (2015) refer to a 'prevention paradox', where shifts in norms and attitudes towards violence against women are undermined by structural gender inequality, while at the same time increased levels of violence against women and other forms of backlash can occur if structural changes towards greater gender equality are achieved without attitudinal and normative changes. Lindvert (2002) demonstrates how a focus on redistribution in Nordic countries at the expense of recognition contributed to the neglect of men's violence against women in the pursuit of social and economic gender equality in the public sphere (see Chapter 2).

In the context of international relations, Elias and Beasley (2009) note that some critical forms of scholarship overemphasise material relations and neglect discursive formations. Drawing upon Gramsci (1971), they argue for the importance of materialist *and* discursive analyses to understand globalisation. Similarly, Hearn (2014a, 2015) has explored the intersection of materialist and post-structuralist approaches and developed what he calls a material-discursive approach to violence and violence prevention. Such an approach acknowledges the role of language, culture and discourse in constructing and reproducing the world, while at the same time locating discourse and culture in specific material conditions.

Community attitudes and social norms must be situated within the structural contexts that reproduce them. Any comprehensive analysis of men's violence against women must address both the cultural and structural dimension of the problem. While challenging patriarchal ideologies and hegemonic beliefs that support violence are insufficient in themselves to prevent violence against women, they are nevertheless an important part of violence interventions if they are able to move beyond the individual level of attitude formation to the wider institutional and public level of dominant ideologies and the structural level of unequal gender relations within which men's violence against women is embedded.

5 | HOMOSOCIALITY AND PATRIARCHAL PEER SUPPORT AMONG MEN

Introduction

Dominant expressions of masculinity that are linked with men's violence against women are generated through men's relations with other men. This means that to understand why men are violent towards women, we must understand how men are situated in relation to other men. Violence against women is a vehicle by which men locate themselves in relation to other men and a way in which men reproduce a particular form of masculine self (Hearn and Whitehead 2006). Men demonstrate their manhood in relation to other men more than in relation to women. This also explains men's violence towards other men as well as violence towards women (Whitehead 2005; see Chapter 8).

In this chapter, I explore how men's relations with other men are framed in the context of homosocial bonding (Flood 2008b), fratriarchy (Remy 1990), mateship (Pease 2001) and male peer support (DeKeseredy and Schwartz 2013). I examine men's relations with other men in the context of male-dominated sites of sports, locker rooms, fraternities, the military, workplaces and male peer cultures. The chapter does not attempt to provide a comprehensive overview of all the sites of homosociality and male bonding. Rather, the aim is to illustrate the ways in which homosocial bonding in specific gender regimes reproduces the wider patriarchal gender order and perpetuates men's violence against women.

Homosociality, fratriarchy and the reproduction of patriarchy

Homosociality generally describes social bonds between people of the same sex, although in critical masculinity studies it has been used to emphasise the significance of relations between men in reproducing hegemonic masculinity and men's dominance (Haywood et al. 2018). Through their friendships and bonds, men build close-knit networks to defend their power and privileges. As men's domination of women is maintained by the solidarity and homosocial relations between men, it is important to understand relations between men as part of the process in which patriarchy is reproduced.

Kimmel (1994) defines masculinity itself as a form of homosocial enactment, whereby men scrutinise other men to rank them and to accept them into traditional manhood. Hence, men are 'rewarded' when they boast about their accomplishments by gaining approval from other men. Men seek to improve their ranking on the masculinity scale to be accepted as 'real men'. Consequently, for Kimmel, homophobia is not only an irrational fear of gay men or of being perceived as gay; it is also a more generalised fear that other men will judge you for not being a real man. All men are under pressure to measure up to traditional notions of manhood to avoid being called out as feminine.

Eve Sedgwick (1985), through an analysis of English literature, illustrates how homosocial relations between heterosexual men are enhanced through their sexual desire for women. Sedgwick suggests that homosociality between men, while non-sexual, is connected to forms of male desire. Men seek closeness with other men, while at the same time they fear this desire for closeness may turn into homosexual desire. In Sedgwick's view, there is a tension between heterosexual men's desire to form close relationships with other men to sustain their power and the deep fear of homosexuality. It is this tension that forms the basis of the way heterosexual men treat women and gays. Hence, to bolster their heterosexuality, men express their hatred towards homosexuals and women.

Homosociality is one of the ways that men reproduce patriarchy and the hegemonic masculinity that sustains it. Male bonding, as an expression of broader structural relations, plays a key role in transmitting patriarchal values and maintaining patriarchal power relations (Bird 1996; Hammarén and Johansson 2014; Wadham 2016). Bird (1996) identifies three dimensions of homosociality, among heterosexual men, that reproduce patriarchy: emotional detachment, competitiveness and sexual objectification of women. While men seek close relationships with other men, they have to avoid emotional expression and emotional attachments. They also need to be ready to compete with other men and are not to reveal any vulnerabilities that men may take advantage of. Finally, they should boast about their sexual relations with women through the objectification of women's bodies.

One way of framing homosociality between men is that of fratriarchy, which refers to male power associated with brotherly alliances and groups (Tallberg 2003). Isenberg (2013) defines it as a fusion of patriarchy and fraternity, whereby men rule through fraternities and brotherhood. The concept was first developed by Remy (1990) to describe forms of male domination by young men. Remy notes that close relations between men under fratriarchy are disconnected from women and the responsibilities of caring for children. Fratriarchy is seen as a useful way of describing the domination of women by young men who do not currently have children or family responsibilities. Pateman (1988) outlined a similar configuration of male power that she called 'fraternal patriarchy'. This was a new form of patriarchy that was premised upon fraternal bonds between men that arose from brotherhood rather than the kinship relations that characterised patriarchy. Although the premise of fratriarchy is the existence of egalitarian and supportive bonds between men, the reality is that notions of brotherhood are characterised by competition and hierarchical relations of power (Tallberg 2003).

Mateship and homosocial bonding among men in Australia

Mateship is a peculiarly Australian form of homosocial bonding between non-Indigenous men that espouses equality, fraternity and solidarity (Murrie 2007). Mateship is part of the Australian male heritage; it originated in colonial days and was (and still is) glorified in war and sport. An important element of mateship has always been that the company of other men is preferred to the company of women (Bell 1973). Australian mateship developed in the context of what was experienced by European colonisers as the harsh reality of bush life for men without female companionship. The central elements are that mates are 'exclusively male, not female, they share a particular sceptical camaraderie in doing things together [and] there is a lack of emotional expression other than sharing jokes' (Edgar 1997: 79). Mateship implies the unspoken understanding that a mate will always support you. Thus, your mates would never inform on you to the police, no matter what crimes you may have committed. For many Australian men, mateship implies that loyalty to one's mate is a higher virtue than observance of the law.

While bonds between men have often been used as a basis for male solidarity in many countries, Australia is perhaps the only country where the romanticisation of male bonding provides so useful a basis for national ideology. It is more than just an Australian version of male bonding; rather, such bonding has formed the basis of myths of national identity among Australian men. Bell (1973) noted that while male comradeship is common in most cultures, the Australian version seems to exaggerate this institution, 'almost as if Australian men were constantly in a state of emergency where they needed one another' (pp. 8–9).

While mateship is often presented and promoted as healthy, wholesome and positive, Marston (1994) draws attention to a number of aspects of mateship that are unhealthy, oppressive and destructive. While the idea of mates staying together is presented as one of the virtues of mateship, it can be used to justify violence against women, gays and Indigenous people. In fact, dominant Australian manhood and masculinity were and are constructed against the image of 'others' who are different.

In this context, Bell (1973) argued over 45 years ago that an understanding of mateship is important to an understanding of female and male relationships in Australian society. He said that frequently the personal satisfaction of mateship for the man are achieved at the cost of marital satisfaction for his female partner. Marston (1994) similarly argues that mateship limits the potential of men and their relationships with women and other men.

A number of writers have historically commented on the emotional poverty of Australian masculinity. Colling (1992), for example, says that mateship embodies toughness and a disdain for 'weak emotion'. Meanwhile, Webb (1998) regards the celebrated culture of silence and emotional repression as the main issue facing Australian men. In fact, silence is seen as the essence of traditional mateship, as evidenced in the nature of men's relationships that emphasise sport and communal drinking.

Australian men are renowned for their dedication to drinking beer. Drinking in the company of other sporty and gambling men has come to be seen as being archetypically Australian. Dixson (1982) says that 'heavy drinking is a symbol of mateship and solidarity' (p. 169). Thus, drinking beer has become part of the mateship subculture. Beyond the expression of mateship in sport and communal drinking, there are more troubling aspects of this Australian form of male bonding.

Gang rape is more prevalent in Australia than in America or Britain. Almost 25 years ago, Looker (1994) suggested that this was connected to the intricacies of relationships between men in Australia and the affirmation of an aggressive form of masculinity. She cites a convicted rapist:

There's ... a sense of camaraderie about a gang bang, where you have
a good mate and you will share a woman with a good mate. It's ... a
very binding act with you and your friend, with you and your mate.
The sense of camaraderie would be possibly the biggest aspect of it.
You do everything together.

(Looker 1994: 218)

Similar studies of gang rapes in North America found that group sexual assault was both a public demonstration of men's dominance and a
celebratory drama involving, for the men, an atmosphere of recreation
and fun (Franklin 2004). Recent media reporting on rape by footballers who used gang rape as a 'bonding' experience suggest that little has
changed (Vertuno 2017).

This aspect of male culture is elucidated by Carrington (1998), who
retraces the police investigation into the rape and murder of a 14-year-
old girl at a beach party in an Australian town in 1989. She describes
what happens when shame and mateship mix with a small-town mentality. The police responsible for the murder investigation reported
that a 'wall of silence' hampered their investigation. This silence was
seen to be related to 'a rigorous adherence to the ethic of not dobbing
in a mate' (Carrington 1998: 99).

Homophobia is also a dominant feature of Australian masculinity,
with widespread condemnation of homosexuality by men evidenced by
the hostility and violence shown towards gay men. Tacey (1997) says
that homophobia is the most recently discovered aspect of Australian
mateship. While 'men adore their mates, there will be no obvious caring, no touching, no outward display' (p. 135).

While male bonding is an important prerequisite for the development
of masculine identity in Australia, many men fear that if the bonding
is too close, it will destroy heterosexual identity and become confused
with homosexuality (Webb 1998). Nevertheless, as suggested earlier,
mateship and homosexuality have a very close homosocial proximity.
Certainly, there are affinities between mateship as a social relationship
and homosexuality as a sexual relationship. Dixson (1982) even suggests that mateship involves sublimated homosexuality. More recently,
Durber (2006) has argued that the emotional closeness between men
through mateship allows for forms of same-sex sexualised pleasure outside the framework of being gay.

Masculinity and the culture of violence in sport

Sport as a social institution is interconnected with power relations, not only between groups within a nation state, but also between nation states. The rise in the interest in sport in recent years can be understood as a response by many men to what is perceived to be a crisis in gender relations. Sport provides an opportunity for men to elevate the male body as superior to women's bodies, and hence maintain their control over women (Messner 1992). Thus, when masculinity is threatened, men may turn to the homosocial world of competitive sport to restore their sense of superiority over women. As the title of Nelson's (1994) book suggests, *The Stronger Women Get, the More Men Love Football*.

Contact sports encourage dominance, physical aggression and toughness, extreme competitiveness, and insensitivity to the pain of others. Contact sports naturalise and glorify injurious and violent contact on the field, and are thus implicated in violence against women off the field (Dyson and Flood 2008). Numerous studies in Canada and the United States demonstrate links between men who participate in contact sports and higher levels of violence towards women (Burstyn 1999; Crossett 2000; Curry 2000; Sabo et al. 2000; Fleming et al. 2015). The fostering of aggression in sport encourages young men to think that the capacity for violent behaviour is an essential part of what it is to be a man (Sabo et al. 2000).

In a co-authored study of factors influencing community attitudes to violence against women in Australia, my co-author and I (Flood and Pease 2006) found secondary evidence of links between sporting subcultures, violence-supporting norms and violence against women. While there was no equivalent Australian empirical research on male athletes and violence against women, we hypothesised that the masculinist subcultures of Australian Rules football and professional rugby, which also involved male bonding, high male status, aggression and toughness, would suggest similar likely outcomes to studies in North America.

Sport is an arena in which violence between men is normalised and even rewarded. Many men are attracted to contact sports because of the opportunities they provide for violent confrontations and affirmations of being a 'real man' (Curry 2000). Sport certainly provides men with the opportunity to display speed, stamina and physical strength, all of which are associated with hegemonic masculinity. While success in competitive contact sports is associated with physical domination and the sanctioned use of violence, it is not surprising that professional athletes will be violent off the field as well as on the field (Welsh 1997). When sporting peer cultures endorse physical violence on the field, it increases the likelihood that individual sportsmen will engage in violence against women (Crossett 2000).

According to Welsh (1997), it is inevitable that violence in sport will spill over into athletes' off-field relationships. Violent expressions of masculinity are constructed through the encouragement of aggression, physicality and domination in sport, where the athlete's body is used a 'weapon' to dominate opponents. When this aggression on the field is combined with the sense of entitlement that is fostered through the elevated status of the athlete, misogyny and aggressive sexuality flow over into men's relations with women. The celebrity status associated with being an elite athlete engenders a sense of entitlement and a lack of accountability for behaviour off the field. When this is combined with excessive alcohol and drug use and 'groupie' culture, players' sexual relations with women often lead to sexual assault and rape (Dyson and Flood 2008).

McBride (1995) frames male contact sports, such as football, as male territorial games, and explores links between contact sports, war and men's violence against women. Contact sports, like war and violence against women, are all seen as symptoms of a masculinist psychic economy and predicated on the use of violence against others. Violence against women, in his view, is an inevitable outcome of male territorial games where men compete with each other for dominance. McBride is aware that in drawing a connection between football and men's violence against women, he is challenging a male ritual that is almost universally loved by men. Thus, he expects a significant backlash by men to the suggested association between the two activities. However, he argues that football and other contact sports are a central part of patriarchal culture. For many men, football is not just a tangential leisure activity; it is rather an essential component of what it means to be a man. In playing football, as in conducting war, men are affirming that they are men.

Sporting culture, disrespect for women and sexualised violence

It is still an acceptable and desirable practice for men in contact sports to express sexist and misogynistic attitudes towards women. Patriarchal peer cultures where there is group-based disrespect for women, aggressive male behaviour, sexualised discussion and consumption of pornography have been shown to have a high-level association with men's violence against women (Rosen et al. 2003). Such factors are present in professional sports teams where male bonding and loyalty to other men intensify sexist and misogynist behaviours towards women.

One aspect of homosocial bonding in sporting culture is the men's locker room. This is where fraternal bonds between men are fostered. Lyman (1987) has observed how fraternal bonds between men in the locker room are encouraged through sexist joking and sexualised talk about women. In Lyman's study, the men justified their sexist humour on the basis of the special bond that it created between them. Sexist and sexualised joking generated a kind of intimacy that addressed the latent aggression and tensions they otherwise experience with each other. Such joking is seen as a form of play, and any concerns about aggressive attitudes towards women are dismissed. Thus, men create a special bond between them that is at the expense of women.

Curry (1991) suggests that men's talk about women as objects and their shared stories of sexual conquests encourages a rape culture where aggressive anti-female behaviour and expressed disdain towards women are normalised. The representation of women as sexual objects provides opportunities for men to talk about their sexual conquests as a way to gain approval from other men and masks their sense of insecurity around intimacy with women. However, such a practice impoverishes men's sexual and emotional relations with women.

Further to the place of sexualised talk and sexist joking among men, Flood (2008b) illustrates how the bonds between men shape their sexual relationships with women. That is, men's homosocial bonding influences the kind of sexual relationships men have with women, the meanings they give to their sexual relations and the ways in which they talk about them. Flood gives examples of watching tabletop dancing, strip shows and pornographic movies, and group visits to brothels as practices that reproduce the bonds between men.

The men in Flood's study reported that when having sex with a woman, they imagined how they would talk about it to their mates. Boasting to other men about one's sexual exploits was a common practice among the men. For these men, heterosexual sex was itself not only a form of masculine affirmation, but also a means for further male bonding. This could go as far as having sex with the same woman and even include gang rape.

Nelson (1994) says that male contact sports 'set the stage' for men's violence against women. When we hear how male players talk about women, it is not surprising that these men become involved in sexual assault and gang rape. Although she was writing in the United States in the 1990s, Nelson's observation about newspapers reporting continually on male athletes being arrested for sexual assault and violence against women applies equally well to Australia at the time of writing.

Physicality for men has come to mean an expression of male dominance in that it involves coercion, force and the ability to subdue others. It is thus not a huge step for this physicality to spill over into group rape. Interviews with rapists report that the main rewards of gang rape for the rapists are camaraderie, cooperation and friendship that is fostered by the sexual aggression and violence. Crossett (2000) goes so far as to suggest that men's contact sport is a rape culture.

Male bonding, spectator sports and men's violence against women

While most men do not have the physicality required to play professional football, they are able, as spectators, to vicariously experience the pleasure of physical mastery and aggression as they watch the game (Nelson 1994). It is said that male viewers find violent sports imagery exciting, and some sports commentators foster this by honing in on violent clashes between teams (Sabo et al. 2000). Violence between men on the sports field is ritualised and even celebrated in commercial sports journalism. Rather than being an unwanted element, violence on the field appears to be central to contact sports.

Women's refuges have noted incidents of men's violence against women increase following major football games such as the Super Bowl in the United States (Sabo et al. 2000). There appears to be a link between some forms of spectatorship of sports and men's violence against women. Recent research in Australia (Livingston 2018) has found an association between State of Origin football matches and men's violence against women. Informed by the research in North America about links between football matches and sexual assault and domestic violence, Livingston interrogated police reports of recorded assaults on the evenings of State of Origin matches in New South Wales. He found a significant increase in violence against women on the nights of State of Origin matches compared with other evenings. Digging deeper into the statistics, he discovered that violence against women was more likely to be perpetrated by male fans of the losing teams. For die-hard fans, their self-esteem is tied to the success or otherwise of their teams. They will bask in the glory of a winning team and share in the despair of a losing team.

Fraternities and sexual violence against women

Residential university colleges in the United States are called fraternities and are largely comprised of young undergraduate men living on campus. In research conducted by Loy (1992), patriarchal relations among men in fraternities were found to be closely related to high levels of men's violence against women. In later research (Loy 1995), the pursuit of status through physical prowess and competition in male-dominated groups in fraternities were found to be correlated with gang rape of women and interpersonal violence. Sanday's (2007) research into gang rape in fraternities found that the sense of entitlement and male privilege that male fraternity members feel are major causal influences on violence against women. Furthermore, men experience a strong bonding with other men through their aiding and abetting of sexual assault against women.

Recent research in Australia (Gebecki et al. 2017) on sexual harassment and sexual assault at universities found that most incidents of sexual assault in university settings occurred at a university or residence social event. The results of the national survey indicated high levels of sexual assault in university residences and residential colleges. The report noted that female students described a university culture where male students felt entitled to sex and access to women's bodies. Residential colleges were described by female students as being accepting of sexual harassment and sexual assault as a 'normal' part of university life.

Homosociality and men's violence against women in the military

Another key site of homosocial male bonding that fosters tolerance of violence against women is the military. In the review into the treatment of women in the Australian Defence Force, Broderick (2012) found that mateship and the bonds between men was what male recruits liked most about the army. Male bonding is closely associated with the solidarity experienced during military combat, where it enables men to endure the stresses of deployment and war. While fraternity in the military is seen as essential to foster strong teamwork among men, it also encourages an 'us' and 'them' mentality, which tends to inferiorise others, especially women. Initiation practices promote a sense of exclusiveness, and ensure obedience, as those who are unable to withstand the brutalisation drop out of the services (Wadham 2013).

The homosocial bonding between men also contributes to the high levels of violence against women in the military. Violence within the military that is outside of war is not aberrant or pathological, as often argued by high command, but rather an inevitable outcome of violent initiation practices such as hazing and the brutality of military culture, which reproduces men's dominance (Wadham 2016). Rosen et al. (2003) point out that the peer bonding processes involved in promoting group cohesion in the military fosters a form of hypermasculinity that includes the denigration and objectification of women through the use of sexist language and the consumption of pornography.

Wadham (2016) demonstrates that sexual harassment and violence against women in the military is a direct outcome of increasing numbers of women in military services. Such violence and harassment arise from the perceived threat that women pose to men's solidarity and closeness, which are seen as necessary for cohesion.

Homosociality and the reproduction of men's dominance in workplaces

Research in organisations demonstrates that men's dominance at work is maintained through informal male networks that are colloquially referred to as 'old boys' clubs' (Tallberg 2003; Flood and Pease 2006; Holmes and Flood 2013; Fisher and Kinsey 2014). Men exclude women from key decision-making through male-only work groups and male-focused pursuits that deter women's involvement. Male bonding in workplaces defends and bolsters male privilege and entitlement, and emphasises men's accomplishments at the expense of women's achievements.

As a group, men have developed various strategies to try to keep women out of some workplaces or to contain them in their place once they have entered the organisation. One of the ways in which they do this is by emphasising sex boundaries in friendship patterns and group relations (Pease 2002). Single-gender work cultures reflect and enhance job segregation and help to preserve conventional views of proper masculine and feminine behaviour, while creating an environment for male bonding (Bradley 1989). Such bonding reinforces gender inequality in the workplace by giving men access to practical sources of information and contacts while subordinating women (Cockburn 1983). So, 'while masculinity remains dominant in the workplace, homosociability ... will continue to provide a powerful basis for resistance to the presence of women' (Franzway et al. 1989: 145).

Another strategy used by men to 'keep women in their place' is the use of sexual joking and obscene language. Trading obscene stories is a commonplace practice when men gather. To be equal, women must tolerate and be prepared to join in when sexual innuendo and jokes are used around them.

Flood and I (Flood and Pease 2005) previously outlined how women's exclusion from and subordination in workplaces and institutions is also sustained through men's collective social relations. We analysed how men's networks contribute to the discursive and structural processes involved in gender inequality in organisations and workplaces. Men excluded women from informal work-related networks and gave greater acknowledgement to men's presence than women. Furthermore, in occupational and professional training, they created exclusively male in-groups by using 'men' as a generic language to refer to all employees and excluding women from bonding experiences.

Tallberg (2003) also investigated the relationship between men's networks and gendered power, with a particular focus on the role of homosociality in reproducing men's privilege in workplaces. He demonstrates how male homosociality dispossesses women of organisational power and allocates privileges and rewards among men. Fisher and Kinsey (2014) illustrate the ways in which male bonding plays out in academic workplaces. Men talk about sex, alcohol, cars and sport to connect with other men and to exclude women, enabling them to obtain and hold on to power. Some men use the chemistry they feel with each other to determine who they associate with to foster success. This is a form of what Martin (2001) refers to as 'mobilising masculinities' to build all-male networks and homosocial bonds.

Men often experience greater comfort when they are solely with other men, as they cultivate and nurture opportunities for all-male work groups.

Male peer support and men's violence against women

Male homosociality is also implicated in men's informal peer group support for violence against women. Research demonstrates that participation in all-male peer groups increases men's tolerance for violence against women, and furthermore provides direct support to men who perpetrate violence against women. Since the 1970s (Dobash and Dobash 1979; Bowker 1983; DeKeseredy and Schwartz 1993, 2013), studies have found that the more that men spend time with male friends, the greater the likelihood of them perpetrating violence against their wives and female partners. DeKeseredy and Schwartz (2013) found that male peer groups that encourage sexism and dominance influence men towards committing violence against their female partners. Secondary research conducted by Flood and I (Flood and Pease 2006) on the factors influencing 'community attitudes' towards violence against women found that sexism and misogyny in male peer groups had a strong influence on men's likelihood to perpetrate violence against women.

DeKeseredy and Schwartz (2013) developed the male peer support theory to explain how young men's abusive peer attachments were correlated with men's violence against women. They argued that male support motivates men to abuse women and encourages men not to tolerate women's challenges to their authority. They provide considerable empirical evidence to support their theoretical model with reference to studies in colleges and universities, men's violence against women in families, men's dating relationships, sports teams, and men's rights organisations.

In the early version of the theory, they focused primarily on individual factors. However, in later versions of the model, they explored the association of male peer support groups with wider patriarchal social relations (DeKeseredy and Schwartz 2013). Bowker (1983) suggests that men's homosocial networks constitute forms of patriarchal cultural violence that functions at the symbolic level. Thus, individual behaviours of men are an expression of wider patriarchal forces at the cultural level (see Chapter 4).

We are frequently reminded that the majority of men do not physically assault women and that most men are well-meaning. However, if most men are not physically violent, how do we explain the high levels of violence and misogyny in the world? Some men say that they have not been invited to become part of the solution. Other men are reluctant to get involved in violence prevention work. What is clear is that men's silence in response to men's violence against women and their lack of active engagement in anti-violence work supports other men's abusive and violent behaviour (DeKeseredy and Schwartz 2013).

Research conducted by Towns and Terry (2014) in New Zealand found that the men they interviewed were reluctant to talk about any difficulties they were having in relationships with women because it would leave them vulnerable to other men's potential ridicule and the threat of violence. It was also difficult for these men to challenge a male friend they knew who was being violent to his intimate partner. To challenge a mate was to 'wreck the system' of male bonding that connected the men to each other. The discomfort the men talked about in potentially challenging their mate was seen as a sufficient reason to discourage them from interfering in what they regarded as a private matter. The requirements and expectations of mateship discouraged the men from challenging their male friends, and the consequences of this inaction was collusion with the violence their male friends were perpetrating.

What was particularly interesting in Towns and Terry's research was that this loyalty to men did not only manifest itself in terms of close friendships. It was also evident in men feeling a need to take the side of men more generally, when, for example, violence against women's awareness campaigns named men as perpetrators. Even though these men did not consider themselves to be violent or abusive and wanted to separate themselves from other 'bad' men, they still felt the need to challenge the notion that domestic violence was primarily about men.

Conclusion

There is something about the segregation of dominant group members that solidifies their sense of superiority and leads to the inferiorisation of those who are less powerful. Thus, in all male groups, whether they be in sports, the locker room, university colleges and fraternities, the military, or male-dominated workplaces, women are denigrated and objectified. The implications for eliminating violence and challenging patriarchy are that male-dominated organisations and male peer group cultures need to be addressed to demonstrate to men how their complicity in forms of homosocial bonding reproduce a culture that allows men's violence against women to flourish.

While this chapter has demonstrated the various ways in which male homosociality is implicated in men's patriarchal practices, the question is raised about whether men can form anti-patriarchal bonds that do not subordinate and oppress women. Furthermore, to the extent that men can overcome their emotional stoicism with other men and become less reliant upon women for emotional support, they may lessen the burden on women to provide care and emotional labour to men (Flood 2007). Stoltenberg (1993) argues that one of the ways for men to improve their relationships with women is to break with homosocial practices among men that exploit women.

Hammarén and Johansson (2014) distinguish between hierarchical homosociality and horizontal homosociality. It is hierarchical homosociality that strengthens men's power and maintains men's privilege and dominance that has been reviewed here. Horizontal homosociality, in Hammarén and Johansson's view, is premised upon more inclusive relationships between heterosexual men that encourage emotional closeness between men and are not forged to exploit women. They argue that horizontal homosociality can potentially rupture hegemonic masculinity and male power. However, this latter form of homosociality is underdeveloped, and there is little evidence of heterosexual men forming connections with each other that undermine the hegemony of men. The potential for men to break their complicity with patriarchal male bonding and to develop more caring dispositions towards women is explored in Chapters 11 and 12.

6 | COERCIVE CONTROL AND FAMILIAL PATRIARCHY

Introduction

It is important to distinguish between public and private patriarchy. Whereas public patriarchy is based on men's control over institutions in the public sphere, private patriarchy refers to men's control of women and children in the home (Walby 1990). DeKeseredy and Schwartz (2013) differentiate between social patriarchy, where male domination is enacted in the public realm, and familial patriarchy, which refers to men's control over women in families and domestic settings. These two levels of patriarchy, which can be referred to as macro- and micro-patriarchal systems, are interconnected. Interpersonal dynamics between men and women must be seen in the context of the macro-patriarchal order.

Dragiewicz (2011) also notes that patriarchy is expressed at interpersonal levels between members of a family. This is manifested in the sexual division of labour and power in the home, where women still carry a disproportionate level of responsibility for childcare and housework. Rosen (cited in National Institute of Justice 2000) says that it would be interesting to map familial patriarchy to different forms of violence against women. While various studies have researched the relationship between patriarchal ideologies of men in families to the perpetration of violence (Smith 1990; Tonsing and Tonsing 2017), the framing of patriarchy in this book refers to more than just the attitudes and motives of individual men. It also includes the authority and power structure of families and the connection of families to the wider gender order.

From family violence to power and control

There is an ongoing dispute about how to name and theorise men's violence against women in the family. For feminist researchers and activists, and profeminist allies, it is important to connect men's violence against women in the family to other forms of violence against women in the patriarchal gender order. However, family violence researchers and practitioners regard intimate partner violence as one of many forms of family violence, which includes elder abuse, child abuse and violence between siblings. In their view, men's violence against female partners is not qualitatively different from these other forms of 'family violence' (Lawson 2012).

Almost 30 years ago, Walker (1990) raised the juxtaposition of the words 'family' and 'violence' in family violence. She observed that the concept of 'family violence' deflects focus away from the criminal justice system towards welfare, health and social services. Patriarchal family relations are thus not problematised. The conceptual frame of 'family violence' allows professional discourses and interventions to take precedence over the sociopolitical framing of men's violence against women. What is addressed in family violence prevention is not men's authority and power in families, but their abuse of that authority and power.

In contrast, feminist analyses see men's violence against women in the home as a manifestation of male power whereby men reproduce and maintain their authority and power over women. Feminists argue that men's drive for control and dominance is central to an understanding of men's violence. Many men believe that they are entitled to exercise power over women and that they can use violence to punish women if they fail to accommodate to this power (McGregor and Hopkins 1991).

A power and control wheel developed by research with 200 abused women is an important tool in understanding what are regarded as more subtle forms of men's violence. In the model developed by Pence and Paymar (1993), educational classes focus on physical and sexual violence, and eight forms of power and control, including intimidation, emotional abuse, isolation, minimising the abuse, using children, using male privilege, economic abuse and threats. The power and control wheel of violence provides a framework for understanding the various forms of abuse that can occur within a family. The model is premised upon men's entitlement and privilege, which allows various forms of power and control to be utilised (Rossiter 2011).

The rationale for extending the definition of violence to include emotional and psychological abuse, financial control, and patriarchal expectations about women's domestic labour has been the belief that more women will recognise these forms of controlling behaviours as violence and will seek support. Ashcraft (2000) points out that including emotional abuse and domestic control as forms of domestic violence is a part of a strategy to encourage reflection on other elements of abusive relationships within the family that might otherwise be considered 'normal'. However, she raises questions about the success of this strategy of educating the community about the widespread abuse of women in families. While there is increasingly general disapproval of men's violence against women in the family, she notes that very few people accept the notion that more general forms of controlling behaviours that are prevalent in families constitute domestic violence.

Ashcraft observes that many women recognise dissatisfaction in their relationships with men. However, they are reluctant to define the problem in terms of violence or abuse. As a result of not being able to identify the situation as violent or abusive, they are unable to name the injustices they experience. She proposes a new language of domestic control, which includes physical violence and other forms of inequality in relationships such as domestic distortion, domestic domination, domestic dodging and domestic neglect. Ashcraft argues that the concept of violence loses its meaning if we try to encompass all forms of gender injustice and oppressiveness within it. Stark (2007) similarly suggests that by conflating all forms of abuse as violence, we are less able to distinguish the multiple layers of women's oppression. There is, of course, the risk that in not regarding other forms of abuse and exploitation as violence, their relationship to physical violence may be neglected.

The power and control wheel has been integrated with many cognitive behavioural counselling programs for violent men (Tolman and Edelson 1995; Robertson 1999; Dankwort and Rausch 2000). The Duluth model has been described as a 'gender-based cognitive-behavioural' approach to counselling that locates violence within the context of power and control (Gondolf 2007). However, in this respect, power and control, which were originally conceptualised in terms of gender inequality and male dominance, have been reframed as interpersonal issues related to sex role socialisation. As Francis and Tsang (1997) observe, this reframing of men's violence aims to make power and control more responsive to education and therapy.

Price (2012) also argues that the power and control wheel, which has been used extensively to describe diverse forms of violence against women has contributed to the limited definition of violence against women as being only an interpersonal dynamic in the home. Power and control by the male partner is disconnected from the wider institutional and cultural supports for men's violence against women, and consequently disconnects the private from the public. Defining violence against women primarily as domestic violence hides the structural and institutional forms of violence related to law, the state and culture that women in marginalised communities experience.

'If women do it too, how can violence be about gender and patriarchy?'

The issue of women's violence is raised by family violence researchers and men's rights activists to negate the relevance of a feminist analysis of domestic violence and to challenge the significance of gendered dynamics in abuse. Such proponents challenge the gendered framing of violence by arguing that the problem of violence is a 'human' problem. They do so by arguing that men and women are equally violent, that women are responsible for the violence that is perpetrated against them and that society tolerates violence by women more so than violence by men. Men's rights campaigns against feminist framings of violence aim to divert attention away from men's responsibility for violence and the patriarchal context that fosters violence.

The feminist and profeminist response to women's violence often takes the form of challenging the research methodology of the conflict tactics scale (CTS), which is used by those advocating a gender-neutral perspective to supposedly demonstrate that domestic violence is symmetrical (Straus 1990). As many critics note, the CTS measures incidents of violence rather than coercion and control, ignores various forms of abuse and severity of injuries, does not take into account the circumstances under which violence occurs, assumes violence is family-based, and ignores the reasons why people use violence (Schwartz and DeKeseredy 1998; Kimmel 2002; Taft et al. 2002). This strategy has been important to contextualise women's violence and to challenge the exaggeration of this violence by anti-feminist proponents who are more interested in negating feminism than addressing the needs of male victims.

Strategies against the backlash have not been effective, however, in negating the widespread perception in the community that women are equally as violent as men (ANROWS 2017). The backlash against feminist analyses of domestic violence that portray violence in the family as gender-neutral has become increasingly more accepted in mainstream understandings of domestic violence.

All instances of women's violence are used by anti-feminists to repudiate gender analyses of violence. The challenge for feminists and profeminist allies is how to take women's violence seriously without it being used by men's rights advocates to de-gender violence and to obscure men's violence (Berns 2001). There is an understandable reluctance to acknowledge women's violence in the context of anti-feminist backlash and the lack of responsibility that men have taken for addressing men's violence. However, strategies for challenging the anti-feminist backlash need not deny the reality of women's violence.

Feminist perspectives on women's violence tend to locate women's experiences in the context of victimisation and gender inequality (Mottram and Salter 2015). There is research to indicate that many women who are perpetrators of violence in the family are themselves victims of violence (Enander 2011). However, not all violence by women against men is a form of defence against a violent male partner. Some feminists have also explored women's experiences of both power and powerlessness in heterosexual relationships, which involves moving beyond solely structuralist analyses of women's violence that portray women only as victims (Ali and Naylor 2013; Cannon et al. 2015; Mottram and Salter 2015).

These feminists are concerned that attempts to minimise women's violence or explain it solely in relation to women's victimisation and self-defence negates women's agency and their capacity to enact violence in forms other than self-defence (Baird 2010; Ali and Naylor 2013; Cannon et al. 2015). Cannon et al. (2015) express concern that the structuralist feminist paradigm, which suggests that women only ever enact violence as a form of self-defence, denies women agency and does not do justice to women's varied motivations for violence. They challenge the notion that women are necessarily powerless in the face of men's privilege and argue that women do exercise power in the context of gender inequality.

Patriarchy influences and shapes both the victimisation of women and men and the perpetration of violence by both men and women. bell hooks (2000) argues that emphasising men's violence against women over other forms of violence by men and women obscures the range of patriarchal violence. Such a focus also allows this one form of patriarchal violence to be portrayed as anti-male.

Even if the studies that purport to show women's violence against men as being equal to men's violence against women were valid (and they are not), it still would not mean that gender was irrelevant to understanding the perpetration of violence in the family. Anderson (2005) demonstrates that such an argument rests upon an individualist approach to gender, and fails to understand the relationship between violence and gender through interactional and structural analyses where gender is enacted and structurally embedded.

It is the conflation of the sex categories of male and female with patriarchy that enables anti-feminists to argue that women's violence negates a feminist and gendered analysis of violence. Patriarchy does not only refer to men and does not only impact on violence perpetrated by men. Women too are shaped by patriarchal gender relations and patriarchal values (Dragiewicz 2011).

In seeing gender beyond the sex categories of male and female, we need to locate men's and women's behaviour in the context of masculinities and femininities, both of which may be embodied by men and women. This means that while power and violence is connected to masculinity, women as well as men can embody and practise it, and consequently enact violence associated with it (Cannon et al. 2015). Edwards (2006) also notes that in acknowledging that violence is not predicated on maleness, but masculinity, it offers an explanation of women who are violent as they may have internalised elements of masculinity. The masculinisation of women can be explained by locating them in the context of patriarchy and the cultural values that promote the idea that some people have the right to dominate others. Women, as well as men, may internalise these values and so enact violence towards children as well as to other women in lesbian relationships (White and Kowalski 1994). However, women are likely to be far more conflicted in their use of patriarchal power, as this contradicts other discourses about being a woman. This may explain why so fewer women abuse patriarchal power when they have it compared to men.

Stark (2010) says that in the strategy of challenging gender parity in violence, we have ignored the argument about gender parity in abuse. He argues that one of the consequences of separating violent acts from their historical and social context is that all violence is seen as equally abusive. For Stark, the focus should be less on countering the statistics of who hits who how often, and more on what is different about men's violence and women's violence. Stark (2007) argues that there should be less focus on inequality in capacity for violence between men and women, and more attention to the unequal access men have to material and social resources that enable them to gain advantage and privileges in power struggles in families. One can acknowledge that some women may use violence as a tactic in family conflict. However, this is qualitatively different to the way in which men use violence to control women's lives.

It is clear that accounts of women's violence do not negate a gendered understanding of domestic violence. Notwithstanding the overwhelming proportion of male perpetrators of violence, it is also the case that if we only use gender to study men as perpetrators and women as victims, we will miss many of the gendered dimensions of violence. Gender is more than the sex category of the perpetrator; all violence is gendered, whether it is perpetrated by men or women (Anderson 2009). If women's violence is not acknowledged and theorised, conservative critics and anti-feminist men's groups will gain more widespread support.

Reconciling family violence perspectives with power and control theories?

In response to debates about the significance of gender in understanding violence, some theorists argue that it is possible to develop typologies that incorporate both feminist and family violence approaches. Johnson (1995, 2008) is the most popular advocate of the typological approach. He developed his typology in response to the conflicting research by feminists and family violence theorists noted earlier. Johnson legitimates both perspectives and purports to have resolved the debate between the two contrasting approaches.

Johnson (1995) initially argued that there were two distinctly different forms of domestic violence, what he then called 'patriarchal terrorism' and 'common couple violence'. Johnson and Leone (2005) later expanded these distinctions to four categories to include violent resistance and mutual violent control, where in the latter both partners were endeavouring to control the other through violence. At the time of the expansion of his typology, Johnson and Leone renamed his earlier categories as 'intimate terrorism' and 'situational couple violence'. In renaming patriarchal terrorism as intimate terrorism, Johnson (2008) argued that not all coercive control was perpetrated by men, nor was it necessarily based in patriarchal attitudes and structures.

Johnson (2008) argues that what differentiates intimate terrorism from situational couple violence is the presence or otherwise of a motive to control a partner. While intimate terrorism aligns with the feminist analysis of violence against women in the home, where the violence is intended to control one's partner, situational couple violence is said to only be concerned with controlling a specific situation. However, as Anderson (2008) notes, it is unclear how this distinction can be made when controlling a situation must involve in part some attempt to control the partner.

For Johnson (2008), situational couple violence does not have underpinnings of power and control, and it is ungendered. Rather, violence simply emerges from arguments that escalate out of control. The model advanced by Johnson adopts a view of situational couple violence as predominantly anger-based, which has largely been discredited as a coherent framework for understanding men's violence (Rossiter 2011).

While Johnson (1995) says that he wants to defend feminist analyses, the reality is that his typology tends to reinforce the prevailing view that men's violence against women is primarily a relationship issue, as most violence against women is presented by those who use this typology as situational couple violence (Dutton and Nicholls 2005; Steegh 2005; Baird 2010). Dutton and Nicholls (2005) use Johnson's distinction between 'patriarchal terrorism' and 'common couple violence' to challenge the feminist analysis of men's violence against women as being characterised by coercive control. They argue that only 1 in 200 men arrested for violence against their partner would be identified as a patriarchal terrorist.

In contrast to claims to the contrary by Johnson and other domestic violence researchers noted earlier, Frye et al. (2006) argue that even if such a distinction was valid, situational couple violence is likely to be *less* frequent than intimate terrorism. Meier (2007) expresses concern that if situational couple violence does not constitute the majority of cases of domestic violence, it is likely that family violence courts may trivialise domestic violence as mutual when it is more likely to be a form of intimate terrorism. The introduction of typologies of violence has allowed male perpetrators of violence in the family to argue that incidents of violence against their partners were aberrant or situational when they are not (DeKeseredy and Dragiewicz 2009). Furthermore, rather than two completely separate forms of violence, so-called situational couple violence could evolve into intimate terrorism over time (Zoe 2013). All experiences of violence against women should be regarded as serious and potentially dangerous.

Stark (2006) identifies behaviourist underpinnings to Johnson's distinction between feminist and family violence researchers. Rather than understanding coercive control as a political structure that is embedded with social power, Johnson views coercive control simply as an interpersonal act that can be measured alongside acts of physical violence. However, this removes coercive control from the structural and discriminatory systems that give it power, and instead transforms it into an individualised act of volition by an individual man.

In the early stages of the women's movement, men's violence against women in the home was linked to patriarchal marriage and male domination in the wider society. However, as noted earlier, a shift has occurred, even in some feminist circles, whereby men's violence is seen as a set of controlling behaviours by men unrelated to the social and political context of gender relations. The rise of educational and therapeutic groups for violent men further consolidated the interpersonal focus of control outside of structural gender inequalities.

From domestic violence to coercive control

Stark (2007) argues that it is important to distinguish violence from coercive control, and that the latter is a particular form of injustice against women that is not captured by the language of violence. He refers to coercive control as a form of micro-regulation of women's behaviour to pressure them to conform to traditional gendered expectations. Coercive control is often enacted by abusive men without resorting to physical assault. For Stark (2007), the focus should be on the dynamics of power and control in relationships, irrespective of whether such control accompanies physical violence or not.

Stark (2010) is less concerned with who perpetrates violence and is more focused upon how violence in families reproduces gender inequality. Thus, for Stark, the focus of intervention should be structural inequalities between men and women. By locating coercive control in the context of structural gender inequality, it undermines men's rights claims that domestic violence is symmetrical, as women are not structurally in a position to exert coercive control.

Stark (2007) notes that much physical violence and abuse arises out of situations where a man feels justified in punishing his partner for what he perceives as a transgression, or using violence to prevent such an anticipated transgression from occurring. Empirical research with perpetrators of violence supports the notion of coercive control as a tactic to get women to do what men want them to do (Kuennen 2007). However, what is important to emphasise in Stark's concept of coercive control is that it is not the motives of individual perpetrators that is paramount. Rather, it is the situated power attributed to men from the wider unequal gender arrangements that enables such control to be enacted to subordinate women. Men do not need to be conscious of using violence instrumentally to control women for coercive control to take place, although they are still responsible for the consequences of their actions.

Stark (2007) argues that coercive control should be the main focus of intervention in domestic violence, rather than physical violence. Although the concepts of power and control have been influential in feminist activist and profeminist counselling circles, they have not influenced mainstream violence prevention policies. The current framing of domestic violence is premised upon incident-specific and physical injury-based definitions. Government interventions to address domestic violence are mainly focused upon physical abuse. Such a framing has obscured or minimised the dynamics and effects of coercive control (Stark 2007). The forms of non-physical abuse such as emotional and psychological abuse, which are elements of coercive control, generally do not constitute a crime, and thus the criminal justice system is unable to effectively respond to them (Williamson 2010).

Stark (2007) argues that while some progress has been made in addressing physical violence, less has been achieved in preventing the coercive control that underpins not only physical violence, but also the processes by which men undermine women's personhood and autonomy in personal life. The vulnerability of women to coercive control in private life is connected to their subordinate location within the wider relations of power in society. Thus, any movement to prevent domestic violence must transform the structural dimensions of gender inequality within which violence is situated.

Coercive control is more common in countries where patriarchal, legal, religious and cultural customs have been challenged and greater levels of equality for women have been achieved (Stark 2007). Coercive control is less necessary in cultures where the subordination of women is legitimated by external patriarchal controls. Thus, coercive control is both shaped by women's equality at the public level but sustained by gender inequalities at the private level. Stark (2007) identifies this as a paradox. The gains made by women to live independently are also the basis of men's incentive to engage in coercive control. For Stark, this escalation of coercive control in the context of greater formal gender equality is a 'tragic irony' in sexual politics.

As discussed in Chapter 2, the relationship between greater gender equality in the public realm and men's violence against women in the private realm is complex and contradictory. There is a tension between those who argue that increased gender equality will lead to a reduction in men's violence against women and those who note that men will resist threats to their male privilege in the public realm by escalating violence against women in the private realm.

There is a third view, which suggests that many men who have little power in the public realm will endeavour to control women in the household as a form of compensation for their lack of public power (Stark 2007). Hunnicutt (2009) notes that it is the least powerful men who often feel the need to resort to violence to reassert their masculinity. More powerful men do not need violence as a strategy to control women or to confirm their masculinity, as their privileged position is reinforced in other ways. When gender inequalities are structurally entrenched, violence against women is not necessary to sustain gender inequality.

Beyond coercive control

Stark (2007) argues that adopting his theory of coercive control will end the debates about gender symmetry in domestic violence. However, Anderson (2009) suggests that Stark draws too heavily upon Johnson's typology of domestic violence to distinguish between physical violence and coercive control. Stark seems to accept Johnson's premise that the enactment of violence in the context of 'situational couple violence' is not gendered. However, if we accept that gender operates on the levels of structure, interaction and identity, how do these disappear in so-called 'situational couple violence'? Why are they only present in coercive control? What is needed, as Anderson (2009) argues, is an understanding of how gender is enacted and embedded in all forms of violence between men and women in the family.

Walby and Towers (2018) also challenge the view argued by Stark and Johnson that gender asymmetry is only confined to the more extreme levels of domestic violence. They argue that all violence by men against women is coercive and controlling, and unlike Stark and Johnson they do not exempt any violent act from coercive control, irrespective of the motivation of the perpetrators of the violence and whether it is intended or unintended.

Anderson (2009) notes a contradiction in Stark's argument. While on the one hand, as previously discussed, Stark argues that coercive control increases in the face of greater formal equality for women, he also argues that the solution to ending coercive control is ending structural gender inequality. This raises the question of whether the achievement of full structural gender equality would also lead men to use coercive control to try to restore patriarchal privileges.

This is the problem of articulating only a structural view of gender inequality. It may also go some way in explaining the continued enactment of violence against women in the home in Nordic countries, as noted in Chapter 2, where greater levels of formal gender equality have been achieved. As discussed previously, this necessitates an attention to multiple levels of gender, and multiple levels of patriarchy, if we are going to effectively address both men's physical violence against women and their enactment of coercive control strategies. What is missing in most analyses of violence against women is how the multiple levels of gender and patriarchy interact to reinforce men's violence against women.

Stark (2007) suggests that part of the motivation for exercising coercive control is the cultural connection between masculine identity and being in control. However, he is concerned that too much of a focus on men's individual motivations for violence and control will take the focus off the political and structural dimensions of control. At the same time, though, as Anderson (2009) points out, a sole focus on the structural and cultural dimensions of gender inequality does not address how the wider structure and culture impacts on the behaviour of individual perpetrators of violence. Gender also functions at the interactional level of enactment and performance. This level of gender is relevant in understanding the gendered dimensions of men's micro-regulation of women's behaviours. Such behaviours by men also link to the structural level of gender inequality, which is recreated by men's enactments.

We must draw upon a multilevel understanding of gender as involving structural inequality, cultural beliefs, organisational practices, interactional behaviours, personal identities and sense of self to address the gendered dimensions of coercive control.

Domestic conflict over housework as political struggle

Addressing family violence and coercive control will not in themselves necessarily address the power imbalances in heterosexual relationships, especially those connected to housework and childcare. In some ways, the current focus on family violence may distract from the political manoeuvring in relationships and families. As noted earlier, one strategy to link physical violence to power and control has been to expand the definition of what counts as violence to enable more subtle forms of gender inequality and gendered abuse to be scrutinised. I recall an occasion when I was observing a men's behaviour change program where the facilitator was endeavouring to convince one of the male participants that his refusal to do a fair share of the housework was a form of domestic violence, as it was one of the rungs on the power and control wheel. The participant was not convinced, and neither was I. It was clearly an example of male privilege and exploitation, but was it domestic violence?

Ashcraft's (2000) notions of domestic dodging, domestic distortion and domestic neglect, noted earlier, may have been more effective language categories to convey the gendered exploitation that was being challenged. Domestic dodging involves a range of strategies men use to get out of housework, including performing duties poorly and planning activities to conflict with housework times. Domestic distortion involves maintaining that the unequal division of labour is either economically necessary or a matter of personal style. Domestic neglect involves being absent from home activities and failing to consult one's partner about important issues.

As noted in Chapter 3, Walby (1990) identifies domestic work as one of the key sites of patriarchy. It is here where men exploit the domestic labour of female partners. In a classic article, Hartmann (1981b) advanced the concept of the family as a locus of political struggle, where men's and women's interests were expressed in various forms of conflict, with a particular focus on housework and money. She challenged the prevailing view at the time that the family was not a place where men exercised power over women, and argued that housework and women's labour was a continuing source of conflict between men and women. For Hartmann (1981b), the time spent on housework by women was a good indicator of the manifestation of patriarchy in the home.

McMahon (1999) applies a materialist analysis to household work, arguing that men perceive it to be in their interests to maintain the current division of labour. He draws upon Delphy (1984), who introduced the concept of the domestic mode of production to describe how housework functioned alongside the capitalist mode of production to produce goods and services for men. For Delphy, the domestic mode of production provides an economic base for women's subordination.

In the 1970s, there was optimism that women's entry into the paid labour force would lead to increased equality between men and women in the home. Writing in 1999, McMahon was critical of what he called the 'gradual optimism' of writers who were confident that men and women would develop more egalitarian relationships in the home. Twenty years later, his pessimism about change is borne out.

There have been numerous empirical studies of the division of domestic labour. Across the years, the conclusion is the same: women still carry the major burden of housework and childcare (Thebaud 2010; Davis and Greenstein 2013; Fahlen 2016; Rousseau 2016). This is so whether wives and female partners work in the paid labour force or not. Men's increased involvement in housework has not matched women's increased participation in the paid labour force (Fahlen 2016). Men's increased involvement is generally restricted to particular activities such as drying the dishes, maintaining the garden, changing light bulbs and fuses, and taking out the rubbish (Stark 2007). Women continue to do the majority of housework, even when paid work hours are equal (Fahlen 2016).

Although some men are responsive to women's concerns about the inequality in the domestic division of labour, most men are resistant and they devise various strategies to get out of doing a fair share of housework (Kynaston 1996). The sense of male entitlement to personal services and domestic work has not been eroded after 40 years of second-wave feminism.

Many women continue to make demands on men to participate more in housework, although many women also conclude that there is more work involved in getting male partners to do their share than there is doing the work themselves (McMahon 1999). Many writers have documented the various strategies that men use to avoid domestic work, intimidation and violence among them. Mainardi (1970) illustrates the political struggle between men and women over housework in a classic article. Whenever her male partner responded with excuses to a request to do a fair share of domestic work, Mainardi analysed the patriarchal premises of each response. Almost 50 years later, men's rationalisations have not changed.

Consistent with the notion of the family as a site of political struggle (Rousseau 2016), a change in the distribution of housework is connected to the willingness, or otherwise, of women demanding change from male partners (Davis and Greenstein 2013). There is evidence that housework and childcare responsibilities are major sources of conflict between heterosexual couples (Ruppanner and Geist 2018). In the ongoing context of gender inequality in the division of domestic work, women have become less tolerant of the double shift and experience a growing sense of injustice that leads to increased levels of conflict over housework. Such conflict unsettles marital relationships and leads to great dissatisfaction among women, and often leads them to initiate separation and divorce (Kynaston 1996).

Quite apart from the presence of physical violence or coercive control, women are still carrying the major responsibility for rearing children and undertaking housework to serve the interests of individual men. Gender equality in the public sphere will not be attained while there is injustice in the home, as the gendered division of housework contributes significantly to wider gender inequalities in society (Fahlen 2016).

Conclusion

Although some writers observe a major shift occurring from private patriarchy to public patriarchy, men's practices in the private realm of the family are still significant in reproducing or challenging patriarchy. Public patriarchies are founded upon men's power and control in families, and the family remains an important structure of patriarchy.

Hearn (1987) suggests that it is in the private world of the family and domestic arrangements where men face their most difficult challenges. It is here where issues of sexuality, violence, nurture and procreation are addressed. Men can change their practices in relation to fatherhood, caring, heterosexuality and violence. They can diminish hierarchical sexual relations, reformulate caring, do their fair share of housework and abandon violence.

Van Den Berg (2015) demonstrates that when men participate equally in the household, they are less likely to be violent. He cites research from Norway (Holter et al. 2009) that shows the incidents of violence are considerably higher in households where men are not involved in housework and childcare. Similarly, the conclusion from the *State of the World Fathers Report* (Heilman et al. 2017) is that there is a relationship between men's limited contribution to care work and the likelihood of them being violent in the home. In Chapter 12, I explore the limitations and potential of men becoming more engaged in care work in the home and in the wider society.

7 | PATRIARCHAL MASCULINITIES AND MASCULINE SELVES

Introduction

It is important in emphasising the structural and cultural dimensions of patriarchy that we do not lose sight of men's subjectivities. We need to understand the psychic and emotional investments that individual men have in current patriarchal arrangements. Patriarchy not only structures institutions, but also shapes men's sense of themselves. As hooks (2004) notes, patriarchy is embedded in men's psyches. It involves intra-psychic processes that give meaning to men. Thus, this 'psychological patriarchy' must be challenged alongside the material, discursive, homosocial and interpersonal levels of patriarchy.

As patriarchy is embedded in men's subjectivities and identities, and is enacted in men's personal practices, we need to consider the limitations and potential of personal change for men. Much of the work on preventing men's violence against women and engaging men in violence prevention is focused on the personal level of men's attitudes, self-definitions and behaviour. However, the conceptualisation of masculinity and the subject implicit in many men's behaviour change programs for violent men and programs engaging men in violence prevention is inadequate in explaining the links between masculinity and violence. A more adequate conceptual framework for understanding masculinity and masculine selves is essential to determine the limitations and possibilities for change in men's subjectivities and practices.

The premise underpinning men's behaviour change programs, for example, is that men are wholly responsible for their violence and that they can change their attitudes and behaviour. However, as Hearn (2014b) notes, individual responsibility and choice are consistent with neoliberal notions of individualism and rational and autonomous behaviours that ignore the structural and social forces shaping gender relations.

At the same time, a sole focus on structural dimensions of gender inequalities ignores the agency of individual men who enact the violence and the agency of men who are complicit with the violence. While Snider (1998) acknowledges that ending men's violence will require change in the structures of patriarchy, she also outlines the importance of counter-hegemonic strategies that challenge violence at the micro level. It is important to understand the ways in which domination and violence are embedded inside the individual. We need to explain how patriarchal power at the structural level of society is connected to the violence of individual men. One of the reasons for studying masculinity is to understand how patriarchal ideology shapes and constrains men's sense of self. We need to find ways to encourage the development of male subjectivities and men's selves that reject domination. This means that we need to know more about how masculinities are formed through material and cultural forces and about how micro-level processes construct masculine subjectivities.

Hegemonic masculinity and men's violence against women

Connell (2002) argues that the concept of hegemonic masculinity is useful in analysing violence by shedding light on communities where violence and physical aggression are culturally embedded and idealised among men. Certainly, there is research which demonstrates that men's violence against women is encouraged and endorsed by men's adherence to hegemonic forms of masculinity (Gallagher and Parrott 2011; Smith et al. 2015).

Hegemonic masculinity is 'the form of masculinity which is culturally dominant in a given setting' (Connell 2001: 9). Such masculinity is idealised and promoted as a desirable attainment for boys and young men to strive towards. It is presented as heterosexual, aggressive, authorative and courageous (Connell 2000a). For Connell (1995), hegemonic masculinity involves gender practices that legitimise patriarchy by reproducing the dominance of men and the subordinate position of women. It is thus one of the ways in which patriarchal power is maintained by consent. It perpetuates gender inequality and encourages men to live up to hegemonic ideals about what it is to be a man.

If hegemonic masculinity is one of the foundations of patriarchy, it has to be addressed in some way. To focus solely on equal rights and structural changes ignores how men's advantages and privileges are defended and reproduced. Although men benefit from what Connell (1995) calls 'the patriarchal dividend', which arises from their dominant position in the gender hierarchy, they have a choice about whether they act to reproduce their privileged position or whether they actively struggle against their dominance. It is this notion of choice that encourages profeminist activists to educate men about the costs for women and men of patriarchy and to inspire them to change their personal and political practices.

In response to critics, Connell and Messerschmidt (2005) note that the concept of hegemonic masculinity has been oversimplified and misused. Hegemonic masculinity is best understood as a configuration of practices that perpetuate men's patriarchal power over women rather than as a set of traits. Masculinity is something that has to be accomplished in specific social contexts. Men do masculinity under specific constraints and with varying degrees of power (Messerschmidt 1993).

What is under-theorised in contemporary gender studies is the relationship between hegemonic masculinity and patriarchy. Is hegemonic masculinity the only form of masculinity that reproduces patriarchy? I prefer the language of patriarchal masculinities, as non-hegemonic forms of masculinity may also reproduce patriarchy, as well as those forms of masculinity that purport to be egalitarian. Hearn (2014b) looks beyond the link between hegemonic masculinity and men's violence, which legitimates patriarchy to acknowledge how complicit masculinities condone patriarchy and subordinate masculinities compensate for men's lack of power. By focusing solely on hegemonic masculinities, it can let men who embrace non-hegemonic masculinities 'off the hook' from the role that they play in reproducing patriarchy (Hearn 2012b). Most men do not recognise themselves in this framing of hegemonic masculinity, and thus they are able to argue that it is other men who are oppressive and violent (Forsberg 2010). They regard themselves as 'good men' who are progressive, caring and egalitarian towards women. Consequently, they do not see themselves as reproducing patriarchy in their attitudes and practices.

Complicit masculinities and men's violence against women

Connell (1995) defines complicit masculinities as those men who do not meet the normative standard of hegemonic masculinity but nonetheless benefit from it in various ways. Complicit masculinity is typified by the majority of men, who, while not meeting the criteria of hegemonic status of demonstrating the worst excesses of hegemonic masculinity, do not challenge either the patriarchal gender order or men's violence against women (Mills 1998). Complicit masculinities reinforce the patriarchal dividends for men without necessarily being in the hegemonic position (Connell 1995).

In relation to violence against women, complicit masculinities maintain the structures and ideologies that produce men's violence (Mills 1998). One might refer to these men as perpetuators of violence. One of the dynamics of hegemony is that it operates through consent rather than force. This means that men who do not use violence to control women nevertheless contribute to oppressive gender relations through their complicity with these unequal gender regimes (Morrell et al. 2013).

The important component of complicit masculinity is that while most men are not able to embody hegemonic masculinity ideals, they nevertheless support them and judge other men's behaviour against them. Thus, men's violence, as a more oppressive form of gendered power, is supported by larger numbers of men who are complicit with it.

The implications of placing complicit masculinity in the foreground is to acknowledge that it is not only violent men who needed to be addressed by violence prevention campaigns, but also those larger numbers of men who, while not physically violent, support the culture within which such violence is enacted (Pease 2008).

Hearn (2012b) suggests that complicit masculinity may be a greater problem than hegemonic masculinity. So-called 'ordinary men' who fit Connell's notion of complicit masculinity may constitute the most hegemonic form of masculinity because it is so widespread. Thus, complicit men may ironically achieve hegemonic status by distancing themselves from hegemonic masculinity (Scheff 2003). As most men are complicit in their support of hegemonic masculinity, they actually constitute another form of dominant masculinity.

Many women are also complicit with hegemonic forms of masculinity. To the extent that women adhere to what Connell (1987) calls 'emphasised femininity', which involves an acceptance of women's subordinate position, they also act in ways that reproduce hegemonic forms of masculinity. When women expect men to be economic providers and protectors and believe that men should be dominant and in control, they also perpetuate patriarchal gender relations (Morrell et al. 2013). Thus, dominant forms of masculinity are not only reproduced by men; they are also actively constructed by women as well in their roles as sexual partners, wives, mothers, co-workers and friends. Consequently, various forms of femininity encourage men and women to be compliant with patriarchy.

Marginalised masculinities and men's violence against women

Hegemonic masculinity needs to be understood in relation to masculinities that are marginalised by class and race and subordinated by sexuality. The concept of marginalised masculinities illustrates how the diversity of masculinities is marked by hierarchy and exclusion (Connell 2000a).

Connell (1995) notes that working-class men do not have the same access to the patriarchal dividend as middle- and upper-class men. As working-class men have less power at work, they are more likely to feel the need to be a patriarch at home and to express their masculinity through domestic control. If their authority and power are further threatened, they are likely to use violence to affirm their masculinity and re-establish control over their partner (Messerschmidt 1993). This explains in part why men who lack power, or whose power is threatened, enact violence towards women. Consequently, masculinities do not need to be hegemonic to be harmful or violent. Herek (1987) has demonstrated that abusive and violent behaviours are often enacted among marginalised men who use violence and coercive power as a compensation for their relative powerlessness in the wider economy.

Hegemonic masculinity does not capture all of the forms of men's dominance and power. While hegemonic masculinity is often linked to white and class-privileged men, they may not need to rely upon violence or force to control women (Groes-Green 2009). They are often able to rely on consent and accommodation of women to their power, while marginalised men establish their superiority more forcefully through violence and other forms of abuse.

In this context, associating hegemonic masculinity with violence does not capture the masculinity–violence link, as white class-privileged men may have less need to enact physical violence against women to exercise control over them. When men perform their roles as provider and protector of women, many women consent to men's power and authority. Thus, emphasising the link between hegemonic masculinity and violence may neglect the ways in which marginalised masculinities enact aggressive sexuality and physical violence (Groes-Green 2009).

Psychoanalytic engagements with masculinity

Psychoanalytic theorists have raised concerns about hegemonic masculinity's lack of ability to explain how gender identity is constructed. Jefferson (2002) argues that Connell's emphasis on the structural dimensions of gender takes attention away from understanding the psychic aspects of men's lives. Psychoanalytic perspectives are said to provide an opening into the psychic complexity of men's lives and ways of overcoming resistance to change. For Gadd (2000), men's resistance to challenges to their dominance can be understood as unconscious attempts by men to defend themselves against psychic threats to their experience of vulnerability. Thus, in this view, men's violence can be understood as a way of men warding off feelings of weakness.

Feminists have utilised psychoanalytic theory to understand the connections between men's power and men's identity. Juliet Mitchell (1974) provided an early feminist-informed psychoanalytic view in which she regarded the symbolic power of the fathers as being located in the unconscious as a key dimension of patriarchy. From a psychoanalytic perspective, masculinity is reproduced by denying the feminine (Frosh 1994). Jukes (1993), a psychoanalyst who works with violent men, argues that because men feel such enmity towards women, they feel a need to control and dominate them.

Feminist psychoanalysts, such as Chodorow (1978), argue that many of men's abusive behaviours can be located in the suppression of emotions, especially empathy and compassion, as these are in conflict with the expectations associated with men's dominance and power. For psychoanalytic theorists, it is the defensive and fragile male psyche that is at the heart of men's resistance to challenges to their dominance. Consequently, for Chodorow (1978), democratising the gendered division of labour in the care of children would eliminate the contrasting socialisation into masculinity and femininity and the gender binary that flows from that contrast. She argues that men's involvement in childcare would change the personality structure of men, and that eventually over time it would eliminate men's dominance over women (see Chapter 12).

Chodorow's account has been criticised on numerous grounds. For Segal (1987), infantile attachment to the mother is only one aspect of the formation of masculinity, and Chodorow's theory underemphasises the importance of social and ideological structures outside the family. In Segal's view, violence and discrimination against women result from structural inequalities of power between men and women rather than internal psychic dynamics in men. Similarly, for McMahon (1999), Chodorow does not adequately take into account men's agency in the maintenance of patriarchy and fails to recognise the extent to which the division of labour is in men's interests.

Psychoanalytic understandings should not be seen as being necessarily in opposition to structuralist accounts of men's violence and they do not need to psychologise what are sociopolitical problems. Rather, they can shed insight into the defences and projections of men as they engage with challenges to their privilege and power (Gadd 2002).

Naranjo (2018) talks about the patriarchal mind, which involves violence, absence of caring, and repression of instincts and intuition as being at the heart of what he defines as social pathologies. Although there is no mention of hegemonic masculinity, his outline of what he calls the 'patriarchal complex' mirrors critical discussions about masculinity. For Naranjo, the healing of interpersonal and social pathologies requires the healing of the patriarchal mind. Patriarchal society, in this view, is reproduced through the patriarchal psyche of individual men. While Naranjo's emphasis on changing individual men's subjectivities as the prerequisite for transforming political and social institutions tends towards psychologism, he is correct in stating that changes in social and political structures will not in themselves address the deeply embedded patriarchal desires of individual men.

Craib (2011) argues that changing men's subjectivities and changing social and political structural inequalities are two completely different projects. In this view, transforming social institutions will not necessarily change individual men, although it is likely, he says, to increase men's anxieties. It seems clear that the project of transforming patriarchal gender relations will involve a degree of pain for men. It will be what Rowan (1989) calls a 'wounding' experience. This is certainly consistent with my own personal experience of change in response to women's demands for gender equality.

While combining these different perspectives creates some tensions, psychoanalytic insights can assist in explaining the ways in which dominant forms of masculinity are constructed and sustained. Patriarchal masculinity is deeply embedded in the ego and the superego (to use psychoanalytic terms). Thus, transformation and change require more than just a change in consciousness and behaviour by men.

The emotional turn in masculinities

Living up to traditional notions of masculinity and what it means to be a man requires men to suppress their emotions. Seidler (2007) argues that in focusing on men's power alone, men's vulnerability is neglected. Even powerful and privileged men often experience vulnerability, although it is rarely acknowledged. If we only focus on men's power, we will be unable to understand how masculinity also contributes to men's pain.

Some hyper-masculine men have a history of personal trauma, and engaging with men's vulnerability may open up new ways of understanding masculinist practices among men (Jewkes et al. 2015b). However, in recognising men's pain and emotional suppression, we have to be careful not to overly psychologise men's dominance. Men's need to dominate others is not solely a result of their emotional deficits (Messner 1997). Focusing on the costs for men of patriarchy and dominant forms of masculinity may shift the focus away from the unearned advantages and privileges men receive.

The question is whether it is possible to explore men's vulnerabilities and emotions without sliding into men's rights framing of men as victims. Farrell (1993) has argued that men's feelings of powerlessness are indicators that men are actually not powerful or privileged. However, the personal insecurities of powerful and privileged men do not negate the social analysis of their power and privilege. Rather, it is the construction of patriarchal forms of masculinity that lead men to pursue particular forms of power that paradoxically create feelings of powerlessness and insecurity (de Boise and Hearn 2017).

The capacity for men to enact dominance, strength and superiority seemingly requires a high level of emotional detachment, as any form of emotional expression is seen as feminine and weak. For many men, avoiding what are perceived to be feminine behaviours, values and sensibilities is an essential part of maintaining men's dominance and subordinating women (Smith et al. 2015). Consequently, men detaching themselves from their emotions is important in reproducing gender inequality (Arxer 2011).

Seidler (2007) says that the emphasis in dominant forms of masculinity on independence and self-sufficiency makes it difficult for men to acknowledge emotions of fear and vulnerability because such emotions threaten their identity as men. This inability to experience vulnerable emotions can easily lead men to express anger and violence to affirm their manhood. For Seidler, violence is a reaction to feelings of vulnerability and inadequacy. While this understanding should not be used to justify or excuse men's violence, he argues that it may provide an opening to address the relationship between men's emotional life and their exercising of power and control.

Scheff (2006) also argues that men's suppression of emotions creates a greater propensity for violence. The lack of ability to acknowledge shame, vulnerability and emotional issues leads to anger, aggression and violence. For Scheff, it is important for men to be able to express the full range of emotions, including those of vulnerability, if they are to achieve a balanced emotional life.

Acknowledging that there may well be unconscious pain and alienation in men's lives, and that these suppressed experiences may influence men's harassment, violence and abuse, does not necessarily negate a structural analysis of patriarchy and men's material interests in maintaining it. bell hooks (2004) has commented that it is important to acknowledge how men are also wounded by patriarchy and that the focus on men's power and privileges should also acknowledge men's pain. She argues that men need to come to terms with the ways in which patriarchy has emotionally diminished them as part of a pathway towards their rebellion against patriarchy. When men are brutalised by patriarchy, they are more likely to adopt forms of patriarchal masculinity to cover up their pain and suffering. Thus, it is important to acknowledge the ways in which men are also damaged by patriarchy to encourage them to develop pathways to full emotional well-being. This will involve men understanding the ways in which patriarchy is embedded in their psyches.

Can masculinity be reformed?

Connell (1995) depicts masculinities as historically and culturally situated and embedded in social relations of particular societies. She emphasises that the hegemonic form is not a type of masculinity per se, but is rather whatever type of masculinity is dominant in a given context at a given time. This means that it is conceivable that hegemonic masculinity could be transformed from a negative and destructive form to a positive and egalitarian form. Some theorists argue that hegemonic masculinity in Sweden, for example, where substantive gender equality has been achieved, is egalitarian and not oppressive towards women (Jewkes et al. 2015b).

Is the dominant form of masculinity, or any form of masculinity for that matter, necessarily oppressive? Morrell et al. (2013) argue that it is possible to envisage a form of hegemonic masculinity that does not involve the domination of women and other men. They thus posit the achievement of non-oppressive forms of masculinity as one of the key objectives of profeminist work. Brod (1998) believes that this is essential because if profeminist men have to leave their masculinity behind, they will be unable to sustain their commitment to profeminist politics. He argues that profeminist men need to have a positive vision for themselves as men to effectively engage with feminism.

Many profeminist activists who are aiming to change the ideals of dominant forms of masculinity talk about 'gender-transformative' approaches to change (Barker et al. 2007; Jewkes et al. 2015b). Macleod (2007) notes that men's alternative forms of subjectivity are generally contained within the boundaries of masculinity. While profeminist men proclaim more peaceful and progressive forms of masculinity, they are nevertheless still forms of masculinity. So, rather than undoing or exiting masculinity, they are simply shifting from one form of masculinity to another.

However, creating more gender-equal men will not in itself disrupt the gender binary as it does not challenge the division between masculinity and femininity that upholds the patriarchal gender order (Schippers 2007). Consequently, the masculine–feminine binary is maintained, and while it is in place masculinity will always be positioned as superior. The focus on changing masculinity then pushes the project of transforming patriarchal social relations into the background.

Given that masculinity is constructed against femininity (Bourdieu 2002), the question is raised whether there is a form of masculinity that is not at the expense of women. If one of the functions of hegemonic masculinity is to ensure that so-called 'masculine' qualities are valued above so-called 'feminine' qualities, it is hard to imagine how any form of hegemonic masculinity could not involve a devaluing of what is regarded as feminine. The hegemony involved in masculinity is likely to ensure that it legitimates the interests of men as the dominant group (Arxer 2011).

While masculinity and femininity remain as gender-specific qualities for men and women, respectively, a hierarchical relationship involving men in the superordinate position and women in the subordinate position will remain. Thus, masculinity must always be constituted as superior to femininity (Schippers 2007). One of the main challenges in struggling for changes in gender relations is whether or not it is possible to move beyond the binary of gender.

The problem is that if men define their gender identity through some form of masculinity, all attempts to redefine or reconstruct masculinity towards non-violence or gender equality means that men are still defining themselves as not being a woman. Thus, non-violent and equitable forms of masculinity are seen to embrace values and behaviours that are different from those available to women. For Greig (2002), to create non-violent social relations between men and women, the logic of gender itself must be challenged, for it is premised upon hierarchical social relations.

A number of commentators have identified various ways in which men can respond to challenges to their patriarchal privilege by inventing new ways of being a man that appear to address feminist concerns but actually reproduce their privileged position (Montez de Oca 2012; Bridges 2014; Matthews 2016). Men may change their masculinity and their sense of themselves as men, but unequal gender relations remain. It appears that some alternative forms of masculinity may seem to challenge patriarchy, and yet men are able to maintain their positions of privilege within changing conceptions of masculinity. Men may take on elements of femininity and present softer and more progressive versions of masculinity, while at the same time holding on to power (Matthews 2016).

Is masculinity a distraction?

From the early days of masculinity studies, many feminists expressed concerns about the potential of research into masculinities becoming more focused on men's interests than feminist agendas. While the focus on masculinity within critical masculinity studies has been on how it legitimates patriarchy, some commentators have expressed concern about the dangers in shifting the analysis from patriarchy to masculinities

(Acker 1989; McMahon 1999; Macleod 2007; Hearn 2012b). It has certainly contributed to a decline in the language of patriarchy in gender studies more generally and masculinity studies in particular.

Masculinity is ultimately seen to be located within individual men and it is often used to refer to male sex role characteristics of men. Such a framing draws predominantly from psychology and social psychology (Robertson et al. 2016). Often, when linked to men's abusive practices, it is attributed with causal power in that it is masculinity that is seen as the primary cause of men's dominance and violent practices in the world. It can thus be used to explain and excuse men's behaviour. When we frame masculinity as a cause of men's violence, we take responsibility away from the men who perpetrate it. This can lead to a focus on changing masculinity at the expense of men changing their behaviour. McCarry (2007) questions whether reconstructing masculinity will necessarily lead to the elimination of men's violence.

Given the focus in critical masculinity studies on masculinity as a range of practices, some critical gender theorists shift the focus to the acts men perform to reproduce gender inequality. Schrock and Schwalbe (2009) suggest that one of the consequences of focusing on masculinities is, as noted earlier, that it is masculinity that is used to explain men's behaviour. Masculinity in this context is disconnected from men's agency. Rather than focusing on masculinities, they emphasise the importance of examining how men's practices reproduce gender inequality. Schrock and Schwalbe (2009) refer to these practices as 'manhood acts'.

While hegemonic masculinity may be useful in understanding some elements of men's violence against women, it does not address men's material and structural power over women (Hearn 2014b). Hearn (2012b) also argues that the concept of masculinity obscures the material practices of men. Men focus too much on reforming their masculinity rather than transforming their practices.

Some critical gender theorists argue that it is possible to achieve gender equality without individual men having to change their subjectivities or their practices (MacInnes 1998; Whitehead 2002). MacInnes (1998) argues that masculinity is not a character trait or an aspect of men's identity, but is rather an ideology. As such, for him, it does not make sense to suggest that men need to change their masculinity as part of the struggle for gender equality. He argues that changing men's personal identities is unlikely to have any impact on social change and that it retreats from a concern with social forces and structures of gender inequality. The focus, for MacInnes, should be on equal rights as opposed to the reforming of masculinity, which he argues is a conservative dead end.

At the same time, a focus on changing structural relations of power without changing men will not address the need for men to build and maintain equitable relationships with women. The challenge is how to address the personal, interpersonal, homosocial, cultural and structural dimensions of men's violence simultaneously.

Conclusion

All men who are raised within a patriarchal society will be exposed to pressures about what it means to be a man and how men are expected to behave. Invariably, these pressures will be internalised and will shape men's attitudes and practices in relation to women. While some men may come to resist such pressures and seek to establish respectful and equal relationships with women, this will involve them 'going against the grain'. For many men, however, they may not be conscious of the extent to which the expectations of patriarchy have been internalised within their psyches. It is thus necessary for men to understand patriarchy and its influence on their lives if they are to find a way of challenging it.

The catch cry of 'the personal is political' in second-wave feminism emphasised the importance of interpersonal and personal experiences as important arenas of political struggle. It was thus important not only to transform structural relations of power, but also feelings, attitudes, beliefs and practices of individuals as well (de Boise and Hearn 2017). This has important implications for men's engagement with patriarchy.

It is generally agreed that profeminist men should endeavour to 'walk the talk' in gender politics, and that it would be hypocritical for men to challenge patriarchy at the public level while reproducing it at the personal level (see Chapter 12). Thus, it has become important to understand how men's identities reproduce gender inequalities and to develop practices to change those identities to support a trans-formation of patriarchy (Ashe 2007).

While it would be naive to argue that reconstructing the self alone is likely to achieve gender equality, to ignore the subjectivities and prac-tices of individual men as part of the struggle against patriarchy is also problematic. Why does the politics have to polarise the struggle for personal change against the collective struggle for structural changes in gender relations? Demanding changes in men's subjectivities and personal practices does not negate demanding public support for gender equality at material and ideological levels. It does not require an either/or political response, but rather a multilevel engagement with all of the dimensions of patriarchy.

It is argued here that symbolic, discursive, structural, interactional and psychic dimensions of gender are not exclusive or contradictory in relation to each other, as is so often argued. Any lasting change to address the violences of men will require changes in structural and cultural relations of gender and changes in individual men's lives.

PART THREE

LINKING MEN'S VIOLENCE AGAINST WOMEN TO OTHER VIOLENCES BY MEN

8 | GENDERING MEN'S PUBLIC VIOLENCE AGAINST MEN

Introduction

Although men are the primary perpetrators of most violence in the world, it is still contentious to explain such violence with reference to gender, masculinity and patriarchy. Very few violence prevention policies explicitly name men as perpetrators in the framing of the intervention, although it is implicit that they are the target of such policies. When gender analyses are used in understanding violence, the focus tends to be primarily upon women as victims, sometimes with an acknowledgement (usually as a footnote) that most of the perpetrators are male.

In response to backlash criticisms by anti-feminist commentators who ask, 'What about the men?', violence prevention organisations in Australia maintain that violence against women is substantially different to violence against men (Melbourne Research Alliance to End Violence against Women and Their Children 2018; Our Watch 2018). They do so on the basis that most violence against women occurs in the home, while most violence against men occurs in public settings. They also suggest that while the patterns and dynamics of violence against women are gendered, they imply that violence against men is not gendered. These explanations are used to legitimate a focus on addressing violence against women to the exclusion of violence against men. However, the premise of this chapter is that there are commonalities in the violence that men enact towards women and the violence they enact towards other men (Archer 1994a; Fleming et al. 2015; Heilman and Barker 2018).

Men's violence against men as gendered violence

Men are not only the vast majority of perpetrators of violence; they are also more likely than women to be victims of men's violence (Polk 1994; Barker 2005; Fleming et al. 2015; Heilman and Barker 2018). This applies to homicide and lethal violence, as Polk (1994) demonstrated almost 25 years ago, and which continues to be the case

(Flynn et al. 2016; Heilman and Barker 2018). With the exception of domestic violence, men are also more likely than women to be victims of non-fatal violence by other men (Barker 2005; Fleming et al. 2015).

There is often silence about men mostly being the victims of men's violence. A number of commentators have noted that male-on-male violence is not considered a form of gendered violence (Tomsen 2008; Seymour 2012; Fleming et al. 2015). In a study conducted by Seymour (2010), while participants regarded 'domestic violence' as a form of violence by *some* men that was unacceptable, men's violence towards other men was perceived as normal and something that virtually all men were involved in. Where domestic violence was understood as men abusing gendered power over women, violence between men was not considered to be a gender issue. Gender and gender power were only seen to be significant when women were the victims of men's violence.

Men's violence against women is increasingly publicly condemned by governments, while much of men's violence against men continues to be accepted and normalised in most cultures (Flood 2007; Seymour 2010, 2018a). While some forms of men's violence are condemned and punished, other forms of violence by men are legitimated and endorsed. The term 'gender-based violence', for example, is often assumed to mean only men's violence against women, whereas others argue that it also encompasses, or should encompass, men's violence against men as well (Greig 2002; Carpenter 2006; Dolan 2014; Wojnicka 2015).

It is understandable that there would be concerns in shifting the focus from women as the primary victims of men's violence due to the fear that this will lead to a de-gendering of violence and will undo the prioritising of women and girls in violence prevention programs (Ward 2016). Also, some of the arguments that include men as victims of 'gender-based' violence are based upon criticisms of feminist framings (Dolan 2014). However, when the focus is only on female victims of men's violence, the gaze is shifted away from the practices of men who do violence both to women and to other men. This shift takes attention away from the links between men's violence against women and girls and men's violence against men and boys. Furthermore, it limits our understanding of gendered power and how such power is enacted and constituted through policies of the state (Nayak and Suchland 2006).

Linking men's violence against women and men's violence against men

Over 30 years ago, Morgan (1987) explored the links between different forms and levels of violence, from men's interpersonal violence in the home to men's collective levels of violence in gangs and warfare. He noted that some forms of violence by men are legitimated and normalised in society through an acceptance of an aggressive, competitive and hierarchical culture. Such legitimated violence between men takes' many forms, including fighting and violence between young men in groups, men's violence on the sporting field, and violence between men in war. One could also add institutional rituals in university fraternities, the military, sporting clubs and workplaces that promote male-to-male violence.

At the time of Morgan's publication, Kaufman (1987) also situated men's violence against other men within what he calls a 'triad of men's violence', where the other forms of men's violence are directed towards women and at men themselves in terms of self-harm. More recently, Heilman and Barker (2018) identified the connections between patriarchal masculine norms and eight forms of men's violent behaviour: intimate partner violence, physical violence against children, child sexual abuse and exploitation, bullying, homicide and other violent crime, non-partner sexual violence, suicide, and war. They argue that focusing only on one form of violence in violence prevention neglects the links between the causes of perpetration. Consequently, strategies to address one form of men's violence are likely to fail if they ignore the other forms of violence by men.

Archer (1994a) observes that the structural power that legitimates men's violence against women and the power struggles between men are interrelated. It is important to note that while some forms of violence between men are largely conceptualised in terms of mutual combat between equals, other forms of men's violence perpetrated against men take place in the context of hierarchical power relations between men that are similar to those between men and women. Such conflicts are often shaped by power struggles between different forms of masculinity, including marginalised, subordinate and hegemonic forms (Tomsen and Crofts 2012).

There is also considerable empirical evidence that men who enact violence towards women also commit violence towards other men outside the home (Archer 1994b; Jones 2013; Pain 2014). Thus, men's violence against women in the home is associated with the use of violence by men more widely. Similar patriarchal gender norms shape men's violence against men as those that influence men's violence against women (Fleming et al. 2015). However, almost all engagement with violent men is focused on the perpetration of violence against female partners.

The ideological beliefs held by men who are violent towards women are the same beliefs informing men's violence towards men. Such beliefs include a traditional understanding of manhood and masculinity, achieving and maintaining status through risk-taking and fighting, and a view of women as property. Such values promote interpersonal conflict between men and men's control of women, both of which support violence to achieve these ends (Archer 1994a).

Part of the resistance to seeing men as victims of men's violence is that the image of men as vulnerable does not correspond to the hegemonic view of men as powerful and dominant. Thus, to see men as experiencing harm in itself challenges the traditional hegemonic view of men, which itself is at the heart of men's violence (Wojnicka 2015). When men are victimised by other men, their framing of victimisation as being weak and helpless leads them to experience shame and isolates them from support and help (Stanko and Hobdell 1993). Supporting such men, and engaging them in prevention against men's violence, is an important strategy in overcoming a patriarchal gender order.

While some commentators have made the case for the gendered character of men's subjection to violence (Barker 2005; Flood 2007; Dolan 2014), little consideration has been given to the gendered nature of men's perpetration of violence against other men. Thus, the focus is on men as victims of such violence rather than the gendered nature of men's perpetration of violence against other men.

Theorising men's violence against other men

Patriarchy is not only a gender order that involves men's domination over women; it also involves hierarchies among men whereby some groups of men dominate other groups of men. In this context, violence is both a mechanism for imposing power over men and men resisting such power. While masculinity is most often discussed in the context of men's relations with women, men demonstrate their manhood more in relations with other men. Men use violence in policing other men (Whitehead 2005). Barker (2005), for example, notes that young men and boys in Africa are socialised into forms of masculinity that involve violence and abuse of other men. Men's violence against other men is connected to the importance among many men of maintaining status within all-male groups and as a vehicle for proving one's masculinity.

A number of writers point out that masculinity is primarily performed for an audience of other men (Kimmel 1994; Polk 1994; Tomsen 2008). Tomsen (2005) is one of the few masculinity scholars to explore the gendered basis of men's violence against men. Many men interviewed by Tomsen talked about how they used violence against other men to impress women and enhance their masculine status by punishing other men who failed to conform to traditional masculinity.

Whitehead (2005) identifies two ways in which men affirm their masculinity through violence against other men: displaying courage against a rival man, and humiliating another man by negating his masculinity. Many incidents of violence between men are related to conflict over honour and the risk-taking involved in crimes. Men's violence against men involves a range of situations, including friends, acquaintances and strangers (Polk 1994). Much of the violence between men escalates from relatively minor altercations arising from jostling and insults. Men are quick to respond to any challenge to their honour. Thus, in most forms of male-on-male violence, there is some form of perceived challenge to the perpetrator's masculinity (Connell 2014).

Intersectionalising men's violence against men

It is now widely recognised that an intersectional analysis is important in understanding and addressing men's violence against women (Sokoloff and Dupont 2005; Murdolo and Quazon 2016; Beringola 2017). Such an analysis has important implications for men's violence against men. All men under patriarchy have power and privilege in relation to women. The hierarchy of power between men, however, also means that some men are dominated by other men, as is the case with immigrant men, young and old men, disabled men, gay men, men of colour and working-class men.

Men who are members of privileged groups are more likely to be perpetrators of violence against other men, while men who are marginalised by class, race, ethnicity, religion or able-bodiedness are more likely to be victims of men's violence (Wojnicka 2015). Men who do not conform to the dominant conception of heterosexual masculinity, such as gay, bisexual and queer men, as well as transsexual and transgender people, are more vulnerable to men's violence. Heterosexual men who are not members of the dominant white Anglo male group, such as asylum seekers, refugees, Aboriginal men or men who are members of minority religions, are more likely to become victims of men's violence. Furthermore, disabled men, homeless men and men in shelters or prisons are also more likely to experience men's violence. Finally, older men and younger men are more vulnerable to violence than middle-aged men and are also more likely to be living in institutional care settings where they are vulnerable to violence by male staff members (Wojnicka 2015). This is not to deny that marginalised men can also enact violence against privileged men, just as women can enact violence towards men.

The concepts of hegemonic, subordinated and marginalised masculinities illustrate the ways that men are structurally positioned in unequal relations, whereby some men have power over other men (Messerschmidt 1998). Marginalised men have limited opportunities to attain traditional forms of masculinity (Whitehead 2005). Thus, men who are subordinated by class and race and who are excluded from traditional forms of male power may enact physical violence as a way of affirming their masculinity in the face of their structural erosion of power. Such men may not be able to obtain paid employment that affords many men with status and power. For them, physical violence may be one of the few means to achieve some form of masculinity within the particular context of their lives (Fleming et al. 2015).

Kimmel (2013) refers to these men as experiencing 'aggrieved entitlement'. These men are angry because they have either lost or not been able to attain status and resources to which they feel entitled. Montoya (cited in Greig 2000) argues that men are most prone to violence when they feel least powerful. Most mass killings are carried out by men who experience themselves as having lost out in the system (Barker 2016). Experiences of marginalisation and disadvantage foster anger and hostility towards others who are scapegoated and blamed for white men's loss of privilege (Treadwell and Garland 2011).

These arguments highlight the complexities of gendered power relations. Men's structural and collective advantages do not always translate smoothly to the lives of individual men. Moving beyond individual incidents of male-on-male violence to an understanding of social divisions between men reflected in different locations in hierarchies of power and different and competing masculinities enables us to see clearly the everyday violences in relations between men.

Public violence by men

Violence in the private realm of the family is separated out from violence in the public realm. Most forms of public violence are perpetrated by men and boys, but this is rarely acknowledged as such. So-called 'king-hit' violence, perpetrated by men, most often against other men, is currently a matter of concern in Australia (Connell 2014). What is notable in much commentary about one-punch assaults in Australia is that these are framed as the 'coward punch' and are regarded as unfair, so as to differentiate them from other forms of male violence that are acceptable or even honourable (Flynn et al. 2016; Seymour 2018a).

Men's sense of their masculinity is connected to their use of violence. Physical violence between men in public spaces often occurs in the aftermath of insults and verbal threats (Archer 1994b). Men are expected to be able to defend themselves against threats to themselves, their possessions and 'their women'. Thus, even minor insults can often escalate into physical violence, as men have to find a way of saving face and not being seen to back down.

It is often the case when men's status or power is threatened that they use violence to exercise power and re-establish their position among other men. Sometimes seemingly trivial events such as spilling a beer or being perceived as flirting with another man's partner may be sufficient to evoke male-on-male violence (Carrington et al. 2010). So-called 'alcohol-related' violence is primarily about the performance of masculinity, especially among working-class men (Lindsay 2012).

Drinking alcohol and fighting are two key markers of traditional masculinity. While alcohol itself cannot be seen as a cause of men's violence, drinking alcohol is often associated with the perpetration of violence (Connell 2014). Drinking often makes men feel stronger and more masculine and it encourages the inclination towards fighting (Canaan 1996). Men who drink to intoxication are at a particularly high risk of either becoming violent or being a victim of another man's violence (Lindsay 2012). Rogan (2015) demonstrates, through the men he interviewed, that such risky drinking is informed and shaped by men's understanding of masculinity, whereby they expressed their masculine identity through their drinking practices.

Youth violence or violence by young men?

Youth violence is another field where there is little acknowledge-ment that most of the violence is perpetrated by young men against other young men. Thus, although young men are significantly over-represented in all forms of youth violence, analyses and interventions rarely acknowledge masculinities and unequal gender relations (Fleming et al. 2015).

Similarly, the literature on school violence often fails to consider why it is only boys who perpetrate violence on their classmates. Kantola et al. (2011) point out that in Finland and the United States, media reporting of school shootings neglected gender analyses. Terms such as 'gang violence', 'youth violence' and 'teen violence' lack a gendered analysis of who is perpetrating the violence (Kimmel and Mahler 2003).

Boys are more likely than girls to experience bullying in schools, and such bullying reproduces hegemonic masculinity. These boys who are most likely to be subjected to bullying are those that do not conform to traditional masculinity. Boys will often engage in hyper-masculine behaviours to reinforce their own often fragile sense of masculinity (Vojdik 2014). Tonso (2009) draws parallels between the Montreal massacre and the Columbine school shooting as two forms of public violence by men where male perpetrators used violence to re-establish their position within social hierarchies that they believed had reduced their privilege. In both cases, internalised male supremacy that was unfulfilled was the catalyst for the sense of entitlement that enabled the perpetrators to enact deadly violence. All perpetrators felt a sense of injustice because their privileged positioning was usurped by others. The supremacist belief that some should have rights over others and the legitimacy of violence as a means to reassert privilege combined to justify the violence. Just as men's great propensity to commit violence is related to them trying to live up to a traditional model of manhood, so is men's greater vulnerability to such violence, as they involve them-selves in dangerous situations. They are, in Barker's (2005) words, 'dying to be men'.

Most homicides among young men are gang-related. Men are far more likely than women to be involved in gangs, and such gangs often promote codes of behaviour that emphasise violence, hostility towards women and an exaggerated sense of male honour (Barker 2005). Hagedorn (1998) commented 20 years ago that most of the sociological research at that time on male gangs had neglected gender. With few exceptions (Treadwell and Garland 2011; Baird 2012; Armstrong and Rosbrook-Thompson 2017), this is still the case.

Hate crimes by men

Most hate crimes involving racist and homophobic attacks are further forms of men's violence. While all men are presented as being invulnerable, gay men and non-white men both have to carefully negotiate their vulnerability in homophobic and racist societies (Stanko and Hobdell 1993).

In the United States, black men are most likely to be victims of police violence (Barker 2016). Messerschmidt (1998) documents how lynching of African American men was a response by white men to the erosion of their dominance. Lynching was a mechanism of these men doing a form of white supremacist masculinity in an attempt to restore their dominant status.

Violence against gay men is another form of gender-based hate violence. Research in Australia on anti-gay homicides reveals that almost all of the killings are by male perpetrators (Tomsen 2013). Gay-identified men and women have been on the receiving end of homophobic violence largely by men for many years. Anti-homosexual homocides are often defended on the basis of allegations of a homosexual advance, where such an advance is experienced by some men as such an affront to their masculinity that violence is argued as a justified response (Tomsen and Crofts 2012).

Homophobic violence is premised upon a hierarchy of masculinities. Normative heterosexuality is a central characteristic of a patriarchal gender order (Greig 2002). Men who commit violence against those men who are perceived to be gay are often endeavouring to prove their heterosexuality and their masculinity (Flood 2007). Kantola et al. (2011) argue that gay-bashing is less to do with prejudice against non-heterosexual sexual identities and more to do with the perceived failure to conform to hegemonic masculinity. Just as inequalities between men and women facilitate men's violence, so do power hierarchies among men. If men do not prove themselves to be powerful and strong, they will be victimised by other men, as is the case of gay men and others who do not conform to traditional norms of masculinity. Men are encouraged to prove themselves to be 'real men' by showing contempt for non-heterosexual men. In this sense, men's violence is as much about hierarchies among men as it is about dominance over women (Fleming et al. 2015).

Sexual violence against men in war

Men, of course, are more likely to be involved in armed conflict and wars (see Chapter 9). There is also a gendered dimension to the killing and torture of men in military and political conflicts. Carpenter (2006) notes that male civilians are more likely than female civilians to be singled out for execution. She also examines the forced recruitment of adult men in wartime as a form of gendered violence, as it results from culturally constructed gender roles.

Much sexual violence against men occurs in war and conflict settings. Sexual violence by men against men includes mental and physical abuse, castration, rape and enforced sex with other men (Vojdik 2014). Such violence against men is often neglected and no analysis is offered to understand this violence as a gendered practice. Feminist campaigns against sexual violence and rape in war have focussed only or primarily on female victims (Colombini 2002; Grey and Shepherd 2012; Vojdik 2014). Feminists are accused by some critics as being indifferent to the suffering of men (Carpenter 2006; Dolan 2014).

Many of the critiques of feminist accounts of sexual violence that focus only on women do not recognise the gendered nature of men's sexual violence against men (Vojdik 2014). Thus, they end up taking a critical stance towards feminism and gender analyses rather than enriching such analyses. Feminist theory and critical masculinity studies provide the necessary insights to make sense of sexual violence against men. As such, they offer an important alternative to those who argue that to address men as victims requires moving beyond feminist and gender analyses of sexual violence.

Men's sexual violence against other men needs to be understood as another gendered weapon of war, as such violence empowers particular groups of men. Perpetrators of sexual violence against men feminise male victims while valorising themselves as masculine in the frame of dominant masculinity. Violence against men in war and conflict settings is a means of asserting masculine domination over men, in the same way that such power is used over women. Men's sexual violence against men is also about masculine power and domination, and thus serves similar purposes to men's sexual violence against women (Vojdik 2014). Thus, sexual violence against men is related to sexual violence against women. In Vojdik's (2014) view, men's sexual violence against women and men is mutually reinforcing. Challenging sexual violence against men involves the same focus on hegemonic masculinity as challenging sexual violence against women.

A masculinities theoretical perspective enables us to theorise the interconnections between the enacting of power by men as individuals with the institutionalised male power in the workplace, the military, the state and the global social order. It provides a vehicle for theorising the use of masculinity to attain ethnic power at the national and global level (Vojdik 2014).

What about women's violence against men in patriarchy?

When men are considered as victims of violence, it is the public debate about women's violence to men that is most highlighted. The One in Three Campaign in Australia challenges the focus on men as perpetrators of violence towards women by arguing that women's violence against men is ignored (One in Three Campaign n.d.). This is way out of context, given the relatively small amount of female perpetrators of violence to men. Such men generally do not acknowledge men's violence against other men.

The number of acts of physical violence by women against men are miniscule compared to the levels of violence enacted by men against other men. Thus, by recognising the gendered power relations between men and the violence against men by men that flows from them, it will shift the gaze from the very public but far less common problem of men as victims of women's violence in the home (Wojnicka 2015).

In the minority of situations where the perpetrator of violence is female, the violence is still a form of power and control, and reflects hegemonic masculinity in a patriarchal society (Greig 2002; see also Chapter 6). Women can be socialised into adopting hegemonic forms of masculinity, especially women in the military, who may participate in sexual violence against male prisoners. Women are also masculinised by military training, which partially explains their involvement in sexual violence against women and men in war (Vojdik 2014). Thus, all forms of violence, whether perpetrated by men or by women, are connected to patriarchal and oppressive gender relations.

Conclusion

The main argument of this chapter is that men's violence against other men is not separate from men's violence against women. The implication of the interrelatedness of different forms of men's violence is that strategies to address one form of men's violence need to address other forms of men's violence (Fleming et al. 2015). Consequently, we cannot eliminate men's violence against women without understanding and addressing men's violence against men. Also, a number of writers have noted that men who are violent towards women are more likely than other men to also be violent towards other men (Vojdik 2014; Fleming et al. 2015; Jewkes et al. 2015b). One can understand all of these forms of violence as patriarchal violence (Barker 2016).

In failing to gender and condemn men's public violence against other men, we are encouraged to accept and even celebrate contemporary expressions of masculinity that foster such violence. Such an acceptance normalises men's violence towards other men and leads to tolerance of symbolic and cultural forms of men's violence (Sundaram 2013). We need to gender men's violence against men in the context of patriarchy to ensure that it is not seen as a natural and normal part of manhood.

9 | GENDERING MILITARISM, WAR AND TERRORISM

Introduction

There is a strong link between masculinity and war (Connell 2000b; Hutchings 2008; Hearn 2011; Cockburn 2012a; Duriesmith 2017). At one level, the masculinity–war nexus is obvious. Men make up the majority of state leaders who are involved in engaging in wars, in addition to being the majority of personnel in the armed forces.

The military emphasises violence as a natural part of masculinity and what it is to be a man (Harders 2011). Rationality, physical courage and aggression are essential characteristics of both masculinity and war (Hutchings 2008). Hegemonic masculinity informs military culture and encourages all men in the military to enact particular masculine practices that are conducive to war (Eichler 2014). For some commentators, masculinity is a significant cause of war, while for others the practice of war requires the production and reproduction of particular kinds of men (Hutchings 2008). Either way, dominant forms of masculinity enables war to take place and provides meaning and legitimates the conduct of war. The characteristics of hegemonic masculinity, including rational calculation, absence of emotion, stoicism, discipline, risk-taking and technological mastery, all provide sustenance for the value systems that underpin the military and the conduct of war (Hutchings 2008).

Militarisation promotes hegemonic masculinity and maintains men's dominance in society. Military thinking is imbued with masculine values. Thus, becoming militaristic involves inculcating traditional notions of masculinity and manliness (Ruddick 1989). The military is perhaps the most masculinist of all social institutions, notwithstanding the fact that women perform key administrative and servicing functions within it (Hearn 2011). Militarised masculinity embodies control, dominance and violence. It is premised upon men's sense of entitlement to control women and the protective ethos that obscures this control (Adelman 2003; Bevan and MacKenzie 2012).

Militarism needs to be understood in the context of patriarchy. It is clear that patriarchal power relations are embedded in militarisation and war. Cockburn (2012a) outlines how militarism and masculinism strengthen patriarchy. She notes that feminist activists are often more comfortable using the language of patriarchy than feminist academics, who sometimes find the term too confronting. Enloe (Cohn and Enloe 2002) argues that it is impossible to talk about militarism without talking about patriarchy. She observes the preference for concepts such as 'gender hierarchies', 'gender divisions' and 'discrimination', as these terms are less threatening. However, these terms do not allow us to understand the ways in which certain forms of masculinity are valorised at the expense of women and marginalised and subordinated men.

Masculinity, militarism and peacekeeping

In recent years, it has been noted that new forms of war are emerging (Kaldor 2006; Duriesmith 2017). These new wars raise questions about whether the masculinity–war nexus is also changing. Kaldor (2006) argues that masculinity in the new wars has transformed from that of warrior to policeman, which in her view is a positive shift. Peacekeeping is seen as an alternative to the use of military force. However, to what extent are the qualities and skills fostered as part of military training providing peacekeepers with the competencies to enact peaceful resolutions of conflict situations? Peacekeeping requires men to reject much of the socialisation associated with being a soldier. While they are deployed to have a military role, they are not to be militaristic (Lopez 2011). This development has led to what some commentators call 'peacekeeping masculinities' (Bevan and MacKenzie 2012). While such masculinities are meant to reflect altruism, neutrality and capacity to resolve conflicts, Bevan and MacKenzie (2012) point out that peacekeeping practice is not a benign neutral project and it is intimately connected with power.

Duncanson (2009) explores the way in which peacekeeping may reproduce military masculinities and ways in which it may undermine them. On the one hand, peacekeeping is seen by many soldiers as less manly than involvement in combat. However, adhering to manliness undermines what they have learnt about effective peacekeeping strategies. Consequently, many soldiers endeavour to frame peacekeeping behaviours as masculine and consistent with traditional military masculinity. This is done by arguing that peacekeeping is more challenging and dangerous than combat and by drawing upon masculinity to embed peacekeeping with controlling the use of force and impartiality (Duncanson 2009).

Consequently, notwithstanding the requirements of peacekeeping, hyper-masculinity continues to influence peacekeeping activities. Whitworth (2004) suggests that this is because men feel a need to compensate for not being able to fulfil the ideals of warrior masculinity. This may go some way to explaining the high level of sexual exploitation by peacekeepers of local women (Whitworth 2004; Consortium on Gender, Security and Human Rights 2010; Westendorf and Searle 2017). Aggression and violence by peacekeepers raises questions about whether soldiers can create peaceful environments (Duncanson 2009). There is thus some doubt about whether the masculinity of peacekeepers will challenge the dominant culture of military masculinities.

It should be noted that there is also a racial dynamic operating here, with white peacekeepers travelling to the Global South and asserting their masculine supremacy by racialising locals. There is both a colonial logic and a masculinist logic under the guise of 'partnering' and 'advising'. Western soldiers position themselves as liberal warriors educating the 'other', who are in turn feminised and infantilised as they are accommodated to masculinist and colonialist discourses (Welland 2015).

Militarism and men's violence against women

When we situate public, nationalised and global violence in the political, cultural and social relations of a patriarchal gender order, we are able to see the relationship between men's violence against women and militarism. Men's interpersonal violence can be linked to nationalist and global violence in the public sphere (Hammer 2003).

Exploring interconnections between diverse forms of men's violence challenges the traditional separation of inter-state and interpersonal violence. The overall level of violence in a society comprises militaristic violence, state violence, violent resistance to the state and interpersonal violence (Walby 2012). One can frame these different forms of violence as a continuum, from the international, national and community levels to the more personal level in the private sphere (Purkayastha and Ratcliff 2014). Jones (2013) argues that international violence and violence against women in the home are 'one and the same'. When societies engage in military violence overseas, men's violence against women in those societies is validated on the home front.

Hudson et al. (2008) demonstrate clear links between the security of states and the security of women. State violence, for example, has been shown to lead to higher levels of men's violence against women. At the same time, the gender inequality that underpins men's violence against women explains nationalistic violence. Nationalism is one expression of patriarchy. Caprioli (2005) demonstrates that states with the highest levels of gender inequality are most likely to rely upon military force to settle disputes, whereas states with greater gender equality are less likely to resort to military violence.

Sela-Shayovitz (2010) also demonstrates links between the levels of militarisation in a society and the rates of men's violence against women. She notes that where men have access to weapons through their military connections, they sometimes use them against their female partners. This link is further validated by Adelman (2003), who reports high levels of violence against women in military communities in contrast to men's violence within the civilian population.

Militarism has ongoing consequences for women during peacetime as well as during war. Vojdik (2002) illustrates how the process of creating the male soldier involves fostering forms of hyper-masculinity that are reliant upon the denigration of women. The lack of armed conflict between states does not equate to a peaceful society. Cuomo (1996) claims that anti-war resistance occurs when violence erupts between states. However, the preconditions of violence are woven into so-called peaceful societies through the ongoing presence of militarism in those societies. Constant military presence in societies creates the precondition for military conflict and has ongoing consequences for gender relations in everyday life.

Militarism encourages the use of aggression and violence for achieving political and economic ends and facilitates violent forms of masculinity (Center for Women's Global Leadership 2011). Militarism thus perpetuates not only war and public violence, but also men's violence against women in the home. The norms of military cultures in relation to masculinity, women, violence and sexuality have been shown to be supportive of rape, sexual harassment and violence against women in the home. Militarism influences both the perpetration of violence against women and how it is understood, through the legitimation to use violence to achieve goals and through its promotion of gender hierarchies (Adelman 2003). Thus, there are common sociocultural norms and psychological processes in the use of violence by men in the home and militaristic violence during war. Cockburn (2012a) notes the similarity of women's experience of men's violence in war and their experience of men's violence in peacetime. Some women anti-war activists have become involved in challenging men's violence in the wider society as a result of their anti-violence against women campaigns.

Masculinity and the just war tradition

'Civilised' societies set boundaries on how far humans should go in harming others. At the time of writing (April 2018), there was moral outrage about the Assad regime's use of chemical weapons against its own population in Syria. At the same time, however, there was acceptance of the use of traditional weapons to maim and kill others. Supposedly, ethics and values are intended to limit the degree of violence against others in war (Barry 2010). There are ongoing moral and political discussions about good and bad wars and just and unjust wars. It is important to utilise the masculinity–war link to inform these discussions.

The notion of a 'just war' is a war that is morally justifiable; that is, it frames the right to go to war. In the liberal tradition, just war theory informs international legal frameworks that seek to regulate the humane conduct during war, with specific reference to non-combatants and civilians and the humane treatment of those who are not engaged in hostilities. Such principles should also guide the scale of military response to the level of the threat that is posed (Slim 2015). Mann (2014) argues that we need just war theory to differentiate between different forms of violence. In her view, pacifism is not realistic enough to address the issue of conflict between states.

Within this context, some military personnel talk about 'good aggression'. Good aggression is seen as the productive and proper use of force to serve the nation. Instances where aggression and violence are enacted by men with honour and courage in fighting against overwhelming counter-forces satisfy this criterion. Such men are governed by notions of civility and control in the exercise of aggression and violence. The use of controlled aggression and violence is posited for soldiers to differentiate themselves from so-called uncivilised use of violence where there are no constraints. However, the image of a just and honourable violence is at odds with the reality of warfare, where violence often crosses over these limits (Locke 2013).

There are numerous feminist criticisms of just war theory. Peach (1994) argues that just war theory's conception of human nature is premised upon essentialism, sexism and pessimism. Just war theory has allowed the intentional killing of innocent civilians under special circumstances (Neu 2015). The just war tradition relies upon masculinist framings of ethics and the consequences of war. The focus on abstract notions of universal rights and justice and acceptance of traditional gender roles of men as combatants and women as helpless victims reproduces particular assumptions about war and gender (Krcek 2012). Also, its realist premise that wars are inevitable because human beings are naturally aggressive is based upon masculine values that obscure the human capacity for empathy and ethics of care (Hun 2014).

Feminists are divided about whether just war theory can be reformed or not. Feminists who adopt a pacifist position argue that war is never an acceptable option under any conditions (Vellacott 1993). Other feminists argue that just war theory can be reformulated to incorporate feminist analyses and insights (Peach 1994; Elshtain 2001, 2003; Malone 2004; Kinsella 2006). However, there is an alternative to pacifism and a gendered just war theory, which is advocated here.

The justification of war in just war theory fails to grapple with more fundamental questions of ethics and morality (Neu 2015). Just war theory assumes that wars are isolated events that occur when states decide to engage in military conflict with other states. In establishing war as a special event, the normal moral rules governing the use of violence are seen to no longer apply; pre-existing conditions are not part of the moral equation. However, wars are a result of a wider range of pre-existing situations that are escalated at key points. By utilising just war theory only after the declaration of war, ethical considerations about the militarisation of a society prior to war are ignored (Cuomo 1996).

Howell (2018) raises the important question of whether the concept of militarisation itself limits our understanding of how pernicious the military encroachment into civilian life has become. She suggests that there is an implication that a pure civilian space untainted by militarisation exists. In her view, demilitarisation does not go far enough as it does not address the many ways in which what she calls 'martial politics' has permeated all of our social institutions and normalised relations of power that are warlike in form and expression.

Too often the just ethics of war are framed by those with superior forces who argue that less powerful opponents should meet them on the same moral ground, where they can be more easily defeated (Held 2010). International laws that govern conflict are heavily biased towards the interests of existing states irrespective of their moral standing, whereas those seeking change are held to a higher moral standard (Held 2008). While terrorists are understandably condemned for the intentional killing of civilians, the unintentional killing of civilians caused by the bombing of cities is defended as 'collateral damage'. Held (2010) questions whether the moral distinctions between the two forms of killing can be upheld. Schott (2008) argues against the moral distinction between terrorism and war that is advocated by the just war tradition because it normalises war. War, if conducted within certain moral codes, is legitimated as morally acceptable. In Schott's view, war may be justified in given circumstances, but it can never be just.

Sjoberg (2006) says that wars are humanised by the legitimation of protecting women. Men become warriors and engage in combat to supposedly create a safer world for women. She suggests replacing the ethical principles informing moral victory with what she calls 'empathic war fighting'. The latter approach is concerned with empathy arising from human connectedness and cooperation. While she does not suggest that empathy and emotional connections will end war or gender subordination, she does believe that it is important to move beyond just war narratives about courageous men protecting vulnerable women.

Militarism and the costs for men

It is noted that in militaristic societies, men seem unable to provide emotional support to women. In part, this is due to male soldiers being able to suspend the capacity to care about the suffering of others and enact violence against others if required. Men in the military are socialised to repress their own feelings as well as suppress their feelings for others. Digby (2014) suggests that this explains why there are so many civilian casualties in so-called 'military mistakes'. If there is no empathy for the suffering of others, there will be little attention to detail to ensure that civilians are not killed along with combatants.

For Digby (2014), the emotional costs of militarism for men are not primarily the experiences of war and conflict, but rather the way in which boys and men are socialised in militaristic societies to prepare to serve as soldiers when the time comes. When it comes to masculinity, it is the refusal to acknowledge vulnerability as a fact of human life that has contributed to militarisation and the promotion of nuclear weapons as a deterrent (Cohn and Enloe 2002). If men were able to acknowledge the impossibility of making themselves invulnerable and invincible, they might be concerned with interdependence, and hence acknowledge the importance of ensuring the survival of humankind and the liveability of the planet (see Chapter 12).

Barry (2010) talks about how the language of 'innocent lives' suggests that while it is seen as wrong to kill non-combatants, combatants can be legitimately killed as part of modern warfare. It is acceptable that men as combatants will be killed in wars. Men need to be socialised into accepting this possible outcome as part of the process of becoming a man. This expendability of men's lives is inscribed in international laws where only civilians are required to be treated humanely in all circumstances. Soldiers know that they do not have these protections, and that by involving themselves in war they are killable. When war is accepted as inevitable, the focus is on regulating it rather than preventing it.

Men's lives are thus expendable in war. This is the downside for men of their protector role. To the extent that women accept men as their protectors, they are also culpable in perpetuating men's expendability. Barry (2010) sees men's emotional disconnection from others as a result of being socialised into a form of masculinity that requires men to be able to kill others and to be expendable themselves. As a populace, we all need to allow ourselves to experience the pain and suffering of others that is caused by war. Refusal to do so means that we are more likely to be complicit in the perpetuation of militarism.

If we allow ourselves to observe the casualties of war from the point of view of the victims, we will have to face the horrifying impact of violence on the bodies of real people (Gregory 2015). We will then be less inclined to stand back in the belief that we can use international law to moderate the level of severity of the violence inflicted.

Women, femininities and war

Women who belong to the dominant classes may also promote the maintenance and escalation of militarism and war. While only a minority of women are actively involved in violent conflicts, larger numbers of women actively or passively support military cultures (Harders 2011;

MacKenzie 2015; Henshaw 2016). Many women support the military involvement of their lovers, sons and friends (Ruddick 1989). De Vries and Gueskens (2010) point out that women are not innocent of war and militarism. Women, like men, can accept the values of a patriarchal culture and 'buy into' the reproduction of masculinist power arrangements.

When women support the notion that violence is a legitimate means of achieving one's goals, they are colluding with patriarchal violence. To the extent that women believe that people in authority have the right to use violence to exert control, they are complicit with patriarchy (Hammer 2003). Within the wider system of patriarchal subordination, women have also used torture, violence and abuse in wars. When women do commit violence, we understandably want to explain it as having different motivations. In doing so, we often deny women's agency and focus too much on their subordination by men as an explanation (Sjoberg et al. 2011). It is as if we think that if we allow women agency in relation to their violence, we fear that it may shift the focus off the gendering of violence.

I cannot do justice to the complex issues around women's involvement in militarism and war, nor do I engage in the debate about whether women should be involved in combat or not. For readers who want to explore these issues in more depth, I recommend MacKenzie (2015) and Henshaw (2016) for excellent introductions to these debates. However, I do reject the normative claims about women's essential nature as nurturers and I also reject the arguments that women lack the capacity to be involved in combat. For my purposes here, I am more interested in the question of whether women's increased involvement in combat changes or challenges the relationship between militarism and patriarchy.

Masculinity and the gendered face of terrorism

There is very little recognition in the wider public debates about terrorism that terrorist movements are gendered. The majority of terrorists are men. There is widespread anger in Muslim countries about globalisation, capitalism and imperialism. In the context of social protest, religious fervour serves to fuel the gendered experience of marginalisation that for many Muslim men leads them to feel emasculated. Being unable to fulfil the breadwinner role, marginalised men fail one of the dominant expectations of hegemonic masculinity. Terrorists promise a pathway to enable such men to feel dignity and honour again. Extremist violence becomes a way for marginalised Muslim men to attain a form of masculine honour (Aslam 2012).

A number of commentators have noted that men are most vulnerable to being recruited into terrorist organisations when they have difficulty fulfilling the traditional expectations of masculinity and manhood (Aslam 2012; Ezekilov 2017; Kimmel 2018). Men who are unable to achieve the hegemonic and idealised notion of manhood are marginalised by their peers, and consequently may turn to violence to fulfil expectations of masculinity (Ezekilov 2017).

Ferber and Kimmel (2008) note that terrorists often feel emasculated and terrorist political action often aims to restore what is perceived as damaged masculinity. Men often resort to violence when they feel that their position in society is threatened. Terrorists frequently make reference to ways in which they believe Muslims have been emasculated and diminished by the West (Ferber and Kimmel 2008). Wright (2014) uses the concept of 'thwarted' masculinities to talk about the experiences of men who are unable to attain the standards of hegemonic masculinity. Such men, it is argued, are more likely to commit violence, both in the home and in the public world. Violence is used either to affirm masculinity to compensate for these otherwise masculine attainments or to gain access to the benefits of manhood.

Aslam (2012) explores how Islamic men's experiences of manhood, which are deeply embedded with cultural notions of honour and shame, create troubled masculinities for many Muslim men. When these men are unable to live up to the cultural ideas of Islamic masculinity, they are prone to violence and vulnerable to radicalisation. Aslam argues that masculinity is a significant factor in the rise of militant jihardist Islamism. She also argues that militant jihadist Islamism provides an avenue for many Muslim men to address the sense of masculine inadequacy evoked by the changing sociopolitical context of their lives. It is a way for these men to confirm their manhood where other opportunities to do so are unavailable to them. Terrorism is therefore one way of performing masculinity.

It is also important to acknowledge that terrorism takes many forms beyond that of Islamic extremism in the West. The dynamics of terrorism in non-Western countries where those in power do not embody the values of the West complicate the specifics of the analysis above, as does terrorism by white supremacists in the West. At the same time, regardless of the proponents, the various 'causes' pursued or the vocabulary of the claims, terrorism in all of its forms is connected to the structures of patriarchy and configurations of masculinity (Haider 2016).

Kimmel (2018) calls for a gendered psychology of extremism to explain violent extremist movements. Such a psychology, he says, illuminates how men in terrorist movements are focused on proving and validating their masculinity to other men. Such men frame their emotional experiences of being aggrieved by an ideology of hate and violence. Masculinity does not fully explain the rise of terrorism; extremist politics must also be seen in the context of political, economic and structural forces.

Women, femininities and terrorism

While the vast majority of terrorists are men, women also engage in terrorist acts (Repo 2006). However, despite only a very small proportion of terrorists being women, they receive far more than their share of media attention (Sjoberg and Gentry 2008). When women commit political violence, they are acting outside of traditional gendered expectations. As such, they are often perceived as 'monsters' (Ortbals and Poloni-Staudinger 2018).

Women terrorists are seen to have trespassed into what is regarded as a male domain (Auchter 2012). When women engage in terrorist acts, they depart from the traditional stereotype of women as nurturing and innocent. If women are inherently more peaceful than men, then there is no way to explain the terrorist violence by women as an act of agency. Women's violence must then be understood as a response to pressure from terrorist men. Such women are seen as victimised by their men in terrorist organisations (Auchter 2012). Thus, many feminist commentators suggest that women who conduct terrorism do so primarily because of their exploitation by male terrorists (Auchter 2012; Tervooren 2016; Ortbals and Poloni-Staudinger 2018).

In Tervooren's (2016) view, a representation of women's terrorism as a response to their victimisation by men in terrorist organisations does not enable us to get to the individual motivations of women terrorists. If women terrorists are perceived only as passive victims of terrorist men, their agency in the world is diminished (Ortbals and Poloni-Staudinger 2018). Tervooren (2016) argues that framing women as solely the victims of terrorist violence, and not as perpetrators of it, reaffirms the traditional gender binary and the patriarchal construction of femininity. In Auchter's (2012) view also, the gender binary is the source of women's subjugation. Sjoberg (2009) develops a feminist analysis of women's terrorism that brings women's agency to act into the foreground. For her, it is necessary to develop a feminist approach to women's agency to counter idealised conceptions of women and femininity.

Swati Parashar (2014) provides the most detailed investigation into women's participation in terrorism to date. Focusing on women in Kashmir and Sri Lanka, she outlines both the involvement of women in armed resistance and also their accommodation to and support of Islamist ideology. The complexity of women's experiences, ideologies and motives for their involvement in terrorist activities suggests more nuanced understanding of women's support for terrorism is required than has currently been the case.

Gendering responses to terrorism

Gender is also relevant to how we respond to terrorism, as it is used to legitimise violence and militaristic responses. Repo (2006) examines the type of masculinities embedded in the war on terror. In responding to terrorist attacks, political leaders often emphasise forms of dominant masculinity in framing their exhortations about fortitude, resolve, strength and firmness (Coe et al. 2007).

Governments undertake so-called 'wars on terror' while not addressing women's personal safety in the family. However, there are parallels between the impact of terrorism and war and women's experiences of rape and violence in the home (Phillips 2008). Herman (1997), for example, documents how the experiences of trauma that women suffer in the aftermath of violence mirrors the experiences of the victims of war and terrorism. Both forms of violence aim to induce fear and intimidation (Sjoberg 2009). While terrorism is widely used in reference to what is regarded as illegitimate political violence, little consideration is given to possible links to men's violence against women in the home (Repo 2006). For many women, the experiences of coercion and violence by men during war is similar to their experiences of men during so-called peacetime.

Pain (2014) also explores links between intimate terrorism in the home and public violence in the international arena. Hitherto, global terrorism and men's violence against women in the home have not been seen to be related. However, there is considerable evidence that men's intimate violence against women is influenced by national and global politics. Many men who commit violence in the public sphere against strangers also perpetrate violence against women in the home (Chemaly 2016; Smith 2017). Men who support Islamist ideology are also likely to support the patriarchal beliefs that inform violence against women.

When we separate men's violence in the family from the other forms of violence by men in relation to terrorism, war and civil unrest, we fail to acknowledge the ways in which the state often sanctions or condones some forms of men's violence (Hearn and McKie 2006). Thus, the distinction between interpersonal violence and international violence needs to be contested. Pain (2014) suggests framing domestic violence as 'everyday terrorism'. Such terrorism, with its capacity to instil fear through coercive control, overlaps with other forms of political terrorism. While public terrorism receives considerable attention from governments, intimate terrorism in the home has not produced the same level of concern. Considering men's violence against women as a form of terrorism has the potential to inject a new understanding into policies for prevention. It may also enable us to be more alert to possible public forms of terrorism where signs of propensity for violence are already known through men's violence against their intimate partners (Chemaly 2016).

Pain (2014) also notes similarities to the masculinist protection by men in relation to women in the private sphere and the forms of protection that frame international security. Such latter political responses to the 'war on terror' are related to the politics of fear. Young (2003a) defines masculinism as a form of protection. Male political leaders often position themselves as protectors of a population. Drawing upon Peterson (1977), Young notes that the state's relations to women can be likened to a protection racket, whereby protection from 'others' is guaranteed for a fee. Masculinist protection becomes a form of logic male leaders use to increase surveillance and security measures in the face of anticipated terrorist attacks. Young sees masculinist protection as a benign form of male domination, whereby authoritarian governments use the threat of terrorism to implement harsh security measures.

In contrast to selfish and more brutish forms of masculinity, chivalrous and gallant forms of masculinity also prevail. The latter are premised upon the notion of 'good' men who protect women and others from external threats by 'bad' men (Young 2003b). Masculine protection enables men to position themselves as chivalrous, loving and self-sacrificing in relation to women. Such a form of masculinity is reliant upon there being 'bad' men who women need to be protected from. In this framework, those who are protected are also subordinate to men, as women sacrifice their autonomy to gain the benefits of protection.

De-gendering militarism or demilitarising society?

Increasingly, larger numbers of women are joining the military and becoming more involved in combat situations (Eichler 2014). This raises questions about men's and women's historical links to militarised masculinity. Does women's inclusion in combat roles disrupt militarised masculinities? Digby (2014) notes that war is changing and that such changes open up the possibility that militarism and war could be de-gendered. He suggests that women's participation in combat roles undermines the gendered nature of war and militarism. However, does military masculinity require the male body to be enacted? To what extent, then, can women perform military masculinities? Henry (2017) raises these questions in light of reading Halberstam's (1998) work on female masculinities.

Even though the military in many countries now includes women, gay people and trans personnel, hegemonic masculinity continues to be the ideal for good soldiering (Carpenter 2010). Women in the military, for example, are under pressure to accommodate to masculine values embedded in military culture. While some proponents of women's increased involvement in the military encourage women to challenge the patriarchal underpinnings of military culture and see possibilities for a more democratic and compassionate military (Duncanson and Woodward 2016; Heinecken 2016), others (Cowan and Siciliano 2011; Cockburn 2012b) see little potential for women to transform the misogyny and hyper-masculinity of military culture.

Carpenter (2010) raises the question of what non-militarised masculinity or a post-masculinised military might look like and indicates some of the challenges. We would need to pay the same amount of esteem to caring roles as we do to military services; we would need to de-gender traditional caring roles and we would need to change the relationship between the military services and civil society. Eichler (2014) also considers strategies for undoing the link between militarism and masculinity. The first strategy involves reducing the power of dichotomous hierarchical gender norms within the military and disconnecting militarism from hegemonic forms of masculinity. However, this raises the question of whether it is possible to construct demilitarised masculinities in the armed forces as a strategy to encourage men to reject militarism.

What does it mean to demilitarise a society? For Cockburn (2012a), patriarchal gender relations are one of the main causes of militarism and war. Consequently, any strategy for peace and demilitarisation must involve a transformation of dominant forms of masculinity and the social relations of gender that produce it (Breines et al. 2000). Military violence is also a form of organised violence, so addressing it requires a focus on organisations and the state (Hearn 2011). Addressing violence against women in wars requires the end of wars per se. It is not enough to address particular forms of violence in wars without the prevention of militarism and war itself. Making war safer for women means becoming complicit in the wider system of militarised conflict (Wright 2015).

Notwithstanding women's involvement in war, as noted earlier, the caring roles that are largely undertaken by women have provided the main impetus for women's engagement with peace activism. For peace activism to be successful, larger numbers of men will need to be involved and they will also need to act against everyday violence in patriarchal cultures (Harders 2011). The potential for this engagement is explored in Chapters 11 and 12.

10 | GENDERING GLOBAL WARMING AND ENVIRONMENTAL VIOLENCE

Introduction

A number of scholars have noted the connections between climate change and increased levels of violence around the world (Scheffran et al. 2014; Zimmerer 2014; Wonders and Danner 2015; Bonds 2016; Levy et al. 2017; Theisen 2017). However, most studies focus on the violence coming from less powerful groups as they respond to the turbulence caused by climate change rather than the systemic and structural violence perpetrated by privileged and powerful groups (Solnit 2014). By focusing solely on the violence by those who are impacted by climate change, we overlook the wealthy and powerful groups who promote the continued use of fossil fuels that create climate-related disasters. Climate change is created through the prioritising of corporate profits and economic growth at the expense of environmental well-being (Bonds 2016).

Furthermore, when we discuss climate change as caused by humans, we shift the focus from wealthy white men in corporations and governments in the Global North who perpetrate most of the environmental impacts that contribute to global warming. Wealthy white men from the Global North who dominate political and economic decision-making disproportionately influence decisions that shape the causes and consequences of global warming (Wonders and Danner 2015).

It has been widely noted that environmental disasters have a greater impact on women and children than they do on men (Neumayer and Plumper 2007; Pittaway et al. 2007; Enarson 2012; True 2012; Tyler et al. 2012). Furthermore, numerous studies demonstrate increased levels of men's violence against women in the aftermath of disasters (Scanlon 1998; Enarson 1999; Harris 2011; Enarson 2012; Sety 2012; True 2012; Parkinson and Zara 2013; Pease 2014b; Masson et al. 2016). The disruption of men's role as protectors creates uncertainty and inadequacy for many men. Austin (2016) argues that gender roles are broken down and reconstructed in disasters because the institutional supports for gender role performance are destabilised during disasters. As the workplace, the home and the institutions of the state may be destroyed during a disaster, many men may feel a threat to their dominance. Austin demonstrates how an expression of hyper-masculinity among men could be a response to the loss and stress associated by natural disasters. As men experience a sense of loss in their dominance in work, politics and intimate relationships, they may resort to a hyper-masculinity to restore their hegemonic influence. This may explain in part men's increased levels of violence in intimate relationships with women following disasters.

While it is understandable that the gender and climate change scholarship will focus on women's greater vulnerability to climate-related disasters, and the consequences of them, there is a danger that such work will naturalise women as passive victims. There thus needs to be more focus on the gendering of the processes that create women's greater vulnerability (Wonders and Danner 2015).

Climate change as structural violence

Structural violence is a term that was first introduced by Johan Galtung (1969) to describe forms of legitimised violence exercised by the state that reproduced social institutions. It was often not perceived as violence because the harms it caused could not easily be identified with particular actors. Environmental violence, or violence against ecosystems, is a form of structural violence (Zimmerer 2014; Cueva Salcedo 2015).

Soron (2007) regards so-called 'natural disasters' as expressions of structural violence because the social forces contributing to cataclysmic weather events are obscured. O'Brien (2017) also identifies climate change as a form of structural violence because the changes to the atmosphere created by wealthy and powerful groups in the industrialised world cause pain, suffering and death. Thus, in addition to talking about the violence that flows from climate change, we should also talk about climate change itself as violence (Solnit 2014). Nixon (2011) uses the language of 'slow violence' to describe the incremental ways in which environmental destruction can impact on people across the planet. He notes that this form of violence is generally not viewed as violence because the indirect effects that flow from environmental catastrophies are gradual and are out of sight.

The act of destroying the natural environment is not only a form of violence against the planet, but it also constitutes violence against humans who are dependent on the planet (Lee 2018). This violence takes a number of forms: violence between people over natural resources; environmental policies that lead to violence; violence that flows from environmental disasters such as earthquakes, heat waves, hurricanes and tsunamis; and damage to the environment from humans that threatens their survival. Environmental disasters not only destroy land; they cause large-scale migration, they kill people, and they contribute to wars that further degrade the environment and kill people. Thus, environmental disasters that flow from global warming is a major form of environmental violence.

In a toolkit developed by the Native Youth Sexual Health Network and Women's Earth Alliance (2014), an Indigenous perspective on the land connects destruction of the environment with the impact on the bodies and communities of Indigenous people. Such environmental violence includes toxic pollution and industrial hazards arising from corporate development projects. Structural violence can be conceptualised as a crime because of the impact it has on humans, non-human animals and ecosystems (Wonders and Danner 2015).

White (2005) argues that environmental violence should be recognised as a crime because humans and the environment are being harmed. This harm may be caused directly, thus constituting a primary crime, or indirectly as a secondary crime (South and White 2013). Crimes against the environment involve both conscious actions that impact negatively on humans and non-humans or acts of omission where the failure to act has had destructive ecological consequences (White 2016).

The focus of critical green criminology is on state and corporate environmental crime where business interests collude with nation states to avoid taking actions to address environmental crises (White and Kramer 2015). Although Kremer (2010) distinguishes between environmental crimes by individuals and those by organisations, the focus of critical criminology tends to be on crimes perpetrated by corporations as these are the source of the most destructive environmental crimes. However, it is individuals within corporations that are the culprits, and such culprits are predominantly men. Men are prosecuted more than women for serious environmental crimes, and men who are convicted hold higher-status positions in corporations than women.

Linking men's violence against women and environmental destruction

Horkheimer (1947) and Adorno (1963) have both argued men's domination of nature arises from men's domination over women and other men. Ensler (cited in Hymas 2013) draws connections between men's violence against women and the environmental destruction caused by fossil fuel companies. She argues that the mindset that informs ecological damage is the same mentality that informs the violence perpetrated against women by men. Such a mindset encourages men to disassociate themselves from emotions and to see themselves as dispassionate individuals in pursuit of profit, status and power. To be effective in achieving their goals, men must embrace an emotional callousness and treat the emotions of others with condescension.

Fischer (2005) also notes the interconnections between violence between humans (largely perpetrated by men) and the destruction of nature (also largely perpetrated by men). In his view, the domination of nature contributes to the violences of men through the brutality that it evokes. Men's domination of women and the environment are both premised upon the sense of entitlement and ownership of women and the earth. It is thus necessary to rethink what it means to own.

Patriarchy, hegemonic masculinity and environmental destruction

A number of feminist critics have identified the ways in which masculinist notions of objectivity and rationality have dominated men's attitudes towards nature (Keller 1982; Plumwood 1993; Litfin 1997; Alaimo 2009; Israel and Sachs 2013; Connell and Pearse 2015). Climate change science purports to provide an objective and transcendent scientific perspective on environmental crises (Alaimo 2009). Technocratic and marketised approaches to addressing environmental problems also prevail. Such technocratic and science-based approaches are not seen as a problem if one mistakingly believes that environmental crises are solely a product of ozone disintegration or physical deterioration.

There are clear links between patriarchal social structures and environmental crises and ecological destruction (Stibbe 2006; Gaard 2011; Connell and Pearse 2015; Mellor 2017). Environmental crises arise from social, cultural and political relations and institutions of government and corporations. These relations and institutions are male-dominated and premised upon masculinist assumptions about the social and the natural world (Seager 1993).

Feminist approaches to science demonstrate the ways in which scientific practice is not neutral and reflects and reproduces masculinist power relations. The form of objectivity affirmed by science is seen to be embedded in a form of masculine subjectivity. Keller (1982) suggests an alternative approach, what she calls 'dynamic objectivity', which, rather than a form of detachment, encourages an empathic approach to the world that acknowledges emotions and subjective experiences. While women are often more able to practise dynamic objectivity because of the ways in which gendered differences are socially constructed, men could potentially learn to develop this capacity (see Chapter 12). Feminist science studies have much to offer a renewed understanding of the relationship between masculinity and climate change (Israel and Sachs 2013), and consequently men's relationship with the environment. They encourage men to move beyond the logic of domination and control and the technoscientific framing of climate change.

Western science's approach to knowledge and methodology has been oriented towards dominating nature (Twine 1997). Geoengineering as a strategy to address climate change is an example of a masculinist technical approach to environmental problems (Buck et al. 2014). Fleming (2017) points out, for example, that advocates of climate engineering are predominantly Western, industrialised, rich men who believe that they have the power to 'fix the sky'.

When climate change is framed as a technoscientific problem based on an ideology of the domination and control of nature, there is less focus on the ethical and political issues at stake. A masculinist focus on technical issues neglects the social and gender justice concerns about the impact of climate change on women and vulnerable populations (Boyd 2010). Consequently, there is less attention on challenging the patriarchal interests that are threatened by environmental actions.

Garlick (2011) brings a gendered lens to Marcuse's (1991) notion of one-dimensional man to illustrate the ways in which technological rationality shapes men's relations with nature. Litfin (1997) identifies various assumptions embedded, for example, in earth observation studies that illustrate the ways in which the concept of scientific objectivity is a masculine construct. They include the claimed neutrality of science, science as a source of certainty, and technology as a solution to environmental problems. Such work suggests that technology shapes human relations with nature in a variety of ways, and consequently the forms of masculinity embedded within technology limits a more empathic approach by men towards nature.

While there are links between hegemonic masculinity and masculinist structures, it does not mean that men should be excluded from strategies to challenge these structures. Men should bear the greatest responsibility for challenging environmental disasters because they are largely responsible for perpetrating them (Pease 2016). We must be careful not to see men's power and dominance as reflective of some sort of essence within men. Men's ecologically destructive actions have to be seen in historical and local social contexts. Also, if there is a 'bad' essence in men, there is little scope for transforming men, masculinities and male culture. If male culture and hegemonic masculinity are socially constructed, then they can be transformed. However, men have material interests in maintaining the status quo, and if they are to be part of the solution in addressing environmental crises, they will need to open themselves to the pain that comes from recognising the costs of men's human and environmental destructive actions (New 1996).

Ecofeminism revisited

Ecofeminism emphasises the connections between the treatment of women and the treatment of non-human species and the natural environment (Connell and Pearse 2015). To address the issue of men and nature, it is necessary to revisit the debates about gender and nature through the lens of ecofeminism. There is more than one ecofeminism. It is more appropriate to refer to ecofeminisms in the plural to capture the variety of different perspectives (Sandilands 1999; Marchant 2005; Connell and Pearse 2015). What all ecofeminisms share in common is the importance of linking ecological struggles with feminist struggles (Sandilands 1999).

Cultural ecofeminism, as it was named by some commentators, historically affirmed the importance of creating women-centred politics, art and literature. Emphasis was given to women's spirituality and theology (Daly 1978; Griffin 1978). Sometimes called 'affinity ecofeminism' (Mellor 1996), this perspective emphasised how women's power is connected psychologically and physically with nature. The premise underpinning cultural ecofeminist views is that women's body organs involved in suckling and birthing facilitate specifically feminine nurturing attitudes towards the natural environment (Salleh 1995). From an essentialist perspective, women are natural carers who are able to extend their caring roles within the family to protecting and caring for the earth.

Some ecofeminists embrace the association between women and nature as a source of empowerment. However, different gendered body experiences of nature does not necessarily mean that women have a unique and superior insight into nature. Men's and women's bodily interactions with the environment may contribute in part to different relationships with nature, but this does not mean that women are closer to nature, as some ecofeminists claim. A more nuanced take on women's relationship with nature is the notion that women are not more natural than men, but the material conditions of their lives allow them to experience nature in ways that are different from men (Sandilands 1999).

There are numerous feminist critiques of essentialism in some forms of ecofeminism (Archambault 1993; Jackson 1995; New 1996; Sandilands 1999; MacGregor 2006; Sargisson 2010; Gaard 2011). A number of feminists working on environmental issues argue that essentialist notions about women's connection to nature lets men 'off the hook' from taking action to address ecological crises (Birkeland 2010; Phillips and Rumens 2016). The essentialist premise of cultural ecofeminism makes it difficult for men and women to develop solidarity in challenging environmental destruction (Sandilands 1999).

Further criticisms of ecofeminism focused on the experiences of white middle-class women in North American culture (Sandilands 1999; Phillips and Rumens 2016). It is argued that the differences among women related to class, sexuality, ethnicity and able-bodiedness, as well as transgender, are ignored. In response to early critiques, many ecofeminists have adopted postcolonial, transnational, intersectional and post-structural ideas (Shiva 2016; Foster 2017; Thompson and MacGregor 2017). More recently, they have incorporated post-human insights as well that treat the affinity between humans and the environment in a post-anthropocentric way (Gaard 2017a).

While it is clear that some early ecofeminist activists, especially those who emphasised women's spirituality and women's culture, did embrace essentialist ideas about the 'eternal feminine', it is inaccurate to identify all ecofeminist thought as essentialist. It is more likely that post-structural feminists will reject ecofeminism as a whole, as they are equally critical of structuralist and materialist perspectives as they are of essentialist and biologically determinist views (Thompson and MacGregor 2017).

Gaard (2011) believes that there are many features of ecofeminism that have been misrepresented. While one can reject some ecofeminist claims about women's biological affinity with nature, this does not mean rejecting the links between men's oppression of women and men's ecologically destructive practices. It is important to acknowledge the role that ecofeminism played in analysing the impact of patriarchy and masculinist ideologies and epistemologies on the environment. Even New (1996), who is highly critical of what she sees as essentialism in the work of many ecofeminist activists, acknowledges that there are important links between men's oppression of women and domination of the environment.

Reaffirming materialist ecofeminist analyses

Materialist ecofeminists are concerned that emphasising women's physiological and spiritual affinity with nature neglects the inequalities between women and the material exploitation and oppression of women under patriarchy (Mellor 1992). Not all women are mothers and not all mothers breastfeed. However, because women are less implicated in environmental destruction than men, this does give them a different vantage point from which to view environmental degradation (Archambault 1993).

In opposition to cultural feminists' claims about women's affinity with nature, materialist ecofeminists focus on the links between women's understanding of nature and their experience of oppression and exploitation by men (Connell and Pearse 2015). Materialist ecofeminist approaches focus more on the sexual division of labour that assigns women to caring roles in the family and caring occupations in the public sphere. They emphasise the material conditions of women's lives, and the work that they are prescribed, to establish non-biological links between women and nature (MacGregor 2006). Mellor (2017) examines the conditions of women's work and also the construction of 'Economic Man', whereby men are assumed to be mobile, fit and able-bodied, with no domestic or caring responsibilities. Such men are alienated from the processes of real life. Morita (2007) also, in advancing a materialist ecofeminism, explores the causes of global warming through male domination of the sphere of production. For him, global warming is 'man-made' or 'masculinity-made' because the production sphere is based upon hegemonic forms of masculinity.

Materialist ecofeminisms are grounded in political economy and feminist political ecology. They emphasise the political economy of social relations that impact on the environment and consider the impact of race, class, sexuality and other forms of social divisions on women's and men's experiences.

Ecofeminism, masculinity and nature

Understandably, ecofeminism was focused on women's experiences. If masculine power is the driving force of environmental destruction, then it is understandable that ecofeminists will see women as leaders in the development of a more ecologically sustainable world. Women may be seen to have a different stake in ending the domination of nature because of the connections between the oppression of women and the exploitation of nature (Agarwal 1992). Many men consequently reacted against ecofeminism because it was enacted by women and they could not see a place for themselves within it.

Materialist ecofeminists and feminist environmentalists have long recognised that men's dominating and controlling relationship with nature is connected to hegemonic forms of masculinity. However, understandably, most research on gender and the environment is focused upon the impact of environmental crises on women and what they can do about it. When men and masculinities are discussed, the focus tends to be on the role they have played in environmental degradation. It is now time to understand why men behave as they do and to develop strategies to change them (Hultman 2017).

Some feminists argued that it was difficult for men to challenge environmental destruction because of their internalised superiority (Daly 1978). More recently, however, many ecofeminist writers have argued that men can be involved in ecofeminism and can become gentle, caring and non-dominating (Phillips and Rumens 2016; Gaard 2017b). While men have historically dominated nature, they can potentially be inspired by ecofeminism to challenge masculinist ideologies and hegemonic male power.

If we adopt a social constructionist approach to gender that focuses on history, ideology and social structure, then any special affinity women have to nature will be more likely a result of socialisation and experiences of subordination than any essential connection to nature (Birkeland 2010). Balbus (1982) suggested that it is the different child-rearing practices in Western societies in relation to male children that gives rise to adult men's estranged relationship with nature. In situations where child-raising is less nurturant, it is said to lead to instrumentalist approaches to nature and violence towards women. This means consequently that men's disassociation from nature will also be less a result of a biological deficit in men and more a result of men's socialisation and their experience of privilege and masculine entitlement.

Men's dominator approach to nature is premised upon a false belief that they are separate from nature (Connell and Pearse 2015). Hegemonic forms of masculinity promote an expectation that men enact control over themselves and other men, over women, and over the environment (Schwalbe 2009). For men to be vulnerable to external forces is to challenge their masculinity and their sense of self as a man, as being in control and taking risks are two of the key dimensions of hegemonic masculinity. Such forms of masculinity, or masculinism as Brittan (1989) characterises it, define manhood in terms of the capacity to dominate others and the natural world. Cornall (2010) refers to the masculine mindset as 'the dominator model', which he regards as the cause of environmental problems and ecological disasters. Thus, if we want to address environmental destruction, we must address both the institutional power of culturally powerful men and also the internalisation by men of the dominator model of human consciousness. Similarly, Franz-Balsen (2014) argues that hegemonic forms of masculinity are at odds with ecological sustainability. If this is so, then the promotion of environmental awareness and knowledge about the social impact of global warming will pose a threat to this form of masculinity.

Some forms of masculinity are so fragile that they have to be constantly affirmed and reproduced. If we understand these men's scepticism about climate science as a threat to their masculinity, it may open up the public debate about environmental policies and gender politics (Anshelm and Hultman 2014). The above analysis reinforces the view articulated in the early 1990s that the current patriarchal gender regime will need to change if we are to pursue a more sustainable world (Johnsson-Latham 2007). While gender equality is a prerequisite for sustainable development and disaster risk reduction, it can also be argued that sustainable development is a prerequisite for gender equality (Stoparic 2006). Gender inequality is part of unsustainable development, which in turn drives climate change and increases 'natural' disasters (Leduc 2010).

There is a positive correlation between gender equality and progressive policies on climate change and environmental sustainability (Norgaard and York 2005) This is in part explained by the greater likelihood of women's pro-environmentalism and their increased participation within state policymaking apparatuses. Furthermore, if there are common structural causes of environmental degradation and gender discrimination, greater gender equality will most likely parallel more progressive environmental policies. While this is often cited to promote improvement in the status of women, less attention is given to what it means for progressive gender and environmental politics by men (Pease 2016). What strategies are available, then, to men to create alternative identities? How can men move beyond oppressive relations with nature?

Moving beyond dualism

Plumwood (1993) sees the various forms of oppression, including violence against nature, as stemming from the legacy of Western dualism. She documents the ways in which men have used their domination over nature and women to serve men's interests in patriarchal societies. Privileging men's values over women's values establishes one of the key forms of dualism whereby men's interests are assigned a higher value than women's interests. When men are valued over women and humans are valued over the non-human environment, it creates the mindset that reproduces patriarchal societal structures. In such contexts, women and nature are viewed as the 'other'. Thus, dualism is a key mindset of patriarchal ideology and Western dominance more generally (Mathews 2017).

All forms of dualism involve hierarchies between the polar opposites, where one form is valued above the other (Mathews 2017). For Plumwood (1993), the priority is to dismantle dualistic thinking, so differences between men and women and humans and the non-human environment are not polarised and turned into hierarchies. This will create more egalitarian relations between humans and nature and between men and women. Thus, developing non-dualistic thinking is a necessary step towards eliminating all forms of oppression and environmental destruction.

Conclusion

Men need to eliminate ideological attitudes that have severed their sense of embeddedness in nature. This requires men to break with the view of nature as an object and a commodity that is separate from human beings (Salleh 1995). It is our vulnerability and our corporeal connection to the material world that fosters an ethic of care for the environment (Alaimo 2009). If men's relationship with nature is founded on hegemonic masculinity, then a non-oppressive relationship with nature will require a transformation of dominant ways of being a man, if not a retreat from manhood itself. Men will need to transform their sense of authority over nature and their internalised invincibility.

Following Twine (1997), I believe that encouraging greater emotional and physical vulnerability among men will challenge the denial that causes them illness and stress. This involves men developing emotional connections to nature (see Chapter 12). In a later work, Twine (2001) encourages men to engage more with their bodies to increase their sensual capacities, which will allow them to become more sensitive to nature. This will require men to develop a more emotional response to nature and all living beings (Hall 2005). Men can work within feminist environmentalism by developing a more empathic role in relating to nature that will enable them to move beyond the practices of objectifying and subjugating nature. Men thus need to be encouraged to experience emotional and physical vulnerability in response to nature.

Hall (2005) notes the challenges men will face in responding emotionally to the environment. Men must learn how to express their emotions and concerns about the looming ecological crisis facing the planet. This will involve expressing rage, grief, fear and despair about the environmental challenges we face. For Schmah (1998), giving expression to painful feelings is an important act of self-preservation. It is unemotional passivity and denial about global ecological destruction that is the problem. Expressing emotions as a natural response to environmental crises is often a catalyst to taking action to address these environmental issues. It is only when we feel the pain for our role in environmental degradation that we will feel motivated to act.

The key questions are how do we theorise men's relationship to nature, how do we frame the project for engaging men, and how do we move men towards caring subjectivities and practices (see Chapter 12)? If hegemonic masculinity is founded upon the desire to control nature, then new ecological practices by men will need to challenge not only masculinity, but patriarchy as well.

PART FOUR

OVERCOMING A VIOLENT GENDER ORDER

11 | DISRUPTING MEN'S COMPLICITY IN THE PILLARS OF PATRIARCHY

Introduction

In recent years, there have been numerous articles, books, conferences and government policy statements advocating the greater involvement of men in working against men's violence and towards gender equality. The involvement of men in violence against women prevention has become institutionalised in the philosophies and policies of many international organisations and many governmental and non-governmental organisations around the world. As men have become more prominent in violence against women prevention work, the issue of men's relationship with women against violence services has become a subject of ongoing concern for many feminist anti-violence activists, practitioners and scholars. I have written previously about tensions and dilemmas in engaging men in violence prevention (Pease 2008) and about the importance of men's accountability to women services when men become engaged in anti-violence work (Pease 2017). The focus of this chapter is to argue that to engage men in challenging men's violence against women and in building gender equality, we have to first disengage them from their complicity in the pillars of patriarchy.

The dominant narrative about engaging men

Activists attempting to engage men in violence prevention and gender equality are often at pains to argue that men have much to gain from their involvement (Kaufman 2004; Ruxton 2004; Flood 2005b; Katz 2006; Holter 2014). However, emphasising the positive outcomes for men of their involvement in gender equality and anti-violence work can fail to address the resistances that men have to relinquishing their privilege and acknowledging their complicity in the reproduction of gender inequality.

Men often experience discussions about men's violence and men's abuse of women as a form of 'male-bashing' and as denigrating all men as essentially bad. Thus, it is experienced by men as having to be resisted. Certainly, many men feel defensive when the language of patriarchy is used to describe institutionalised male power. They often experience it as attributing oppressiveness to all men in some form of essentialist way. They rarely see patriarchy as a set of socially constructed power relations that all men participate in.

Katz (2006) has emphasised that he is careful not to adopt an accusatory tone in working with men about violence against women. Flood (2009) adopts a similar invitational approach when he comments, 'Most men are not violent and most men treat women in their lives with respect and care' (p. 17). Flood argues that the claim that most men are not violent is compatible with the point that violence is primarily perpetrated by men. He argues that to link all men with violence infers that 'men's involvements in violence, coercion and control are homogenous and uniform' (Flood 2009: 42). I argue that while all men are linked to violence, these links vary in their character and intensity.

We have to be careful not to position men as being either violent *or* non-violent. Non-violent men are encouraged to challenge the violence of other men. Such men are framed as 'good men' who will protect women from 'bad men'. These 'good men' are often promoted as 'real men' who treat women respectfully and as equals, constructing what Seymour (2012) calls a 'chivalrous masculinity'.

The notion of the 'good man' speaking out is evident in the White Ribbon Campaign in Australia. Good men are positioned as family men who chivalrously protect women from other men who are atypical and deviant (Seymour 2018b). Good men use their male strength to act ethically and challenge other men's violence. Appeals are made to men's sense of honour, and their masculinity is affirmed rather than interrogated. Men are encouraged to 'step up' and in some cases 'man up'. It is assumed that the men who are encouraged to become involved in violence prevention are all 'good' men who are encouraged to challenge the violence and abuse of other 'bad' men (Messner 2016).

Engaging men in violence prevention as 'good' men is a strategy for minimising men's discomfort because it focuses on other men. When it is 'other' men who are the problem, it takes attention away from the privileges and benefits that all men gain from patriarchy. In emphasising physical and sexual violence against women, it neglects the everyday sexism and non-physical abuse that most men engage in.

Of course, men vary in their propensity for, and their use of, violence against women. However, to note this diversity does not require the construction of a dichotomy of violent men against a majority of men who are non-violent and respectful of women. DeKeseredy and Schwartz (2005) note that while there is a kernel of truth to the argument that most men are not violent, it does not follow that men who are violent are deviant or substantially different from other men. It may be more apt to argue that men who do not engage in violence or abuse of women are deviant.

Hearn (1998) has also observed that while men vary in their relationship to violence, it does not follow that there are clearly distinguishable separate types of men. There are both differences and commonalities in men in relation to their potential and actual use of violence against women. Thus, when discussing differences between men, we should always do so in a context of acknowledging the relations of power and dominance over women, which *all* men are enmeshed in.

Engaging men as bystanders without holding them responsible

May (1990) has pointed out that individuals feel no personal sense of responsibility for problems that need to be resolved by collective action. Most men do not regard men's violence against women as something that they should do something about. If they are not physically violent, then they do not see it as their problem. Flood (2009) has also noted that 'most men have done little to challenge the violence perpetrated by a minority of men' (p. 17). In his words, 'While some men are part of the problem, all men are part of the solution' (p. 43). However, if only some men are part of the problem, what is the moral responsibility for other men to be part of the solution (Pease 2011)?

Berkowitz (2004) argues that putting men on the defensive is not effective in working with men. In this view, one should encourage men to be partners in violence prevention without blaming them or criticising them in any way. Marchese (2008) refers to this as a 'reassurance discourse' that creates positive roles for men in violence prevention, as bystanders, as role models, as supporters, as champions and as advocates.

In recent years, bystander intervention programs have become a popular way to engage men in violence prevention. A bystander is someone who observes an act of discrimination or violence and a passive bystander fails to intervene to challenge the offensive behaviour (Powell 2011). Katz (2006), one of the key proponents of the application of bystander theory to violence against women, regards this approach as a way of engaging men in prevention beyond that of framing them as perpetrators or potential perpetrators. While Katz (2006) notes that the common definition of a bystander is a 'description of someone who stands by while bad things happen' (p. 115), he extends the use to include 'someone who is not directly involved as a perpetrator or victim of an act of sexual harassment or violence but is indirectly involved as a friend, or family member' (p. 116). This can also include someone who is in a group, workplace or team.

Advocates for bystander approaches (Katz et al. 2011; Cares et al. 2014; Powell 2014b) argue that it is the implied neutrality of these approaches that will appeal to men because they offer a positive role that does not implicate them in the problem. However, by failing to encourage men to examine how their own behaviour and attitudes may perpetuate gender inequality and violence, these approaches turn attention away from the gendered power relations in which men are all embedded.

When men are engaged as bystanders, they are able to distance themselves from their own complicity in the perpetuation of violence. They do not need to examine their own practices in the world or the practices of other men in their networks who, like them, are positioned as 'good men' (Elk and Devereaux 2014). The language of 'bystander' is that it implies innocence on the part of the bystander, who is framed as external to the situation. All men are implicated in the reproduction of the various levels of patriarchy that facilitates men's violence against women. Consequently, there are no innocent bystanders to patriarchal violence.

While men are encouraged to speak out or to encourage others to challenge the practices, attitudes and policies that contribute to violence (Powell 2011), they are not seen as having any special responsibility to do so because they are men or because of their structural location within patriarchy. When bystander violence prevention programs state that 'Everyone in the community has a role to play in ending sexual violence' and 'Intimate partner abuse is everyone's problem' (cited in Powell 2011: 37), such programs avoid implicating men.

Katz et al. (2011) emphasise that their bystander intervention approach has a social justice focus, and they seek to distance themselves from those bystander programs that have a gender-neutral orientation. However, Katz et al. also discuss the constructive role of female bystanders in interventions to prevent violence. In fact, most bystander intervention programs include both women and men as potential bystanders. Tabachnick (2009) says that the value of bystander intervention is that it regards both men and women as equal partners in prevention.

For Marchese (2008), enlisting men's aid without acknowledging responsibility and complicity creates a false dichotomy of good and bad men, as mentioned earlier. If violent men are seen as aberrant and deviant, we cannot examine the links of these men to the wider culture of hegemonic masculinity and patriarchy of which all men are a part.

In ensuring that men do not get defensive, we avoid the opportunity to challenge men about their responsibility and complicity. Focusing on men's needs and opinions in anti-violence work contributes to the sidelining of women's concerns and views (Marchese 2008). While it is understandable that in a climate that is hostile to feminism, there will be efforts to promote a feminist analysis without appearing to be feminist, the retreat from feminist language means that a gendered analysis is deradicalised in the sense that it moves away interrogating patriarchy and men's structural privilege and power.

Castelino (2010) has developed a feminist audit tool for assessing the consequences of involving men in violence against women prevention work. She is particularly interested in how the role of the women's sector changes when men get involved in violence prevention. She notes that when men are involved, women speak differently about the issue so as not to offend men. Men involved in this work often expect to be seen as good men and they expect women to be grateful that they are involved. Women are thus careful not to blame men or to implicate all men in the issue of men's violence against women. For example, the language in the men's sector is to talk about 'men who use violence' rather than 'men who assault their partners', as the latter is seen to be too confronting and blaming of men. However, Castelino ponders whether feminists are diluting the message and compromising their perspective in this attentiveness to men's concerns. She asks, what are the costs to women in attempts to not alienate men? As Atherton-Zeman (2009) notes, many women report that men involved in violence prevention work continue to be part of the problem and refuse to make their involvement accountable to women.

Casey and Smith (2010) suggest that engaging men in campaigns to stop men's violence against women can be usefully seen as a form of 'ally' development, as in other areas such as white people working against racism and heterosexual people working against homophobia. Becoming an ally against men's violence is not a finite journey. All male allies must accept that their ally status expires at the end of each day and that they must work to renew it on a daily basis (Atherton-Zeman 2009).

If we are to engage men in violence prevention work, we must also encourage them to reflect on their privilege and unearned entitlement as part of that involvement. Casey and Smith (2010) argue that most often the engagement of men in anti-violence work does not challenge men to reflect on their own complicity in relation to the wider culture that supports men's violence. They note that most anti-violence advocates believe that they are 'OK' because they have not themselves been physically violent towards women. In interviews with 27 anti-violence advocates, they found that a common theme among the men was their ignorance of the role that they may have played in reproducing and perpetuating a culture of violence. If well-meaning men refuse to examine their own complicity in reproducing a violence-prone culture, the changes required to bring about an end to men's violence against women will be much slower to develop. Reassuring non-violent men that they are not part of the problem diminishes men's sense of personal responsibility to act.

Learning from critical whiteness studies

I believe that anti-violence work with men can be usefully informed by anti-racist practice and critical whiteness studies, both of which have a clearer political analysis of how all white people benefit from white supremacy and how they are complicit in the reproduction of a racially divided society.

According to Blum (2008), a person is 'complicit in injustice if she benefits from it (even if she did not seek that benefit)' (p. 311). Applebaum (2006) defines complicity as involving 'participation *without* intention' (p. 350, original emphasis). Systemic oppression does not require the intent of individuals. Rather, it is through systemic patterns that are naturalised, normalised and appear to be invisible (Applebaum 2006). Because the structures of privilege are so deeply embedded in society, it is almost impossible for members of privileged groups to escape the receipt of unjust benefits. As Trepagnier (2006) notes, 'No one is immune to the ideas that permeate the culture in which he or she is raised' (p. 15).

Applebaum (2013) refers to two types of complicity. One form of complicity results from unconscious negative attitudes and beliefs that members of privileged groups hold about marginalised people that shape their practices. The second form focuses more on practices and habits of doing whiteness, or gender or class or other forms of privilege. Applebaum (2010) argues that if white people (and by extension all members of privileged groups) want to become allies to challenge systemic racism and other forms of structural inequality, they have to acknowledge their complicity. She is doubtful about allies who espouse their commitment to social justice but avoid a recognition of their own culpability for the perpetuation of oppression.

Thus, it is important to ask the question, 'How might I be complicit in sustaining rather than challenging systemic oppression and white privilege?' (Applebaum 2006: 353). Barton (2010) argues that 'I can only become part of the solution when I recognise the degree to which I am part of the problem, not because I am white but because of my investment in white privilege' (p. 1).

George Yancy (2015a) invited a number of white anti-racist educators and activists to write about how it feels to be a white problem. What are the strategies they draw upon to face their vulnerability and the distress that arises from being exposed about their complicity in white supremacy? How do they remain open to being wounded (Yancy 2015b)?

Most contributors acknowledged that they cannot avoid being a white problem and so they debunk any notion of innocence in relation to racial oppression. Consequently, while they cannot avoid being complicit in white supremacy, they can become more conscious of their complicity and endeavour to enact anti-racist practices against this complicity. Applebaum (2015) says that one of the major challenges white people face is their desire for white innocence. They want to be seen as a good white person to enable them to ignore their complicity with white supremacy. Many white people believe that if they become aware of their white privilege, such awareness is sufficient to exempt them from being part of the problem.

DiAngelo (2018) notes how the language of good and bad white people allows well-intentioned whites to locate themselves on the non-racist side of the binary. If they are non-racist, then nothing is required of them. Racism is a problem for other white people and it is not their responsibility to address it. If white people are challenged about their racism, they interpret that as being framed as a bad person. Consequently, they resist these challenges as it unsettles them and triggers a sense of fragility. To ward off such fragility, they will respond defensively with anger and rage to get those challenging them to back off. In contrast to the project of trying to develop a positive white identity through anti-racism, DiAngelo (2018) argues that white people should strive to be 'less white'. This involves becoming educated about racism, becoming more cognisant about white privilege and becoming less complicit in white solidarity.

Frye (1992) draws parallels between what she calls whiteliness and masculinity. White people cannot cease to be white, but they can reject the values that are associated with being white, including belief in one's own goodness and moral authority over others and denial of culpability in white supremacy. Similarly, while men cannot cease to be male (other than through transgender surgery), they can reject the values associated with masculinity.

Understanding one's own privilege does not necessarily lead to struggles to overcome systemic oppression. Applebaum (2010) suggests that the admission of privilege can deflect members of privileged groups from recognising their complicity in the structures that reproduce oppression. For Applebaum, members of privileged groups must see themselves as having privileged group membership rather than simply seeing themselves as individuals. Otherwise they will be unable to differentiate between individual suffering, which may involve harm, and systemic suffering, which constitutes oppression.

Ironically, the acknowledgement of privilege can lead to an avoidance of recognising people's complicity in the structures that maintain privilege. Levine-Rasky (2010) believes that teaching about privilege as something that is possessed by individuals can obscure the links between the benefits of privilege and the practices by members of privileged groups that reproduce structures of privilege. The focus should be not only on the advantages received by privilege, but also on the processes by which privilege is appropriated (Leonardo 2004).

Much complicity by members of privileged groups is lawful and manifested, for example, in the forms of everyday sexism and everyday racism that aggravates harm but is not criminalised. These forms of everyday oppressive practices create the climate in which physical violence against women, gays and non-white people is legitimated and excused.

Card (2010) uses the language of 'enablers' to describe those men who are not physically violent but are connected to men who are violent without challenging them. All men are complicit to varying degrees in the reproduction of patriarchy. Because men benefit from patriarchy (although not equally), they have less motivation than women to become aware of the costs associated with it. If men do not notice how patriarchy advantages them and disadvantages women, they are likely to regard the distribution of rewards as normal and natural.

As Monteverde (2014) notes, women generally, and feminist women in particular, are also not free of complicity in patriarchal practices and patriarchal structures. When women appropriate masculinist qualities and enact male-identified practices, they, along with men, reproduce patriarchy. Thus, everyone has some level of complicity with gendered power relations, as it is not always possible to live fully in accordance with one's politics and values. What is important is to acknowledge the likelihood that complicity will coexist alongside resistance, and to be ready to face it and address it.

Towards a pedagogy of discomfort

Many attempts to engage members of privileged groups in addressing various forms of inequality try to avoid inducing shame or guilt among those who benefit from unjust systems. Applebaum (2010) says that in understanding complicity in the oppression of others, we should avoid immobilising guilt. This approach suggests that educators should tone down their critiques of structural oppression and encourage members of privileged groups to feel more comfortable.

Those in privileged groups have the most to lose in terms of resources and status in struggles for equality. Many attempts at engaging members of privileged groups in struggles for social justice endeavour to avoid threatening them so as to minimise their resistance. In a discussion of anti-racist practice, Leonardo (2004) talks about the limitation of framing racism as a problem perpetuated by 'bad' whites who are challenged by 'good' white allies. Constructing racism as 'the other' whereby good whites are not implicated will facilitate a sense of comfort for white allies. However, Leonardo (2004) argues that if whites do not feel a sense of discomfort, they will be unable to empathise with the pain and suffering of those who are oppressed by racism. I have argued elsewhere that the same applies to engaging men in campaigns against violence towards women (Pease 2015).

Guilt can be paralysing and it can inhibit critical reflection (Leonardo 2004). However, if one is complicit in perpetuating inequalities, one should feel guilty (Payson 2009). Smith (2013) argues against the notion of creating 'safe spaces' for dialogues between members of privileged groups and members of marginalised groups. Even when members of privileged groups are aware of their privileges, they do not disappear in these dialogues. Like Smith, I am concerned that the accusation of 'unsafe' can be used against people who are marginalised who may express their anger at exploitation and oppression. The question is whether a safe space is possible in the context of enduring structural inequalities.

Challenging privilege and complicity should involve emotions as people connect to their responsibility and culpability in the perpetuation of oppression. Many commentators argue that learning about privilege is painful. Allen and Rossatto (2009) argue that members of privileged groups can only come to understand their privileged positioning through significant emotional experiences. I know this in my own life. The challenge is to ensure that such pain and emotional discomfort leads to change rather than defensiveness and denial. This will require us to move beyond neoliberal notions of individual responsibility.

Beyond neoliberal frameworks of responsibility

If a person is born into systems of privilege and oppression, it does not mean that he or she has no responsibility to challenge them. The structures of inequality are not self-perpetuating. They are rather reproduced by individual participants, especially those who are members of privileged groups (Payson 2009). The burden of responsibility to promote social justice should fall more heavily on those who benefit most from their complicity rather than on those who are non-beneficiaries (Young 2011).

The most common understanding of responsibility is that based on the assumption that society consists of individuals who are unconnected to their historical and social contexts. In this view, perpetrators of racism or violence against women or other abusive practices are prejudiced and ignorant individuals. The approach focuses on the mind of the individual perpetrator. Applebaum (2006) argues that we need to develop new forms of responsibility that are less focused on the acts of individual perpetrators and more focused on identifying the contribution that members of privileged groups make to the structural patterns of privilege and oppression.

Boyd (2004) raises the question of whether the conception of the subject, which underlies the notion of the liberal individual who has moral responsibility for individual actions, obscures systemic oppression and protects members of privileged groups because of the focus on individual intention. In the liberal conception, the individual is isolated from others, exercises rational choice, and is able to transcend structural constraints in the exercise of agency.

The model of responsibility that is based on the premise of the liberal individual conceals the complicity of members of privileged groups in the perpetuation of privilege and oppression (Boyd 2004). There is a need to challenge this concept of the liberal individual if people are to recognise their complicity. This means that it is important to focus less on individual responsibility and more on collective responsibility to challenge the structural dimensions of inequality.

Crowe (2011) has noted the defensive responses of many men to feminism. In addressing such defensiveness, it is tempting for feminists to say to men that it is not their fault and that they are not personally responsible. However, men in general are complicit in the continuing oppression of women. If they are unable to understand their complicity, they will not be able to engage constructively with feminism.

Iris Marion Young and the social connection model of responsibility

Iris Marion Young (2011) made an important contribution to understanding the role of men in the reproduction of patriarchy. Young argued that structural injustice is produced by large numbers of people through their adherence to normative rules and practices. It is one's position within social structures that implicates one in injustice. This is because people are connected to the harm that is caused by these structures. If we are socially connected to the harm, through our involvement in those structures, we have an obligation to challenge the injustice. In Young's view, even if one is innocent of directly perpetrating an injustice, if they are connected to processes that facilitate the injustice, they still bear some responsibility. Consequently, these people have an obligation to work with others to change the structural processes that produce the unjust outcomes.

We need to face the contribution we each make to causal influences that perpetuate injustice and to develop a notion of shared responsibility for the continuation of that injustice. While we all bear responsibility for addressing injustice, the degree of responsibility to act will be shaped by various factors. Thus, the one who has most privilege and most power to influence and membership of powerful groups will bear greater responsibility to act against injustice. While Young does not address the issue of men's violence against women explicitly, her guidelines for shared responsibility have much to contribute to the current debates about engaging men in action against men's violence and gender inequality.

Young (2011) advocates a social connection model of responsibility that challenges the individual notion of responsibility that currently prevails. Men have a responsibility to get involved in challenging men's violence against women if they are causally embedded in processes that produce such violence. That is, as men's actions contribute to the social-structural dimensions of men's violence against women, as moral agents, they should take responsibility for changing the social processes that produce the conditions that allow the continuation of the violence. One's responsibility lies in their complicity in the processes that lead to unjust outcomes. Failure by men who are not physically violent towards women to act against men's violence and abuse of women will lead to the continuation of that violence.

Kutz (2000) also explores the ramifications of individual moral responsibility for collective actions that are mediated by institutional structures. He is concerned with the issue of how individuals can be morally responsible for the practices of others through what he calls 'moral complicity'. If individuals contribute to a collective project, then their participation in that project should hold them accountable to the consequences of that project. In his words, 'No participation without implication' (Kutz 2000: 122). For my purposes here, men's participation in patriarchy implies that all men are implicated in the harms that patriarchy does.

Similarly, May (1992) argues that all men have an underlying moral responsibility to challenge patriarchy because they participate in it. When women are harmed by men's practices, men who did not participate in those practices should feel tainted by them. Furthermore, men who share sexist attitudes share responsibility for the harm that result from those attitudes. Men should feel some shame in, for example, men's complicity in the prevalence of rape through not speaking out against it.

May (1992) also advocates a conception of shared responsibility in relation to men's sexual violence against women. If one is a member of a community in which harm is done, then one should examine whether one's own attitudes and practices may have contributed to a greater likelihood of that harm occurring. This means that members of a community share responsibility for the enactment of those harms even if they did not participate directly in them. Even if one cannot interrupt the practices that cause the harm, one must distance oneself from it and be careful to not be seen to be condoning it.

May and Strikwerda (1994) argue that rape is not only a private act and it is not only the responsibility of individual rapists. In their view, in patriarchal societies most if not all men contribute to the culture of rape, and consequently they should all share some responsibility for the prevalence of rape. As noted earlier, the vast majority of men do little to actively oppose rape, and their silence makes them complicit with the perpetuation of rape. If that is so, all men should feel responsibility and motivation to challenge rape and violence.

Ahmed (2006) cautions that we should be careful not to respond too quickly with answers to the question about what members of privileged people are to do. If people act too quickly, they can avoid hearing the message about their complicity. Mayo (2004), for example, draws attention to the resentment expressed by anti-sexist men who are opposed to rape but who demand a place in Reclaim the Night marches. They need to have acknowledgement from feminists that they are not part of the problem, when the feminist critique is that all men are implicated in men's violence against women. More privilege-cognisant listening on the part of the men about women's experiences may have avoided this outcome.

Feminists have been endeavouring to make the point for many years about how all men are implicated in patriarchy. When individual men oppress or abuse women, they are doing so in the context of the wider institutional structures of male power. Given that all or most men benefit from patriarchy, and if all men are collectively responsible for the harm caused by patriarchy, then every man is partially responsible for the reproduction of that structure that distributes benefits and harms inequitably (May and Strikwerda 1994).

Thus, while not all men are physically violent, all men contribute to the prevalence of violence. Each time an incident of men's violence against women is enacted, men could have made it less likely that this would have happened. It is thus important for men to become aware of how they are implicated in both the wider culture of violence and in particular acts of violence against women. When men develop this awareness, as moral agents, they have responsibility to reconstruct themselves and transform the subjectivities of other men (May and Strikwerda 1994).

Conclusion

The more men participate in patriarchy, the more they feel disconnected from the experiences of others. All men who are raised within a patriarchal society will be exposed to social pressures about what it means to be a man and how men are expected to behave. Invariably, these pressures will be internalised and will shape men's attitudes and practices in relation to women. While some men may come to resist such pressures, and seek to establish respectful and equal relationships with women, this will involve them going against the grain. For many men, however, they may not be conscious of the extent to which the expectations of patriarchy have been internalised within their subjectivities. It is necessary for men to understand patriarchy and its influence on their lives if they are to find a way of challenging it.

Part of the process of understanding patriarchy is to become more aware of the consequences for women and to become conscious of the significance of our own involvement in those processes resulting from our structural location within it. The challenge for men is to work out what it means to be involved in patriarchy. First, we have to acknowledge that patriarchy exists, then we need to find out how it works and how we participate in it (Johnson 1997).

Notwithstanding the deeply embedded internalised domination, men have some agency to act differently against both structural relations and internalised dominance. As Hearn (1987) observes, patriarchy is not just external to men; it exists in men's practices. Hence, men can act differently and against patriarchy at both a personal level of individual behaviour and collectively at the level of public engagement in the state and the wider society. Learning how to participate in patriarchy differently so that we are less likely to reproduce it is a precursor to developing respectful and equal relationships with women.

In the concluding chapter, I explore how a feminist ethic of care can provide the basis for motivating men to break their complicity in patriarchal practices and structures. Fostering caregiving subjectivities and practices among men is an essential part of facing patriarchy and developing a relational self that is based upon nurturance, empathy, vulnerability and political solidarity with women.

12 | FOSTERING A FEMINIST ETHIC OF CARE IN MEN

Introduction

Men's pursuit of manhood and patriarchal masculinity is a major influence on the various forms of men's violence documented in the preceding chapters. The socialisation into hegemonic ways of being a man, and the sense of superiority and entitlement that flow from this, has been shown to limit men's capacity for caring. It has been noted by many commentators that men's limited hands-on experiences of caring have also contributed to men's greater propensity for violence (Ferguson et al. 2003; Lorentzen 2004; Esplen 2006; Hearn and Whitehead 2006; Tronto 2013).

The challenge for feminist and profeminist activists has always been how to name the problem and propose solutions that encourage men to change themselves and the wider patriarchal society. Too often the process of engaging men in violence prevention has allowed men to get 'off the hook' from their culpability in maintaining oppressive gender hierarchies and has not challenged them to make fundamental changes to their subjectivities or their practices. What will motivate men to transform themselves and the social relations of gender they are embedded within?

Many programs engaging men in violence prevention rely upon traditional notions of masculinity. For example, the White Ribbon Campaign in Australia encourages men to 'stand up' and 'challenge' men's violence against women because 'thousands of good men have got your back' (cited in Salter 2016: 10). The 'My Strength Is Not for Hurting' campaign focuses on the use of masculine strength in positive ways to encourage non-violent men to see themselves as real men more so than other violent men (Murphy 2009). 'Man Up' is an international campaign that encourages men to use their strength and power to challenge men's violence and abuse. These campaigns reinforce the notion of 'real men' who are authoratative and protective of women. However, because the notion of traditional masculinity is so embedded with patriarchal values, it is difficult to see how it can be deployed in violence prevention campaigns without undermining their stated objectives. The slogan of 'real men don't hit women' draws upon the very form of masculinity that is at the heart of men's violence against women. It is men who identify most strongly with traditional masculinity who are most likely to be violent towards women (Salter 2016). Suggesting that preventing violence against women is a manly thing to do reproduces patriarchal masculinity.

Most violence prevention campaigns are based on the premise that the prevention of men's violence against women requires men to embrace a new vision of 'what it means to be a man' (see Chapter 7). The argument for using masculinity to engage men is to 'meet men where they are' (Flood 2002–2003). However, can the notion of 'real men' be reclaimed to foster non-violence? Approaches to violence prevention that valorise masculinity reproduce the gender binary that devalues femininity and the feminine that underpins men's dominance and violence against women (Seymour 2018b).

What do we give up when we collude with the very form of masculinity that encourages violence? When we promote strength, bravery and power as masculine virtues, we buy into patriarchal cultural values and become implicated in the reproduction of the gender binary. Part of the process of maintaining a patriarchal gender order requires that men have a sense of their masculine self. What would it mean to encourage men to loosen their connection to masculinity and being a man? Can we encourage men to embrace values and practices that are traditionally associated with the feminine and with women without redefining them as masculine?

Developing an ethic of care as the antithesis of violence

As noted, the exclusion of men from caring roles has been linked to rising levels of men's violence both within the family and within the wider international arena of warfare between nation states. Creating a less violent and more egalitarian world thus requires a shift from the valorisation of hegemonic masculinity to a more caring ethos that is more traditionally associated with women. This means that we need to encourage men not just to undertake more childcare at home, but also to adopt a more caring disposition that challenges the norms of hegemonic masculinity that legitimates violence and gender inequality.

Hearn and Whitehead (2006) argue that to end men's dominance and to create gender equality, it will require moving from a culture of violence to a culture of care. Barker (2005) similarly talks about the importance of promoting an ethic of care among men as a strategy for prevention of violence. He emphasises the importance of young men learning how to become non-violent, respectful and caring in their relationships with women.

A number of ethics of care theorists (Ruddick 1989; Held 2010; Tronto 2013; Robinson 2015) argue that an ethic of care can guide violence prevention not only in the family, but also in the wider international context of terrorism and war. Challenging men's violence against women in the private sphere is the same project as confronting men's military and terrorist violence in the public sphere, as all forms of violence involve a failure to care.

An ethic of care emphasises the pursuit of non-violence over violence as a means of resolving conflicts. For Ruddick (1989), this involves maternal thinking and maternal practices to promote peace. She argues that the practices of mothering could inform the campaigns for peace and non-violence in international politics. In her view, similar moral considerations guide both interventions to stop both men's violence in families and men's military and terrorist violence. Although she is criticised for upholding traditional gender roles and idealising the activities and values of mothering, her philosophical approach provides a framework for engaging men in caring practices and activism for peace.

Breaking the gendered division of care between women and men

Historically, the ethics of care have been gendered as feminine, and some feminist critics have expressed concern that this approach reproduces the association of care with women, and thus entrenches women's caring activities in the gendered division of domestic labour (Glenn 2000; Held 2004; MacGregor 2006; Jordan 2018). In spite of dramatic changes in women's lives following second-wave feminism, women in relationships with men continue to carry the major burden of housework and childcare (Hunter et al. 2017; Ruby and Scholz 2018).

This over-representation of women in caring roles often assumes that this form of work is naturally suited to women, as it is seen to be a reflection of their perceived natural nurturing capacities. It is clear, however, that the association of women with care arises from historical and specific social and political contexts.

The concept of masculinity is disassociated from care and care work (Tronto 2013; Ruby and Scholz 2018). Men's roles in relation to care are framed by the norms and structures of masculinity. Many men consider that they care through providing economically for their partner and children. Men maintain that their major breadwinning activities constitute their contribution to caring for their family. Good fatherhood practice still seems to be primarily measured through the expectation of men providing for and protecting their families (Morrell and Jewkes 2011). Such roles allow men to see themselves as caring without challenging traditional forms of masculinity.

Men's capacity to give priority to their career over caring roles is a reflection of their male privilege and power. Tronto (2013) frames men's avoidance and evasion of care as connected to them having a 'production pass' and a 'protection pass' for getting out of housework and childcare responsibilities. Because of men's protector role and their involvement in economic production, men make the claim that they do not need to be involved in the daily activities of care.

Tronto (2013) has coined the term 'privileged irresponsibility' to describe the process by which men expect others to care for them without any acknowledgement. Such a process allows men to maintain their privileged positioning in the gender order and to be able to ignore the needs of others. Tronto links privileged irresponsibility to what she calls 'epistemological ignorance', whereby members of privileged groups do not have to know about the needs of those who are subjugated.

Hanlon (2009) demonstrates how men avoid and resent caring responsibilities because such responsibilities challenge their masculinity. Hegemonic masculinity is, to use Hanlon's term, 'care-free'. The dominant portrayal of masculinity is rational, inexpressive and unemotional. Doing masculinity requires men to deny their vulnerability, and this makes it very difficult for them to develop nurturing and intimate relationships with others (Hanlon 2012). When men do care, they are under normative pressures to do so in ways that do not challenge their masculinity. Being a carer is associated with femininity and subordination, and it contradicts the expectations of masculinity, which requires men to be dominant. Some men experience caregiving as emasculating because they regard nurturing as feminine and unmanly.

Hanlon (2012) argues that even if men initially seek to maintain their masculinity while providing care, the process of actually doing care will in itself develop in men the emotional and affective experiences that will transform their subjectivities. Doucet (2017) also argues that being at home with children in a primary caregiving role can generate profound changes in men by developing their capacities for attentive care, responsibility for others and non-violence. Such practice of care facilitates a relational sense of self where trust, mutuality and connectedness challenge the autonomous individualism of hegemonic masculinity (Lawson 2007). Relationality facilitates shifts in subjectivities and fosters awareness of the impact of personal activities on others. The issue is whether the nexus of masculinity with dominance can be broken to encompass care and nurturance or whether men's capacity to care and nurture others will require men to break their identification with masculinity.

Fostering caring masculinities?

Proponents of caring masculinities (Gartner et al. 2007; Hanlon 2012; Elliott 2015; Hunter et al. 2017) argue that men can embrace care, positive emotions and relationality as part of a renewed masculinity. The concept of caring masculinity suggests that men who adopt greater sensitivity to others, enhanced emotional expression, and capacity and willingness to undertake domestic work and childcare do not need to reject masculinity. Rather, they create a new form of masculinity that enables them to become 'new men' (Hunter et al. 2017).

Elliott (2015) constructs a theoretical framework of caring masculinities that involves integrating emotions, interdependence, relationality and care into men's identities. Drawing upon feminist care theory, she develops a model that focuses on the practices of care work performed by men. She argues that practices of care can transform masculinities and men's identities into caring masculinities that support gender equality. However, in Elliott's framework, caring masculinities are still based on masculine identities that reconstruct masculinity towards more emotional and relational qualities rather than break with masculine identification per se.

Numerous empirical projects on caregiving men (Doucet 2006; Morrell and Jewkes 2011; Hanlon 2012; Hunter et al. 2017) demonstrate that most male caregivers retain a commitment to many traditional aspects of masculinity that undermine a commitment to gender equality. Morrell and Jewkes (2011), who investigated men's narratives about caring, discovered that none of the men regarded their caring as unmasculine and that their masculine gender identities were able to be maintained. Some of the men were able to do this by framing their caring as alternative gender-equitable masculinities. That is, they were able to reconcile the tension between the traditional expectations of masculinity and their caring practices.

Robinson et al. (2014) note that men in caregiving roles in relation to people with dementia found ways to preserve their masculinity while being engaged in what they understood to be feminine roles. Whenever possible, they emphasised the provider and protector roles previously discussed, even when they were involved in direct care activities. They also talked about the courage they demonstrated in providing care to their partners and reiterated their position as head of the household. All of these rationales for their work sought to associate their caregiving with masculinity. The men also emphasised their task-focused approach to providing care, which drew upon skills they used in their previous work roles.

Hunter et al. (2017) cite research that suggests primary caregiving fathers endeavour to maintain an identity that is linked to either paid work or unpaid community work to enable them to reassure themselves and others that they are still men. It was important for men to maintain a sense of their masculinity in the context of care work. Research by Bach (2017) also discovered that male caregivers were fearful of male subordination to women if they did not maintain a strong sense of masculine self. Similarly, caregiving fathers in Latshaw's (2015) study avoided household tasks they associated with femininity and women, and emphasised what they regarded as masculine housework tasks.

Male caregivers thus emphasise the masculine distinctiveness of their caregiving activities whereby they were able to argue that they enact a masculine style of care that is associated with their maleness and masculinity. The idea of a gender-distinctive form of masculine care that women do not do reinforces gender dualisms that marginalise what are seen as feminine forms of care. Such notions reinforce both hegemonic masculinity and patriarchal gender relations (Jordan 2018). The question is, how do we encourage men to become more engaged in care in ways that do not reinforce the binary opposition of masculinity and femininity?

Transforming masculinity or refusing to be a man?

There is agreement among feminist and profeminist scholars that men need to construct their sense of self outside of frameworks of dominant masculinity so that violence is not equated with masculinity or manhood. The key question is whether masculinity can be reconstructed to allow for a democratic and egalitarian subjectivity or whether such a subjectivity needs to break with notions of masculinity or manhood altogether (Pease 2014c; see also Chapter 7).

Barker (2016) suggests that we need to create non-violent, caring and equitable versions of manhood. The development of caring masculinities is similar to attempts to develop inclusive forms of masculinity that are non-homophobic and involve more emotionally expressive and softer expressions of masculinity (Anderson 2011). These alternative forms of masculinity are optimistic about men's potential to transform themselves towards less exploitative and less abusive masculinities.

Thus, for many masculinity scholars, the focus is on shifting from one form of masculinity to another rather than undoing masculinity. The premise is that we can create more harmonious and peaceful masculinities, which means that men's subjectivity is understood only within the frame of masculinity (Macleod 2007). O'Neill (2015) suggests that these attempts to formulate alternative masculinities allows masculinity scholars to critique patriarchal gender relations, while advancing a way forward for men. However, as some feminist critics warn (Robinson 2003; O'Neill 2015), we have to be careful that heterosexual men advancing alternative masculinities do not remake gender inequality in new and more subtle ways.

Bridges (2014) uses the term 'hybrid masculinities' to describe the incorporation of femininities and marginalised masculinities into the gender identities of privileged men. Such masculinities do little to challenge gender inequality, and in fact reproduce it, while obscuring the process of it happening. He notes how men becoming more emotionally expressive has more to do with styles of masculinities than with challenging men's privileged positioning or transforming men's practices. The reconstructed masculinity appears to be feminist-supportive but actually reinforces both gender inequality through men's continuing patriarchal practices and masculinist gender identities of men.

Eisen and Yamashita (2017) discuss similar concerns with the development of hybrid masculinity where men describe themselves as caring and talk about integrating feminine characteristics into their identities. However, such men were shown to co-opt the notion of caring to gain more status, and consequently to reinforce their gender dominance. While these men wanted to distance themselves from traditional patriarchal men, they did not want to challenge their dominant and privileged positions within gender relations. Eisen and Yamashita's research demonstrates the ways in which some men appropriate characteristics deemed to be progressive to reinforce their power over women and other men. In their view, maintaining some form of masculinity is advantageous to men's interests.

Over 20 years ago, Hearn (1996) asked the question, 'Is masculinity dead?' He noted at the time how the concept of masculinity has roots in psychological research on gender identity and sex roles, and how it refers mainly to the culturally constructed notion of being a man. His concern at the time was that emphasising masculinity focused more on men as victims of gendered power than as active agents of that power, as it neglected the gendered power relations between men and women. By focusing on masculinity as the problem, the political project becomes one of reconstructing or transforming masculinity rather than changing men's behaviours and their privileged social positioning. For Hearn, the focus should be on men's political practices and the social relations of gender.

Since then, Hearn (2004, 2016) has revisited this issue and continues to argue against the language of masculinity and masculinities. He proposes a political and conceptual move from hegemonic masculinity to the hegemony of men, arguing that the focus on masculinity is too narrow. Consequently, the gaze needs to shift to the individual and collective practices of men in explaining men's power rather than the concept of masculinity or masculinities. The problem with the notion of masculinity is that its origins in sex role theory and psychology leads to a psychologisation of gender politics (McMahon 1999). Addis et al. (2010) also note that the concept of masculinity has generally promoted essentialist understandings about gender. They ponder whether it may be at odds with a commitment to eliminating gender inequality. As Hearn (2016) argues, and as many feminists have commented, you can change masculinities without transforming men's privileged and dominant position.

If the socially constructed notions of masculinity and femininity are framed as inherently unequal, it is hard to imagine how they can be reformed towards gender equality. Furthermore, if hegemonic masculinity is seen as the root cause of men's dominance and violence, then the problem is seen as men practising a bad version of masculinity (Schwalbe 2014). If the gender binary is structured as being unequal, it suggests that rather than reconstructing masculinity (one side of the binary), we may need to end the binary of gender altogether.

Stoltenberg (1993) argues that while masculinity purports to describe men's subjectivities and practices, it is actually a mask. For him, the challenge is to refuse masculinity and manhood and create a sense of moral selfhood. Stoltenberg believes the sense of self that is framed by manhood is premised upon the oppression of women and that this is in conflict with a moral sense of self that is based upon justice and equality. So, for Stoltenberg, there is a better self that can be created; it is just not framed by models of masculinity or manhood.

The latter approach means developing an ethical identity among men that is not reliant upon being masculine. Roussel and Downs (2007) argue that the concept of masculinity is essentialist and that masculinity should not be equated with gender. They argue against attempts to reconstruct masculinity and suggest that men should stop being concerned about defining themselves as masculine. Schwalbe (2014) suggests that the notion of a 'new masculinity' or a more inclusive form of manhood does nothing to challenge gender hierarchy. Rather, such softer images make those inequalities more palatable and ultimately more sustainable. However, the costs of preserving such forms of masculinity may not only lead to ongoing violence and war; they may also lead to environmental and planetary destruction.

Doing emotional care work

While some of men's emotions are involved in the reproduction of male privilege and power, these emotions can also be used to motivate men to interrogate their own individual and collective privilege (Pease 2012). Emotions are a site of political resistance to oppression and privilege. Consequently, they have a relationship with social justice and they can play a pivotal role in transforming gender relations. Shame, for example, is an emotion that arises initially when men first become aware of their privilege. Shame is a necessary emotional first step to an acknowledgement of women's suffering.

It has been noted by many feminists that men's emotional relationships with women are shaped by the structures of patriarchy. It is argued that men need to do more 'emotion work' to work towards relations of equality between women and men (de Boise and Hearn 2017). Many women have reported that they experience men's emotional distance as a form of gendered power, whereby men choose to withhold emotions and intimacy as a way of having control over women (Robinson 1996). In the context of how heterosexual men relate to heterosexual women, many men fear that if they are seen to be too emotional, it will undermine their superiority over women because it challenges the hegemonic expectation of male rationality and strength (Coyle and Morgan-Sykes 1998). Some men even talk about loving and intimate behaviour as feminine.

Sattel (1989) argued that many of the theorists who focus on male inexpressiveness misunderstand the origins of men's emotional illiteracy. Their focus on men's inexpressiveness as a form of tragedy does not challenge the social forces that construct these phenomena. For Sattel, men's inexpressiveness is a prerequisite for preparing them for their positions of power and privilege, as it enables men who wield power to reduce their emotional involvement in the consequences of their practices. It enables them make decisions that affect the lives of others and to close their eyes to the pain they are causing. So, men's inexpressiveness is a means to an end rather than an end in itself. It is part of men's capacity to control others, and it can assist them to maintain their power and privileges. When men fail to develop and express their feelings, they are more able to oppress others. Men's emotional indifference allows them to inflict pain on others without having any consequences. Consequently, we must explore the male privilege that resides behind the emotional inexpressiveness that has been associated with white, Western, heterosexual men.

In recent years, there have been a number of books and articles demonstrating that men are showing greater capacity for expressing emotions and arguing that such emotional expression is transforming masculinity (Seidler 2007; Anderson 2011; Holmes 2015). Some commentators suggest that this transformation of men's emotional capacities is leading to increased gender equality. On the surface, it seems that men being more emotional indicates a shift in gender relations because emotions are associated with femininity, which traditional heterosexual men are keen to avoid. Certainly, men's greater emotional expression disrupts some tenets of hegemonic masculinity, as emotions are regarded as unmasculine.

However, as de Boise and Hearn (2017) have observed, men have always been able to cry in some specific settings such as births, funerals and football matches. Thus, emotional expression is not inherently progressive for men. Some ways in which men soften masculinity actually reinforces misogyny and patriarchal practices (de Boise and Hearn 2017). We should be cautious about whether this greater emotional expression by men leads to greater equality between men and women. What is important is to understand how men's emotions maintain or challenge gender inequality.

Lynch and Walsh (2009) refer to the work required to sustain loving relations as 'love labouring' or 'emotional care work'. It involves the investment of energy, time and resources. Lynch and Baker (2009) observe that there are significant inequalities in the doing of love, care and solidarity work, and being in receipt of love, care and solidarity. This inequality, of course, is gendered. So, if we are to achieve equality between men and women in the social relations of emotions, we have to address what Lynch and Baker call 'affective inequality'. To achieve affective equality, I argue that we need to foster a feminist ethic of care in men involving empathy, vulnerability and political solidarity with women.

Practising empathy

To foster an ethic of care in men involves the inculcation of a relational ontology whereby relations with others are regarded as important for the sustaining and structuring of the self. Such a project requires a redefinition of the concepts of agency, autonomy and vulnerability (Apostolova and Gauthier-Mamaril 2018). If we are to learn to live democratically and peacefully with each other, we will need to understand how we are all located in a complex web of interdependencies and intersubjectivities. Thus, men must learn how to construct a relational self in contrast to their adherence to an autonomous self. Developing a relational self involves moving beyond individualised accounts of the world and learning how to empathise with the experiences of others.

Schwalbe (1992) contends that male supremacy constitutes a masculinist self that limits the moral subjectivities of men. This narrow moral self is not linked to men as biological beings, but rather to the ways in which men's subjectivity is shaped by patriarchal social forces. The limited moral responsibility that men exhibit has major consequences, especially towards women. He proposes an ethic of care for men that encourages them to develop empathy and responsibility towards others. An immoral masculinist self that is based on men's privilege and power does not allow men to experience empathy to women's pain. A male supremacist society undermines men's ability to act in a morally responsible way towards women. If men are unable to acknowledge women's pain, they are unlikely to know how they and the society they live in contribute to that pain and what is required of them to address it. The task ahead is to expand the moral self by developing a sense of justice that enables them to see women's pain as unjust. Men must be able to see women's pain as a precursor to seeing how they are implicated in the causes of that pain, and must take responsibility for it. They are then able to draw upon love for justice and care to challenge the patriarchal basis of the masculinist self.

If men are to understand their complicity in the oppression of others, they will need to allow themselves to experience discomfort and emotional distress. It is not enough to know about the oppression of women. We have to experience that knowledge in our bodies and in our hearts. We have to experience emotional responses to the oppression of others (Gilson 2011). Empathy brings feelings into the foreground as a valid form of knowledge. It is what connects us to others and what enables us to care for others (Hemmings 2012). Tong (1997) regards empathy as an epistemic skill that can be learned. Rodino-Colocino (2018) considers what she calls 'transformative empathy' as a starting point for involvement in action for structural change. Men can thus learn to develop a sensibility towards greater connectedness. In fact, a feminist ethic of care must be encouraged in men to break the perceived natural association of care with women.

Becoming vulnerable

In studies of peaceful societies, Howell and Willis (1990) found that where men were allowed to experience fear and vulnerability, there was less propensity towards violence. If the experience of invulnerability is central to masculinity and vulnerability is seen as inherently feminine, then this aspect of dominant gender norms perpetuates the victimisation of women by men. In challenging hegemonic masculinity and patriarchal ideology, we need to focus on the inculcation of invulnerability as an essential part of what it is to be a man. It is the experience of invulnerability that enables men to position themselves as powerful and superior to women (Gilson 2016a). Invulnerability is a form of ignorance as it fosters an illusion of control and closes off the capacity to being affected by the world. It is also what enables those who are privileged to ignore the oppression of others and the various ways in which we are implicated in that oppression.

Thus, men's incapacity to recognise the vulnerability of women to violence arises in part from their own sense of masculine invulnerability. It is men's experience of invulnerability that is connected to dominant forms of masculinity that promote stoicism and toughness that encourage violence towards others. If men cannot recognise their own human vulnerability, and lack the capacity to care for themselves, they are less likely to be able to develop the ethical sensibility to care for others (Cover 2015). Allowing oneself to be vulnerable in an onto-logical sense is more of a challenge for elite white men who adhere to hegemonic masculinity, as men who are subordinated by class, race, sexuality and disability know all too well, along with women, what it means to be vulnerable.

Judith Butler's (2004) work on ethics and vulnerability demonstrates how the process of disavowing vulnerability fuels invulnerability, which is at the heart of violence and war. For Butler, ontological vulnerability is a primary condition of what it is to be human. Recognition of this human vulnerability is essential for developing human connections between people, which are the basis for cooperation. While vulnerability is often negatively associated with weakness and dependency, it is being open to being affected by the world and being able to emotionally engage with the world.

For Butler, it is important to learn how to experience grief and loss associated with violence without becoming motivated to enact further violence in retaliation. This involves learning how to mourn in ways that enable us to act politically to lessen the likelihood of further violence. Butler argues that mindfulness of vulnerability can assist us to develop non-military solutions to international conflicts. Denial of vulnerability increases the propensity for war. To engage in violence and war, we must to some extent deny the human vulnerability of others. We have to fail to acknowledge their human frailty and their personhood.

The notion of ontological vulnerability arises from a recognition of our humanness and our openness to be affected by the world around us. Thus, while vulnerability may limit us in some ways, it also opens us to a wider range of human experiences that are necessary for our long-term survival (Gilson 2011). We need to be open to the notion of being 'wounded' by our exposure to the precariousness of life (Boubil 2018). For men, it also means being open to being wounded by women's pain and suffering.

Developing care in solidarity

Much of the writing on care is relegated predominantly to domestic practices and household work or caring occupations. While the household and paid work are two of the structures of patriarchy and are important locations for the development of democratic gender practices, the focus on care in this chapter extends beyond the family and the workplace.

Beasley (2016) has expressed some scepticism of the value of care and emotions in social change. She is particularly critical of whether the greater involvement of fathers in caring for children, for example, will necessarily bring about gender equality between men and women. In her view, caring and emotional expression do not in themselves challenge gender hierarchies, and in some cases they may uphold men's gender dominance because they are insufficiently engaged with power and the political. Even Hanlon (2012), who is optimistic about the impact of caring practices on men's subjectivities, acknowledges that structural levels of change in political, economic and social arenas are necessary to address gendered inequalities in care.

Miller (2010) articulates a concept of 'cosmopolitan care' that extends beyond familial relations to global and transnational political relations. Transnational and political solidarity work is not usually framed as a form of care. However, the language of care enables us to understand the motivations for people involved in global social justice campaigns. Cantillon and Lynch's (2017) concept of 'affective equality' (noted earlier), as a form of relational justice, goes beyond the usual principles of social justice that are concerned with redistribution, recognition and representation. Such a notion is key if inequalities of care and care relations are to be addressed. Affective equality involves ensuring that the distribution of nurturing through love, care and solidarity relations are equal in both those who provide emotional and other labour and those who receive such labour (Lynch 2010).

Solidarity work refers to caring relations through political work with distant others. Lynch and Walsh (2009) see solidarity work as an essential element of affective equality, alongside love labouring and paid care relations. Such work operates outside of immediate face-to-face relationships, and may involve, for example, political campaigns in relation to refugees and asylum seekers or global campaigns in relation to inequalities between Western and non-Western countries. It is care for the 'distant stranger' that is invoked with the notion of solidarity as care. Scholz (1998) argues that solidarity is a necessary element of care to ensure that care is extended to a wider social and political context. In her view, we need to 'care in solidarity' with those who are outside our familial and collegial contexts.

Political solidarity is a relational concept in that it involves a connection with others (Krishnamurthy 2013). A political solidarity model of social change involves members of a privileged group challenging oppression in solidarity with a marginalised group. The privileged group becomes identified with the cause of the marginalised and develops a relationship of political solidarity with them (Subasic et al. 2008).

Care in solidarity with women provides an alternative framework for engaging men to the dominant narratives previously discussed. Men who aspire to be allies with women do not try to escape their culpability for women's oppression and they do not seek leadership roles within social movements against violence. They do not position themselves as 'good men' and they acknowledge the ways they are implicated in the structures of patriarchy (Duriesmith 2018). This suggests a more modest role for men to avoid the dangers of their involvement in violence prevention, and it requires men to ensure lines of accountability to feminist women's services (Pease 2017).

Conclusion

A key strategy for engaging men in collective action for gender equality and violence prevention is to frame men as having a positive role to play as agents of change. However, to date, as discussed earlier, much of this engagement is to frame men as 'champions', 'bystanders', 'good men' or 'chivalrous men' who are not implicated in the processes and structures of inequality they are encouraged to challenge.

While numerous books, training manuals and articles articulate strategies of engaging men in violence prevention (for an overview, see Flood 2018), the emphasis in this book is that men need to become educated about patriarchy and engaged in significant personal transformation to 'walk the talk' in their personal lives, to become 'aspiring allies' and 'solidarity activists' who work alongside women in an auxiliary role in preventing violence and promoting gender equality.

Men must become, in hooks' (2000) words, 'comrades in struggle' with women for gender equality and a world without violence. Subasic et al. (2008) are interested in the psychological processes that occur in the privileged group members to enable them to define themselves as allies in the political struggle. In the context of men's solidarity with feminist women and their causes, men will be more likely to take action in support of women if they identify with feminism (Wiley et al. 2012). Thus, it is important to encourage men to engage positively with feminist analyses and feminist concerns. A feminist ethic of care provides the framework to guide men in such personal transformation and solidarity activism.

I have written elsewhere about the potential harms that men involved in violence prevention can cause when they do not understand the ways in which patriarchy works and their own complicity in reproducing it (Pease 2017). One of the aims of this book is to provide a resource for men to educate themselves about patriarchy and to challenge them to come to terms with their own place within it, to *face* patriarchy as a necessary step to overcoming it. This will create some discomfort for men, but it also provides men with the opportunity to develop an ethical and relational self that will not only enrich their own lives and the lives of women, but also open men to emotional connections to nature and all living beings. If we are to eliminate men's violence against women and men, and overcome war, terrorism and ecological destruction, we need to open ourselves to love, care and solidarity as political concepts to guide our actions in the world. In the words of bell hooks (2014):

> When women and men understand that working to eradicate patriarchal domination is a struggle rooted in the longing to make a world where everyone can live fully and freely, then we know our work to be a gesture of love. Let us draw upon that love to heighten our awareness, deepen our compassion, intensify our courage and strengthen our commitment.

(p. 39)

REFERENCES

Abrams, J. (2016) 'The Feminist Case for Acknowledging Women's Acts of Violence', *Yale Journal of Law and Feminism*, vol. 27, no. 2, pp. 287–329.

Acker, J. (1989) 'The Problem with Patriarchy', *Sociology*, vol. 23, no. 2, pp. 235–240.

Acker, J. (2009) 'From Glass Ceiling to Inequality Regimes', *Sociologie du Travail*, vol. 51, pp. 199–217.

Adams, P., Gavey, N. and Towns, A. (1995) 'Dominance and Entitlement: The Rhetoric Men Use to Discuss Their Violence towards Women', *Discourse and Society*, vol. 6, no. 3, pp. 387–406.

Addis, M., Mansfield, A. and Syzdek, M. (2010) 'Is "Masculinity" a Problem? Framing the Effects of Gendered Social Learning in Men', *Psychology of Men and Masculinity*, vol. 11, pp. 77–90.

Adelman, M. (2003) 'The Military, Militarism and the Militarisation of Domestic Violence', *Violence against Women*, vol. 9, no. 9, pp. 1118–1152.

Adorno, T. (1963) *The Culture Industry*, Routledge, New York.

Agarwal, B. (1992) 'The Gender and Environment Debate: Lessons from India', *Feminist Studies*, vol. 18, no. 1, pp. 119–158.

Ahmed, S. (2006) 'The Nonperformativity of Antiracism', *Meridians: Feminism, Race, Transnationalism*, vol. 7, no. 1, pp. 104–126.

Alaimo, S. (2009) 'Insurgent Vulnerability and the Carbon Footprint of Gender', *Kvinder, Non Froskning NR*, vols. 3–4, pp. 22–35.

Alexander-Scott, M., Bell, E. and Holden, J. (2016) *Shifting Social Norms to Tackle Violence against Women and Girls*, VAWG Helpdesk, London.

Ali, P. and Naylor, P. (2013) 'Intimate Partner Violence: A Narrative View of the Feminist Social and Ecological Explanations for Its Causation', *Aggression and Violent Behavior*, vol. 18, pp. 611–619.

Allen, C., Swan, S. and Raghavan, C. (2009) 'Gender Symmetry, Sexism and Intimate Partner Violence', *Journal of Interpersonal Violence*, vol. 24, no. 11, pp. 1816–1834.

Allen, J. (1990) 'Does Feminism Need a Theory of the State?', in S. Watson (ed.), *Playing the State: Australian Feminist Interventions*, Allen & Unwin, Sydney.

Allen, R. and Rossatto, A. (2009) 'Does Critical Pedagogy Work with Privileged Students?', *Teacher Education Quarterly*, vol. 36, no. 1, pp. 163–180.

Anderson, E. (2011) *Inclusive Masculinity: The Changing Nature of Masculinities*, Routledge, London.

Anderson, K. (2005) 'Theorizing Gender in Intimate Partner Violence Research', *Sex Roles*, vol. 52, pp. 125–150.

Anderson, K. (2008) 'Is Partner Violence Worse in the Context of Control?', *Journal of Marriage and the Family*, vol. 70, pp. 1157–1168.

Anderson, K. (2009) 'Gendering Coercive Control', *Violence against Women*, vol. 15, no. 12, pp. 1444–1457.

ANROWS (2017) *Are We There Yet? Australian Attitudes towards Violence against Women and Gender Equality*, NCAS Summary Report, Australian National Research Organisation for Women's Safety, Sydney.

Anshelm, J. and Hultman, M. (2014) 'A Green Fatwar? Climate Change as a Threat to the Masculinity of Industrial Modernity', *NORMA: International Journal for Masculinity Studies*, vol. 9, no. 2, pp. 84–96.

Apostolova, I. and Gauthier-Mamaril, E. (2018) 'Care and the Self: A Philosophical Perspective on Constructing Active Masculinities', *Feminist Philosophy Quarterly*, vol. 4, no. 1, pp. 1–14.

Applebaum, B. (2006) 'Race Ignore-Ance, Colortalk and White Complicity: White Is … White Isn't', *Educational Theory*, vol. 56, no. 3, pp. 345–362.

Applebaum, B. (2010) *Being White, Being Good: White Complicity, White Moral Responsibility, and Social Justice Pedagogy*, Rowman & Littlefield, Lanham, MD.

Applebaum, B. (2013) 'Vigilance as a Response to White Complicity', *Educational Theory*, vol. 63, no. 3, pp. 17–34.

Applebaum, B. (2015) 'Flipping the Script … and Still a Problem: Staying in the Anxiety of Being a Problem', in G. Yancy (ed.), *White Self-Criticality beyond Anti-Racism: How Does It Feel to Be a White Problem?*, Lexington Books, Lanham, MD.

Archambault, A. (1993) 'A Critique of Ecofeminism', *Canadian Women's Studies*, vol. 13, no. 3, pp. 19–22.

Archer, J. (1994a) 'Power and Male Violence', in J. Archer (ed.), *Male Violence*, Routledge, London.

Archer, J. (1994b) 'Violence between Men', in J. Archer (ed.), *Male Violence*, Routledge, London.

Armstrong, G. and Rosbrook-Thompson, J. (2017) '"Squashing the Beef": Combatting Gang Violence and Reforming Masculinity in East London', *Contemporary Social Science*, vol. 12, nos. 3–4, pp. 285–296.

Arxer, S. (2011) 'Hybrid Masculine Power: Reconceptualising the Relationship between Homosociality and Hegemonic Masculinity', *Humanity and Society*, vol. 35, pp. 390–422.

Ashcraft, A. (2000) 'Naming Knowledge: A Language for Reconstructing Domestic Violence and Systemic Gender Inequity', *Women and Language*, vol. 23, pp. 1–18.

Ashe, F. (2007) *The New Politics of Masculinity: Men, Power and Resistance*, Routledge, New York.

Aslam, M. (2012) *Gender-Based Explosions: The Nexus between Muslim Masculinities, Jihadist Islamism and Terrorism*, United Nations University Press, New York.

Atherton-Zeman, B. (2009) 'Minimizing the Damage: Male Accountability in Stopping Men's Violence against Women', *XY*, September, pp. 1–8.

Auchter, J. (2012) 'Gendering Terror', *International Feminist Journal of Politics*, vol. 14, no. 1, pp. 121–139.

Austerberry, H. (2011) 'Review of *The Palgrave Handbook of Gender and Healthcare* by E. Kuhlmann and E. Annandale', *Critical Public Health*, vol. 22, no. 1, pp. 109–110.

Austin, D. (2016) 'Hyper-Masculinity and Disaster: The Reconstruction of Hegemonic Masculinity in the Wake of Calamity', in E. Enarson and B. Pease (eds), *Men, Masculinities and Disaster*, Routledge, New York.

Bacchi, C. (1999) *Women, Policy and Politics: The Construction of Policy Problems*, Sage, London.

Bacchi, C. (2004) 'Gender/ing Impact Assessment: Can It Be Made to Work?', *Journal of Interdisciplinary Gender Studies*, vol. 9, no. 2, pp. 93–111.

Bach, A. (2017) 'The Ambiguous Construction of Nondominant Masculinity: Configuring the "New" Man through Narratives of Fatherhood and Gender Equality', *Men and Masculinities*, pp. 1–22, doi: 10.1177/1097184X17715494.

Baird, A. (2010) 'Differences in Types of Intimate Partner Violence: Implications for Public Policy', *Challenge*, vol. 16, no. 1, pp. 1–8.

Baird, A. (2012) 'The Violent Gang and the Construction of Masculinity amongst Socially Excluded Young Men', *Safer Communities*, vol. 11, no. 4, pp. 179–190.

Balbus, I. (1982) 'A Neo-Hegelian, Feminist Psychoanalytic Perspective on Ecology', *Telos*, vol. 52, pp. 115–145.

Barker, G. (2005) *Dying to Be Men: Youth, Masculinity and Social Exclusion*, Routledge, London.

Barker, G. (2016) 'Male Violence or Patriarchal Violence? Global Trends in Men and Violence', *Sexualidad, Salud y Sociedad – Revista Latinoamericana*, no. 22, pp. 316–330.

Barker, G., Ricardo, C. and Nascemento, N. (2007) *Engaging Men and Boys to Transform Gender-Based Health Inequities: Is There Evidence of Impact?*, World Health Organization, Geneva.

Baron, L. and Strauss, M. (1987) 'Four Theories of Rape: A Macrosociological Analysis', *Social Problems*, vol. 34, pp. 467–489.

Barreto, M. and Ellemers, N. (2005) 'The Burden of Benevolent Sexism: How It Contributes to the Maintenance of Gender Inequalities', *European Journal of Social Psychology*, vol. 35, pp. 633–642.

Barrett, M. (1980) *Women's Oppression Today*, Verso, London.

Barry, K. (2010) *Unmaking War, Remaking Men*, Spinifex Press, Melbourne.

Barton, A. (2010) *Going White: Claiming an Identity of White Privilege*, paper presented at the Symposium: Future Stories/Intimate Histories, Australian Critical Race Studies and Whiteness Studies Association Conference, Adelaide, South Australia, 10 December.

Beasley, C. (2016) *What Matters in Social Change? The Uncertain Significance of Caring, of Emotions, in Generating Social Change*, paper presented at the Fay Gale Research Centre, University of Adelaide, 8 April.

Beck, U. (2007) *World at Risk*, Polity, Cambridge.

Bell, C. (1973) *Mateship in Australia: Implications for Male–Female Relationships*, La Trobe University Working Papers, Melbourne.

Bennett, J. (2006) *History Matters: Patriarchy and the Challenge of Feminism*, University of Pennsylvania Press, Philadelphia, PA.

Beringola, A. (2017) 'Intersectionality: A Tool for Gender Analysis of Sexual Violence at the ICC', *Amsterdam Law Forum*, April, pp. 98–109.

Berkowitz, A. (2004) *Working with Men to Prevent Violence against Women: An Overview*, Applied Research Forum, National Electronic Network on Violence Against Women, October.

Berns, N. (2001) 'Degendering the Problem and Gendering the Blame: Political Discourses on Women and Violence', *Gender and Society*, vol. 15, no. 2, pp. 262–281.

Bevan, M. and MacKenzie, M. (2012) '"Cowboy" Policing versus "the Softer Stuff"', *International Feminist Journal of Politics*, vol. 14, no. 4, pp. 508–528.

Bimbi, F. (2014) 'Symbolic Violence: Reshaping Post-Patriarchal Discourses on Gender', *Advances in Gender Research*, vol. 18B, pp. 275–301.

Bird, S. (1996) 'Welcome to the Men's Club: Homosociality and the Maintenance of Hegemonic Masculinity', *Gender and Society*, vol. 10, no. 2, pp. 120–132.

Birkeland, J. (2010) 'Ecofeminism: Linking Theory and Practice', in G. Gaard (ed.), *Ecofeminism*, Temple University Press, Philadelphia, PA.

Blum, L. (2008) 'White Privilege: A Mild Critique', *Theory and Research in Education*, vol. 6, no. 3, pp. 309–321.

Bonds, E. (2016) 'Upending Climate Violence Research: Fossil Fuel Corporations and the Structural Violence of Climate Change', *Human Ecology Review*, vol. 22, no. 2, pp. 3–23.

Borchorst, A. and Siim, B. (2002) 'The Women-Friendly Welfare States Revisited', *NORA: Nordic Journal of Women's Studies*, vol. 10, no. 2, pp. 90–98.

Borchorst, A. and Siim, B. (2008) 'Woman-Friendly Policies and State Feminism: Theorizing Scandinavian Gender Equality', *Feminist Theory*, vol. 9, no. 2, pp. 207–224.

Boubil, E. (2018) 'The Ethics of Vulnerability and the Phenomenology of Dependency', *Journal of the British Society for Phenomenology*, vol. 49, no. 3, pp. 183–192.

Bourdieu, P. (2002) *Masculine Domination*, Stanford University Press, Stanford, CA.

Bowker, L. (1983) *Beating Wife Beating*, Lexington Books, Lanham, MD.

Boyd, C. (2009) *Thinking about Risk: Preventing Violence against Women in Victoria*, unpublished paper.

Boyd, D. (2004) 'The Legacies of Liberalism and Oppressive Relations: Facing a Dilemma for the Subject of Moral Education', *Journal of Moral Education*, vol. 33, no. 1, pp. 3–22.

Boyd, E. (2010) 'The Noel Kempff Project in Bolivia: Gender, Power and Decision-Making in Climate Mitigation', *Gender and Development*, vol. 10, no. 2, pp. 70–77.

Bradley, H. (1989) *Men's Work, Women's Work*, Polity, Cambridge.

Bradley, K. and Khor, D. (1993) 'Toward an Integration of Theory and Research on the Status of Women', *Gender and Society*, vol. 7, no. 3, pp. 347–378.

Breines, I., Connell, R. and Eide, I. (2000) 'Introduction', in I. Breines, R. Connell and I. Eide (eds), *Male Roles, Masculinities and Violence: A Culture of Peace Perspective*, UNESCO, Paris.

Bridges, T. (2014) 'Hybrid Masculinities: New Directions in the Sociology of Men and Masculinities', *Sociology Compass*, vol. 8 no. 3, pp. 246–258.

Brittan, A. (1989) *Masculinity and Power*, Basil Blackwell, London.

Brod, H. (1998) 'To Be a Man or Not to Be a Man: That Is the Feminist Question', in T. Digby (ed.), *Men Doing Feminism*, Routledge, New York.

Broderick, E. (2012) *Review into the Treatment of Women in the Australian Defence Force*, Phase 2 Report, Australian Human Rights Commission, Sydney.

Bronfenbrenner, U. (1977) 'Toward an Experimental Ecology of Human Development', *American Psychologist*, July, pp. 513–531.

Broom, D. (2016) 'Hazardous Good Intentions? Unintended Consequences of the Project of Prevention', *Health Sociology Review*, vol. 17, no. 2, pp. 129–140.

Bryson, V. (1999) 'Patriarchy: A Concept Too Useful to Lose', *Contemporary Politics*, vol. 5, no. 4, pp. 311–324.

Buchwald, E., Fletcher, P. and Roth, M. (2005) *Transforming a Rape Culture*, Milkweed Editions, Minneapolis, MN.

Buck, H., Gammon, A. and Preston, C. (2014) 'Gender and Geoengineering', *Hypatia*, vol. 29, no. 3, pp. 651–701.

Bumiller, K. (2008) *In an Abusive State: How Neoliberalism Appropriated the Feminist Movement against Sexual Violence*, Duke University Press, Durham, NC.

Bunton, R. and Willis, J. (2004) '25 Years of Critical Public Health', *Critical Public Health*, vol. 14, no. 2, pp. 79–80.

Burrell, S. (2014) *The Invisibility of Men's Practices: A Discourse Analysis of Gender in Domestic Violence Policy*, master's thesis, University of Tampere, Finland.

Burstyn, V. (1999) *The Rites of Men: Manhood, Politics and the Culture of Sport*, University of Toronto Press, Toronto.

Butler, J. (2004) *Precarious Life: The Powers of Mourning and Violence*, Verso, London.

Campbell, B. (2014) 'Neoliberal Patriarchy: The Case for Gender Revolution', *Open Democracy*, www.opendemocracy.net/en/5050/neoliberal-neopatriarchy-case-for-gender-revolution/.

Canaan, J. (1996) 'One Thing Leads to Another: Drinking, Fighting and Working-Class Masculinities', in M. Mac an Ghaill (ed.), *Understanding Masculinities*, Open University Press, Buckingham.

Cannon, C., Lauve-Moon, K. and Buttell, F. (2015) 'Re-Theorizing Intimate Partner Violence through Post-Structural Feminism, Queer Theory and the Sociology of Gender', *Social Sciences*, vol. 4, pp. 668–687.

Cantillon, S. and Lynch, K. (2017) 'Affective Equality: Love Matters', *Hypatia*, vol. 32, no. 1, pp. 169–186.

Caprioli, M. (2005) 'Primed for Violence: The Role of Gender Inequality in Predicting Internal Conflict', *International Studies Quarterly*, vol. 49, no. 2, pp. 161–178.

Card, C. (2010) *Confronting Evils: Terrorism, Torture, Genocide*, Cambridge University Press, Cambridge.

Cares, A., Moynihan, M. and Banyard, V. (2014) 'Taking Stock of Bystander Programs: Changing Attitudes and Behaviours towards Sexual Violence', in N. Henry and A. Powell (eds), *Preventing Sexual Violence: Interdisciplinary Approaches to Overcoming a Rape Culture*, Palgrave Macmillan, Buckingham.

Carmody, M. (2009) 'Conceptualising the Prevention of Sexual Assault and the Role of Education', Australian Centre for the Study of Sexual Assault, *ACSSA Issues*, no. 10.

Carpenter, C. (2010) 'What Would a Post-Masculinised Military Look Like?', *Duck of Minerva*, https://duckofminerva.com/2010/12/what-would-post-masculinized-military.html.

Carpenter, R.C. (2006) 'Recognising Gender-Based Violence against Civilian Men and Boys in Conflict Situations', *Security Dialogue*, vol. 37, no. 5, pp. 83–103.

Carrington, K. (1998) *Who Killed Leigh Leigh? A Story of Shame and Mateship in an Australian Town*, Random House, Sydney.

Carrington, K. (2015) *Feminism and Global Justice: New Directions in Critical Criminology*, Routledge, London.

Carrington, K., McIntosh, A. and Scott, J. (2010) 'Globalization, Frontier Masculinities and Violence', *British Journal of Criminology*, vol. 50, pp. 393–413.

Casey, E. and Lindhorst, T. (2009) 'Towards a Multilevel Ecological Approach to the Primary Prevention of Sexual Assault', *Trauma, Violence and Abuse*, vol. 10, pp. 91–114.

Casey, E. and Smith, T. (2010) '"How Can I Not?" Men's Pathways to Involvement in Anti-Violence against Women Work', *Violence against Women*, vol. 16, no. 8, pp. 953–973.

Castelino, T. (2010) *A Feminist Audit of Men's Engagement in the Elimination of Violence*, paper presented at the University of Melbourne, November.

Center for Women's Global Leadership (2011) *Intersections of Violence against Women and Militarism*, Meeting Report, Rutgers, State University of New Jersey, New Jersey.

Charlesworth, S. (2000) 'Not Waving but Drowning: Gender Mainstreaming and Human Rights in the United Nations', *Harvard Human Rights Journal*, vol. 18, pp. 1–18.

Chemaly, S. (2016) 'In Orlando, as Usual, Domestic Violence Was Ignored Red Flag', *Rolling Stone*, 20 June.

Chodorow, N. (1978) *The Reproduction of Mothering: Psychoanalysis and the Sociology of Gender*, University of California Press, Berkeley, CA.

Chung, D., O'Leary, P. and Hand, T. (2006) 'Sexual Violence Offenders: Prevention and Intervention Approaches', *Issues*, no. 5, June, Australian Centre for the Study of Sexual Assault.

Clarke, K. (2010) 'The Paradoxical Approach to Intimate Partner Violence in Finland', *International Perspectives in Victimology*, vol. 6, no. 1, pp. 9–19.

Clegg, S. (2005) 'Evidence-Based Practice in Educational Research: A Critical Realist Critique of Systematic Reviews', *British Journal of Sociology of Education*, vol. 26, no. 3, pp. 415–428.

Cockburn, C. (1983) *Brothers: Male Dominance and Technological Change*, Pluto Press, London.

Cockburn, C. (2012a) 'Gender Relations as Causal in Militarisation and War', *International Feminist Journal of Politics*, vol. 12, no. 2, pp. 139–157.

Cockburn, C. (2012b) *Anti-Militarism: Political and Gender Dynamics of Peace Movements*, Palgrave Macmillan, Basingstoke.

Coe, K., Bagley, M., Cunningham, S. and Van Leuven, N. (2007) 'Masculinity as Political Strategy: George W. Bush, the War on Terrorism, and an Echoing Press', *Journal of Women, Politics and Policy*, vol. 29, no. 1, pp. 31–54.

Cohn, C. and Enloe, C. (2002) 'A Conversation with Cynthia Enloe: Feminists Look at Masculinity and the Men Who Wage War', *Signs*, vol. 28, no. 4, pp. 1187–1207.

Coles, A. (2001) 'Men, Women and Organisational Culture: Perspectives from Donors', in C. Sweetman (ed.), *Men's Involvement in Gender and Development Policy and Practice: Beyond Rhetoric*, Oxfam, Oxford.

Collier, R. (1995) *Masculinity, Law and the Family*, Routledge, London.

Collier, S. (2012) 'Feminist and Gender Neutral Frames in Contemporary Child Care and Anti-Violence Policy Debates in Canada', *Politics and Gender*, vol. 8, no. 3, pp. 283–303.

Colling, T. (1992) *Beyond Mateship: Understanding Australian Men*, Simon & Schuster, Sydney.

Collins, P. (2000) *Black Feminist Thought: Knowledge, Consciousness and the Politics of Empowerment*, Routledge, New York.

Colombini, M. (2002) 'Gender-Based and Sexual Violence against Women during Armed Conflict', *Journal of Health Management*, vol. 4, no. 2, pp. 167–183.

Connell, R. (1987) *Gender and Power*, Polity, Cambridge.

Connell, R. (1995) *Masculinities*, Polity, Cambridge.

Connell, R. (2000a) *Men, Relationships and Violence*, keynote address to Men and Relationships Forum, November, Sydney.

Connell, R. (2000b) 'Arms and the Man: Using New Research on Masculinity to Understand Violence and Promotion of Peace in the Contemporary World', in I. Breines, R. Connell and I. Eide (eds.), *Male Roles, Masculinities and Violence: A Culture of Peace Perspective*, UNESCO, Paris.

Connell, R. (2001) 'Studying Men and Masculinity', *Resources for Feminist Research*, Fall/Winter, pp. 43–55.

Connell, R. (2002) 'On Hegemonic Masculinity and Violence', *Theoretical Criminology*, vol. 6, no. 1, pp. 89–99.

Connell, R. (2005) 'Change among the Gatekeepers: Men, Masculinities and Gender Equality in the Global Arena', *Signs*, vol. 30, no. 3, pp. 1801–1825.

Connell, R. (2012) 'Gender, Health and Theory: Conceptualising the Issue in Local and World Perspectives', *Social Science and Medicine*, vol. 74, no. 11, pp. 1675–1683.

Connell, R. (2014) 'King Hits: Young Men, Masculinity and Violence', *The Conversation*, 31 January.

Connell, R. (2016) '100 Million Kalashnikovs: Gendered Power on a World Scale', *Debate Feminista*, http://doi.org/10.1016/j.df.2016.03.001.

Connell, R. and Messerschmidt, J. (2005) 'Hegemonic Masculinity: Rethinking the Concept', *Gender and Society*, vol. 19, no. 6, pp. 829–859.

Connell, R. and Pearse, R. (2014) *Gender Norms and Stereotypes: A Survey of Concepts, Research and Issues About Change*, Expert Group Meeting, Envisaging Women's Rights in the Post-2015 Context, UN Women.

Connell, R. and Pearse, R. (2015) *Gender in World Perspective*, Polity, Cambridge.

Consortium on Gender, Security and Human Rights (2010) *Masculinities and Peacekeeping*, www.genderandsecurity.org.

Cornall, P. (2010) 'Sustainable Masculinity Is Interwoven with Environmental Sustainability', *Peace and Collaborative Development Network*, 27 April, https://pcdnetwork.org/blogs/sustainable-masculinity-is-interwoven-with-environmental-sustainability/.

Cornish, F. (2015) 'Evidence Synthesis in International Development: A Critique of Systematic Review and a Pragmatist Alternative', *Anthropology and Medicine*, vol. 22, no. 3, pp. 263–277.

Corvo, K. and Johnson, P. (2010) 'Does Patriarchy Explain Intimate Partner Violence? State-Level Correlates of Violence toward Women and Female Homicide', *Family and Intimate Partner Violence Quarterly*, vol. 2, no. 4, pp. 303–314.

Costello, M. (2009) *Australia Says No? Policy, Politics and the Australian Government's Approaches to Male Violence against Women during the Howard Years (1996–2007)*, unpublished doctorial dissertation, Faculty of Education and Social Work, University of Sydney.

Cover, R. (2015) 'Sexual Ethics, Masculinity and Mutual Vulnerability', *Australian Feminist Studies*, vol. 29, no. 82, pp. 435–451.

Cowan, D. and Siciliano, A. (2011) 'Surplus Masculinities and Security', *Antipode*, vol. 43, no. 5, pp. 1516–1541.

Cowburn, M. (2010) 'Invisible Men: Social Reactions to Male Sexual Coercion – Bringing Men and Masculinities into Community Safety and Public Policy', *Critical Social Policy*, vol. 30, no. 2, pp. 225–244.

Coyle, A. and Morgan-Sykes, C. (1998) 'Troubled Men and Threatening Women: The Construction of "Crisis" in Male Mental Health', *Feminism and Psychology*, vol. 8, no. 3, pp. 263–284.

Craib, I. (2011) 'Masculinity and Male Dominance', *The Sociological Review*, vol. 35, no. 4, pp. 721–743.

Crossett, T. (2000) 'Athletic Affiliation and Violence against Women', in J. McKay, M. Messner and D. Sabo (eds), *Masculinities, Gender Relations and Sport*, Sage, Thousand Oaks, CA.

Crowe, J. (2011) 'Men and Feminism: Some Challenges and a Partial Response', *Social Alternatives*, vol. 30, no. 1, pp. 49–53.

Cueva Salcedo, H. (2015) 'Environmental Violence and Its Consequences', *Latin American Perspectives*, vol. 42, no. 5, pp. 19–26.

Culpitt, I. (1999) *Social Policy and Risk*, Sage, London.

Cunningham, A., Jaffe, P., Baker, L., Dick, T., Malla, S., Mazaheri, N. and Poisson, S. (1998) *Theory-Derived Explanations for Male Violence against Female Partners: Literature Update and Related Implications for Treatment and Evaluation*, London Family Court Clinic, London.

Cuomo, C. (1996) 'War Is Not Just an Event: Reflections on the Significance of Everyday Violence', *Hypatia*, vol. 11, no. 4, pp. 30–45.

Curry, T. (1991) 'Fraternal Bonding in the Locker Room: A Profeminist Analysis of Talk about Competition and Women', *Sociology of Sport Journal*, vol. 8, pp. 119–135.

Curry, T. (2000) 'Booze and Bar Fights: A Journey to the Dark Side of College Athletes', in J. McKay, M. Messner and D. Sabo (eds), *Masculinities, Gender Relations and Sport*, Sage, Thousand Oaks, CA.

Daly, M. (1978) *Gyn/Ecology: The Metaethics of Radical Feminism*, Women's Press, London.

Dankwort, J. and Rausch, R. (2000) 'Men at Work to End Wife Abuse in Quebec: A Case Study in Claims Making', *Violence against Women*, vol. 6, no. 9, pp. 936–959.

Davis, S. and Greenstein, T. (2013) 'Why Study Housework? Cleaning as a Window into Power in Couples', *Journal of Family Theory and Review*, vol. 5, pp. 63–71.

Davison, K. (2007) 'Phallocentrism', in M. Flood, J. Gardiner, B. Pease and K. Pringle (eds), *International Encyclopedia of Men and Masculinities*, Routledge, London.

de Boise, S. (2013) 'Patriarchy and the Crisis of Masculinity', *New Left Project*, www.newleftproject.org/index.php/site/article_comments/patriarchy_and_the_crisis_of_masculinity.

de Boise, S. and Hearn, J. (2017) 'Are Men Getting More Emotional? Critical Sociological Perspectives on Men, Masculinities and Emotions', *The Sociological Review*, vol. 65, no. 4, pp. 779–796.

De Vries, J. and Gueskens, I. (2010) *Together for Transformation: Men, Masculinities and Peacebuilding*, Women Peacemakers Program, Alkmaar.

DeKeseredy, W. and Dragiewicz, M. (2009) *Shifting Public Policy Direction: Gender-Focused versus Bi-Directional Intimate Partner Violence*, University of Ontario Institute of Technology, Oshawa, Ontario.

DeKeseredy, W. and Schwartz, M. (1993) 'Male Peer Support and Woman Abuse: An Expansion of DeKeseredy's Model', *Sociological Spectrum: Mid-South Sociological Association*, vol. 13, no. 4, pp. 394–413.

DeKeseredy, W. and Schwartz, M. (2005) 'Masculinities and Interpersonal Violence,' in M. Kimmel, J. Hearn and R. Connell (eds), *Handbook of Studies in Men and Masculinities*, Sage, Thousand Oaks, CA.

DeKeseredy, W. and Schwartz, M. (2013) *Male Peer Support and Violence against Women: The History and Verification of a Theory*, Northeastern University Press, Boston, MA.

Delphy, C. (1984) *Close to Home*, Hutchinson, London.

DiAngelo, R. (2018) *White Fragility: Why It's So Hard for White People to Talk about Racism*, Beacon Press, Boston, MA.

Diemer, K. (2014) *Women's Safety Is a Men's Issue: Men's Attitudes to Violence against Women and What That Means for Men*, White Ribbon Australia, Sydney.

Digby, T. (2014) *Love and War: How Militarism Shapes Sexuality and Romance*, Columbia University Press, New York.

Dixson, M. (1982) *The Real Matilda: Women and Identity in Australia*, Penguin, Melbourne.

Dobash, R. and Dobash, R. (1979) *Violence against Wives: A Case against Patriarchy*, Free Press, New York.

Dolan, C. (2014) 'Letting Go of the Gender Binary: Charting New Pathways for Humanitarian Interventions on Gender-Based Violence', *International Review of the Red Cross*, vol. 96, pp. 485–501.

Doucet, A. (2006) *Do Men Mother? Fathering, Care and Domestic Responsibility*, University of Toronto Press, Toronto.

Doucet, A. (2017) 'The Ethics of Care and the Radical Potential of Fathers "Home Alone on Leave": Care as Practice, Relational Ontology and Social Justice', in M. O'Brien and K. Wall (eds), *Comparative Perspectives on Work–Life Balance*, Springer, New York.

Dragiewicz, M. (2008) 'Patriarchy Reasserted: Fathers' Rights and Anti-VAW Activism', *Feminist Criminology*, vol. 3, no. 2, pp. 121–144.

Dragiewicz, M. (2011) *Equality with a Vengeance: Men's Rights Groups, Battered Women and Anti-Feminist Backlash*, Northeastern University Press, Boston, MA.

Duncanson, C. (2009) 'Forces for Good? Narratives of Military Masculinity in Peacekeeping Operations', *International Feminist Journal of Politics*, vol. 11, no. 1, pp. 63–80.

Duncanson, C. and Woodward, R. (2016) 'Regendering the Military: Theorizing Women's Military Participation', *Security Dialogue*, vol. 47, no. 1, pp. 3–21.

Durber, D. (2006) 'Desiring Mates', *Journal of Homosexuality*, vol. 52, nos. 1–2, pp. 237–255.

Duriesmith, D. (2017) *Masculinity and the New War*, Routledge, New York.

Duriesmith, D. (2018) 'Manly States and Feminist Foreign Policy: Revisiting the Liberal State as Agent of Change', in S. Parasha, A. Tickner and J. True (eds), *Revisiting Gendered States: Feminist Imaginings of the State in International Relations*, Oxford University Press, Oxford.

Dutton, D. (1994) 'Patriarchy and Wife Assault: The Ecological Fallacy', *Violence and Victims*, vol. 9, no. 2, pp. 167–182.

Dutton, D. (2006) *Rethinking Domestic Violence*, UBC Press, Vancouver.

Dutton, D. and Nicholls, T. (2005) 'The Gender Paradigm in Domestic Violence Research and Theory: Part 1 – The Conflict of Theory and Data', *Aggression and Violent Behavior*, vol. 10, pp. 680–714.

Dyson, S. and Flood, M. (2008) *Building Cultures of Respect and Non-Violence*, Australian Research Centre in Sex, Health and Society, La Trobe University.

Edgar, D. (1997) *Men, Mateship, Marriage*, HarperCollins, Sydney.

Edley, N. and Wetherell, M. (1995) *Men in Perspective: Practice, Power and Identity, and Policy*, Prentice Hall, London.

Edstrom, J., Das, A. and Dolan, C. (2014) 'Introduction: Undressing Patriarchy and Masculinities to Re-Politicise Gender', *IDS Bulletin*, vol. 35, no. 1, pp. 1–10.

Edwards, T. (2006) *Cultures of Masculinity*, Routledge, London.

Eichler, M. (2014) 'Militarised Masculinities in International Relations', *The Brown Journal of World Affairs*, vol. 21, no. 1, pp. 81–93.

Eisen, D. and Yamashita, L. (2017) 'Borrowing from Femininity: The Caring Man, Hybrid Masculinities and Maintaining Male Dominance', *Men and Masculinities*, pp. 1–20, https://doi.org/10.117/1097184X17728552.

Eisenstein, Z. (1979) *The Female Body and the Law*, University of California Press, Berkeley, CA.

Eisenstein, Z. (1998) *Global Obscenities: Patriarchy, Capitalism and the Lure of Cyber Fantasy*, New York University Press, New York.

Elias, J. and Beasley, C. (2009) 'Hegemonic Masculinity and Globalization: Transnational Business Masculinities and Beyond', *Globalization*, vol. 6, no. 2, pp. 281–296.

Elk, L. and Devereaux, S. (2014) 'The Failure of Bystander Intervention', *The New Inquiry*, 23 December.

Elliott, K. (2015) 'Caring Masculinities: Theorizing an Emerging Concept', *Men and Masculinities*, vol. 19, no. 3, pp. 1–24.

Elomaki, A. (2015) 'The Economic Case for Gender Equality in the European Union: Selling Gender Equality to Decision-Makers and Neoliberialism to Women's Organisations', *European Journal of Women's Studies*, vol. 22, no. 3, pp. 288–302.

Elshtain, J. (2001) 'The Third Annual Grotius Lecture: Just War and the Humanitarian Intervention', *American University International Law Review*, vol. 17, no. 1, pp. 1–25.

Elshtain, J. (2003) 'Thinking about War and Justice', *The Religion and Culture Web Forum*, https://divinity.uchicago.edu/sites/default/files/imce/pdfs/webforum/052003/commentary.pdf.

Enander, V. (2011) 'Violent Women? The Challenge of Women's Violence in Intimate Heterosexual Relationships to Feminist Analyses of Partner Violence', *NORA: Nordic Journal of Feminist and Gender Research*, vol. 19, no. 2, pp. 105–123.

Enarson, E. (1999) 'Violence against Women in Disasters: A Study of Domestic Violence Programs in the United States and Canada', *Violence against Women*, vol. 5, no. 7, pp. 742–768.

Enarson, E. (2012) *Women Confronting Natural Disasters: From Vulnerability to Resilience*, Lynne Rienner Publishers, Boulder, CO.

Enloe, C. (2017) *The Big Push: Exposing and Challenging the Persistence of Patriarchy*, Myriad, Oxford.

Eriksson, M. (2015) Personal communication.

Eriksson, M. and Pringle, K. (2005) 'Introduction: Nordic Issues and Dilemmas', in M. Eriksson, M. Hester, S. Keskinen and K. Pringle (eds), *Tackling Men's Violence in Families: Nordic Issues and Dilemmas*, Policy Press, Bristol.

Eriksson, M. and Pringle, K. (2011) 'Working with Men in the Gender Equality Paradise? The Case of Sweden', in E. Respini, J. Hearn, B. Pease and K. Pringle (eds), *Men and Masculinities around the World: Transforming Men's Practices*, Palgrave Macmillan, New York.

Esplen, E. (2006) *Engaging Men in Gender Equality: Positive Strategies and Approaches*, Institute of Development Studies, University of Sussex, Brighton.

Ezekilov, G. (2017) 'Gender "Men-Streaming" CVE: Countering Violence Extremism by Addressing Masculinities Issues", *Reconsidering Development*, vol. 5, no. 1, pp. 1–7.

Fabiano, P., Perkins, H., Berkowitz, A., Linderbach, J. and Stark, C. (2003) 'Engaging Men as Social Justice Allies in Ending Violence against Women: Evidence for a Social Norms Approach', *Journal of American College Health*, vol. 52, no. 3, pp. 105–112.

Fahlen, S. (2016) 'Equality at Home: A Question of Career? Housework Norms and Policies in a European Comparative Perspective', *Demographic Research*, vol. 35, no. 48, pp. 1411–1440.

Farrell, W. (1993) *The Myth of Male Power*, Simon & Schuster, New York.

Ferber, A. (2007) 'Whiteness Studies and the Erasure of Gender', *Sociology Compass*, vol. 1, no. 1, pp. 265–282.

Ferber, A. and Kimmel, M. (2008) 'The Gendered Face of Terrorism', *Sociology Compass*, vol. 2, no. 3, pp. 870–887.

Ferguson, H., Hearn, J., Gullvag, O., Lalmert, L., Kimmel, M., Lang, J. and Morrell, R. (2003) *Ending Gender-Based Violence: A Call for Global Action to Involve Men*, Sida, Sweden.

Firestone, S. (1971) *The Dialectic of Sex*, Women's Press, London.

Fischer, K. (2005) 'In the Beginning was the Murder: Destruction of Nature and Interhuman Violence in Adorno's Critique of Culture', *JCRT*, vol. 6, no. 2, pp. 27–38.

Fisher, V. and Kinsey, S. (2014) 'Behind Closed Doors: Homosocial Desire and the Academic Boys Club', *Gender in Management*, vol. 29, no. 1, pp. 44–64.

Fleming, J. (2017) 'Excuse Us, While We Fix the Sky: WEIRD Supermen and Climate Engineering', in S. MacGregor and N. Seymour (eds), *Men and Nature: Hegemonic Masculinities and Environmental Change*, Rachel Carson Centre Perspectives: Transformations in Environment and Society, Munich.

Fleming, P., Gruskin, S., Rojo, F. and Dworkin, S. (2015) 'Men's Violence against Women and Men Are Interrelated: Recommendations for Simultaneous Intervention', *Social Science and Medicine*, http://dx.doi.org/10.1016/j.socscimen.2015.10.021.

Fletcher, P. (2010) 'Dismantling Rape Culture around the World: A Social Justice Imperative', *Forum on Public Policy: A Journal of the Oxford Round Table*, vol. 2010, no. 4, pp. 1–14.

Flood, M. (2002–2003) 'Engaging Men: Strategies and Dilemmas in Violence Prevention Education among Men', *Women against Violence*, vol. 13, pp. 25–32.

Flood, M. (2005a) *Mainstreaming Men in Gender and Development*, paper presented at the AusAID Gender Seminar Series, 8 December.

Flood, M. (2005b) 'Men's Collective Struggles for Gender Justice: The Case of Antiviolence Activism', in M. Kimmel, J. Hearn and R.W. Connell (eds), *Handbook of Studies on Men and Masculinities*, Sage, Thousand Oaks, CA.

Flood, M. (2007) 'Men as Victims of Violence', in M. Flood, J. Gardiner, B. Pease and K. Pringle (eds), *International Encyclopedia of Men and Masculinities*, Routledge, New York.

Flood, M. (2008a) *A Response to Bob Pease's 'Engaging Men in Men's Violence Prevention'*, paper presented at the Forum: 'Men's Role in Preventing Men's Violence against Women', Melbourne, 20 November.

Flood, M. (2008b) 'Men, Sex and Homosociality: How Bonds between Men Shape Their Sexual Relations with Women', *Men and Masculinities*, vol. 10, no. 3, pp. 339–359.

Flood, M. (2009) *Let's Stop Violence Before It Starts: Using Primary Prevention Strategies to Engage Men, Mobilise Communities and Change the World*, notes of a one-day workshop, New Zealand, 28 September–2 October.

Flood, M. (2018) *Engaging Men and Boys in Violence Prevention*, Palgrave, New York.

Flood, M. and Pease, B. (2005) 'Undoing Men's Privilege and Advancing Gender Equality in Public Sector Institutions', *Policy and Society*, vol. 24, no. 4, pp. 119–138.

Flood, M. and Pease, B. (2006) *The Factors Influencing Community Attitudes in Relation to Violence against Women: A Critical Review of the Literature*, paper 3 of the Violence against Women, Community Attitudes Project, VicHealth, Melbourne.

Flood, M. and Pease, B. (2009) 'Factors Influencing Attitudes towards Violence against Women', *Trauma, Violence and Abuse*, vol. 10, no. 2, pp. 125–142.

Flynn, A., Halsey, M. and Lee, M. (2016) 'Emblematic Violence and Aetiological Cul-de-Sacs: On the Discourse of "One-Punch" (Non)Fatalities', *British Journal of Crimininology*, vol. 56, pp. 179–195.

Forsberg, L. (2010) 'Masculinity Studies as Fetish and the Need for a Feminist Imagination', *NORMA: International Journal for Masculinity Studies*, vol. 5, no. 1, pp. 1–5.

Foster, E. (2017) 'Gender, Environmental Governmentality and the Discourse of Sustainable Development', in S. MacGregor (ed.), *Routledge Handbook of Gender and Environment*, Routledge, New York.

Foucault, M. (1980) *Power/Knowledge: Selected Interviews and Other Writings 1972–1977*, Pantheon Books, New York.

Foucault, M. (1991) 'Politics and the Study of Discourse', in G. Birchell, C. Gordan and P. Miller (eds), *The Foucault Effect: Studies in Governmentality*, University of Chicago Press, Chicago, IL.

Francis, R. and Tsang, A. (1997) 'War of Words/Words of War: A Dossier on Men's Treatment Groups in Ontario', *Canadian Social Work Review*, vol. 14, no. 2, pp. 88–103.

Franklin, K. (2004) 'Enacting Masculinity: Antigay Violence and Group Rape as Participatory Theatre', *Sexuality Research and Social Policy*, vol. 1, no. 2, pp. 25–40.

Franz-Balsen, A. (2014) 'Gender and (Un)sustainability: Can Communication Solve a Conflict of Norms?', *Sustainability*, vol. 6, pp. 1974–1991.

Franzway, S., Court, D. and Connell, R. (1989) *Staking a Claim: Feminism, Bureacracy and the State*, Allen & Unwin, Sydney.

Fraser, N. (2001) 'Recognition without Ethics', *Theory, Culture and Society*, vol. 18, nos. 2–3, pp. 21–42.

Fraser, N. (2005) 'Mapping the Feminist Imagination: From Redistribution to Recognition to Representation', *Constellations*, vol. 12, no. 3, pp. 295–307.

Fraser, N. (2009) 'Feminism, Capitalism and the Cunning of History', *New Left Review*, no. 56, pp. 97–117.

Fraser, N. (2013) *Fortunes of Feminism: From State-Managed Capitalism to Neoliberal Crisis*, Verso, New York.

Frosh, S. (1994) *Sexual Difference: Masculinity and Psychoanalysis*, Routledge, London.

Frye, M. (1992) 'White Woman Feminist', in *Wilful Virgin: White Feminism and Women of Color*, Crossing Press, Freedom, CA.

Frye, V., Manganello, J., Campbell, J., Walter-Moss, B. and Wilt, S. (2006) 'The Distribution of and Factors Associated with Intimate Terrorism and Situational Couple Violence among a Population-Based Sample of Urban Women in the United States', *Journal of Interpersonal Violence*, vol. 22, no. 10, pp. 1286–1313.

Fulu, E. and Heise, L. (2015) *What Works to Prevent Violence Against Women and Girls?* Evidence Reviews: Paper 1: State of the Field of Research on Violence Against Women and Girls, What Works to Prevent Violence Program.

Fulu, E., Kerr-Wilson, A. and Lang, J. (2014) *What Works to Prevent Violence against Women and Girls? Evidence Review of Interventions to Prevent Violence against Women and Girls*, Medical Research Council, Pretroia.

Gaard, G. (2011) 'Ecofeminism Revisited: Rejecting Essentialism and Re-Placing Species in a Materialist Feminist Environmentalism', *Feminist Formations*, vol. 23, no. 2, pp. 26–53.

Gaard, G. (2017a) 'Posthumanism, Ecofeminism and Inter-Species Relations', in S. MacGregor (ed.), *Routledge Handbook of Gender and Environment*, Routledge, New York.

Gaard, G. (2017b) *Critical Ecofeminsim*, Lexington Books, Lanham, MD.

Gadd, D. (2000) 'Masculinities, Violence and Defended Psychosocial Subjects', *Theoretical Criminology*, vol. 4, no. 4, pp. 429–449.

Gadd, D. (2002) 'Masculinities and Violence against Female Partners', *Social and Legal Studies*, vol. 11, no. 1, pp. 61–80.

Gallagher, K. and Parrott, D. (2011) 'What Accounts for Men's Hostile Attitudes toward Women? The Influence of Hegemonic Male Role Norms and Masculine Gender Role Stress', *Violence against Women*, vol. 17, no. 5, pp. 568–583.

Galtung, J. (1969) 'Violence, Peace and Peace Research', *Journal of Peace Research*, vol. 6, no. 3, pp. 167–191.

Galtung, J. (1990) 'Cultural Violence', *Journal of Peace Research*, vol. 27, no. 3, pp. 291–305.

Garlick, S. (2011) 'Complexity, Masculinity, and Critical Theory: Revisiting Marcuse on Technology, Eros and Nature', *Critical Sociology*, vol. 39, no. 2, pp. 223–238.

Gartner, M., Schwerma, K. and Beier, S. (2007) *Fostering Caring Masculinities*, Documentation of the German Gender Expert Study, Berlin.

Gavey, N. (2005) *Just Sex: The Cultural Scaffolding of Rape*, Routledge, London.

Gebecki, C., Pomering, R., Flynn, G., Grogan, N., Hunt, E., Bell, J., Raman, K. and Meagher, A. (2017) *Change the Course: National Report on Sexual Assault and Sexual Harassment at Australian Universities*, Australian Human Rights Commission, Sydney.

Gelb, J. and Palley, M. (1996) *Women and Public Policies: Reassessing Gender Politics*, University Press of Virginia, Charlottesville, VA.

Gilson, E. (2011) 'Vulnerability, Ignorance and Oppression', *Hypatia*, vol. 26, no. 2, pp. 308–331.

Gilson, E. (2016a) 'Vulnerability and Victimization: Rethinking Key Concepts in Feminist Discourses on Sexual Violence', *Signs*, vol. 42, no. 1, pp. 71–98.

Glenn, E. (2000) 'Creating a Caring Society', *Contemporary Sociology*, vol. 29, no. 1, pp. 84–94.

Glick, P. and Fiske, S. (2001) 'An Ambivalent Alliance: Hostile and Benevolent Sexism as Complementary Justifications', *American Psychologist*, February, pp. 109–118.

Goldner, V. (1999) 'Morality and Multiplicity: Perspectives on the Treatment of Violence in Intimate Life', *Journal or Marital and Family Therapy*, July, pp. 325–337.

Gondolf, E. (2007) 'Theoretical and Research Support for the Duluth Model: A Reply to Dutton and Corvo', *Aggression and Violent Behavior*, vol. 12, no. 6, pp. 644–657.

Gotell, L. (2010) 'Canadian Sexual Assault Law: Neoliberalism and the Erosion of Feminist-Inspired Reforms', in C. McGlynn and V. Munro (eds), *Rethinking Rape Law*, Routledge, New York.

Gough, I. (2013) *Understanding Prevention Policy: A Theoretical Approach*. LSE Research Online, January, London School of Economics and Political Science.

Government Offices of Sweden (2016) *National Strategy to Prevent and Combat Men's Violence against Women*, www.government.se/feministgovernment@socaildep.

Gracia, E. and Merlo, J. (2016) 'Intimate Partner Violence against Women and the Nordic Paradox', *Social Science and Medicine*, no. 157, pp. 27–30.

Gramsci, A. (1971) *Selections from Prison Notebooks*, International Press, New York.

Gregory, T. (2015) 'Drones, Targeted Killings, and the Limitations of International Law', *International Political Sociology*, vol. 9, pp. 197–212.

Greig, A. (2000) 'The Spectacle of Men Fighting', *IDS Bulletin*, vol. 31, no. 2, pp. 28–32.

Greig, A. (2002) *Political Connections: Men, Gender and Violence*, Working Paper No. I, United Nations International Research and Training Institute for the Advancement of Women (INSTRAW).

Greig, A. (2012) *Mobilizing Men in Practice: Challenging Sexual and Gender-Based Violence in Institutional Settings*, Institute of Development Studies, University of Sussex, Brighton.

Grey, R. and Shepherd, L. (2012) '"Stop Rape Now": Masculinity, Responsibility and Conflict-Related Sexual Violence', *Men and Masculinities*, vol. 16, no. 1, pp. 115–135.

Griffin, S. (1978) *Women and Nature: The Roaring Inside Her*. Harper & Row, New York.

Griffiths, P. (2005) 'Evidence-Based Practice: A Deconstruction Critique', *International Journal of Nursing Studies*, vol. 42, no. 3, pp. 355–368.

Groes-Green, C. (2009) 'Hegemonic and Subordinated Masculinities: Class, Violence and Sexual Performance among Young Mozambian Men', *Nordic Journal of African Studies*, vol. 18, no. 4, pp. 286–304.

Gubin, A. (2004) *Gender Inequality, Normative Violence, Social Disorganization and Sexual Violence against Women: A Cross-National Investigation*, PhD thesis, University of Massachusetts Amherst, February.

Gupta, M. (2003) 'A Critical Appraisal of Evidence-Based Medicine: Some Ethical Considerations', *Journal of Evaluation in Clinical Practice*, vol. 9, no. 2, pp. 111–122.

Hagedorn, J. (1998) 'Frat Boys, Bossmen, Studs and Gentlemen: A Typology of Gang Masculinities', in L. Bowker (ed.), *Masculinities and Violence*, Sage, Thousand Oaks, CA.

Haider, S. (2016) 'The Shooting in Orlando, Terrorism or Toxic Masculinity (or Both?)', *Men and Masculinities*, vol. 19, no. 5, pp. 555–565.

Halberstam, J. (1998) *Female Masculinities*, Duke University Press, Durham, NC.

Hall, L. (2005) *Reflections on the Masculine Hegemon: A Reply to Richard Twine*, www.ecofem.org/journal.

Hall, R. (2004) '"It Can Happen to You": Rape Prevention in the Age of Risk Management', *Hypatia*, vol. 19, no. 3, pp. 1–19.

Hammarén, N. and Johansson, T. (2014) 'Homosociality: In between Power and Intimacy', *Sage Open*, January–March, pp. 1–11.

Hammarstrom, A. (1999) 'Why Feminism in Public Health?', *Scandinavian Journal of Public Health*, vol. 27, pp. 241–244.

Hammer, R. (2003) 'Militarism and Family Terrorism: A Critical Feminist Perspective', *Review of Education, Pedagogy and Cultural Studies*, vol. 25, no. 3, pp. 231–256.

Hankivosky, O. and Christoffersen, A. (2008) 'Intersectionality and the Determinants of Health: A Canadian Perspective', *Critical Public Health*, vol. 18, no. 3, pp. 271–283.

Hanlon, N. (2009) 'Masculinities and Affective Equality: Love Labour and Care Labour in Men's Lives', in A. Biricik and J. Hearn (eds), *Proceedings of Deconstructing the Hegemony of Men and Masculinities Conference*, GEXcel Work in Progress Report Vol. 6, Linkoping University, Linkoping.

Hanlon, N. (2012) *Masculinities, Care and Equality*, Palgrave, Houndmills.

Harders, C. (2011) 'Gender Relations, Violence and Conflict Transformation', in B. Austin, M. Fischer and H. Giessmann (eds), *Advancing Conflict Transformation*, Barbara Budrich Publishers, Opladen/Farmington Hills.

Harding, S. (1986) *The Science Question in Feminism*, Cornell University Press, New York.

Harris, A., Honey, N., Webster, K., Diemer, K. and Politoff, V. (2015) *Young Australians' Attitudes to Violence against Women*, VicHealth, Melbourne.

Harris, K. (2011) 'Compassion and Katrina: Reasserting Violent White Masculinity after the Storm', *Women and Language*, vol. 34, no. 1, pp. 11–27.

Hartmann, H. (1981a) 'The Unhappy Marriage of Marxism and Feminism: Towards a More Progressive Union', in L. Sargent (ed.), *Women and Revolution*, South End Press, Boston, MA.

Hartmann, H. (1981b) 'The Family as the Locus of Gender, Class and Political Struggle: The Example of Housework', *Signs*, vol. 6, no. 3, pp. 366–394.

Hatty, S. (2000) *Masculinities, Violence and Culture*, Sage, Thousand Oaks, CA.

Hawkins, J. (2006) 'Science, Social Work, Prevention: Finding the Intersections', *Social Work Research*, vol. 30, no. 3, pp. 137–152.

Haylock, L., Cornelius, R., Malunga, A. and Kwezilomso, M. (2016) 'Shifting Negative Social Norms Rooted in Unequal Gender and Power Relationships to Prevent Violence against Women and Girls', *Gender and Development*, vol. 24, no. 2, pp. 231–244.

Hayward, R. (1999) *Needed: A New Model of Masculinity to Stop Violence against Women and Girls*, paper presented at the WHO Global Symposium on Violence and Health, Kobe, Japan, 12–15 October.

Haywood, C., Johansson, T., Hammaren, N., Marcus, H. and Ottemo, A. (2018) *The Conundrum of Masculinity: Hegemony, Homosociality, Homophohia and Heteronormativity*, Routledge, New York.

Hearn, J. (1987) *The Gender of Oppression: Men, Masculinity and the Critique of Marxism*, Wheatsheaf, Brighton.

Hearn, J. (1992) *Men in the Public Eye: The Construction and Deconstruction of Public Men and Public Patriarchies*, Routledge, London.

Hearn, J. (1996) 'Is Masculinity Dead? A Critical Account of the Concepts of Masculinity and Masculinities', in M. Mac an Ghaill (ed.), *Understanding Masculinities: Social Relations and Cultural Arenas*, Open University Press, Buckingham.

Hearn, J. (1998) *The Violences of Men*, Sage, London.

Hearn, J. (2004) 'From Hegemonic Masculinity to the Hegemony of Men', *Feminist Theory*, vol. 5, no. 1, pp. 49–72.

Hearn, J. (2009) 'Patriarchies, Transpatriarchies and Intersectionalities', in E. Olesky (ed.), *Intimate Citizenships: Gender, Sexuality Politics*, Routledge, London.

Hearn, J. (2011) 'Men/Masculinities: War/Militarism – Searching (for) the Obvious Connections', in A. Kronsell and E. Svedberg (eds), *Making Gender, Making War: Violence, Military and Peacekeeping Practices*, Routledge, London.

Hearn, J. (2012a) 'The Sociological Significance of Domestic Violence: Tensions, Paradoxes and Implications', *Current Sociology*, vol. 61, no. 2, pp. 152–170.

Hearn, J. (2012b) 'A Multi-Faceted Power Analysis of Men's Violence to Known Women: From Hegemonic Masculinity to the Hegemony of Men', *The Sociological Review*, vol. 60, pp. 589–610.

Hearn, J. (2014a) 'Men, Masculinities and the Material(-)Discursive', *NORMA: The International Journal of Masculinity Studies*, vol. 9, no. 1, pp. 5–17.

Hearn, J. (2014b) 'Why Domestic Violence Is a Central Issue for Sociological and Social Theory: Tensions, Paradoxes and Implications', *Gender, Equal Opportunities Research*, vol. 15, no. 1 pp. 16–28.

Hearn, J. (2015) *Men of the World: Genders, Globalization, Transnational Times*, Sage, Thousand Oaks, CA.

Hearn, J. (2016) 'From Masculinity to Masculinities and Back to Men ... and Fame Too ...', *Discover Society*, no. 30, March.

Hearn, J. and Husu, L. (2016) 'Gender Equality', in N. Naples (ed.), *Gender and Sexuality Encyclopedia*, Wiley-Blackwell, Oxford.

Hearn, J. and McKie, L. (2006) 'Gendered Policy and Policy on Gender: The Case of Domestic Violence', *Policy and Politics*, vol. 36, no. 1, pp. 75–91.

Hearn, J. and McKie, L. (2010) 'Gendered Social Hierarchies in Problem Representation and Policy Processes: Domestic Violence in Finland and Scotland', *Violence against Women*, vol. 16, no. 2, pp. 136–158.

Hearn, J. and Niemi, H. (2011) 'Interventions on, and of, Men in the Finnish State, Civil Society and Media', in E. Respini, J. Hearn, B. Pease and K. Pringle (eds), *Men and Masculinities around the World: Transforming Men's Practices*, Palgrave Macmillan, New York.

Hearn, J. and Whitehead, A. (2006) 'Collateral Damage: Men's Domestic Violence to Women Seen through Men's Relations with Men', *Probation Journal*, vol. 53, no. 1, pp. 38–56.

Heilman, B. and Barker, G. (2018) *Masculine Norms and Violence: Making the Connections*, Promundo, Washington, DC.

Heilman, B., Levtov, R., van der Gaag, N., Hassink, A. and Barker, G. (2017) *State of the World Fathers: Time for Action*, Promundo, Sonke Gender Justice, Save the Children and MenEngage Alliance, Washington, DC.

Heinecken, L. (2016) 'Military Women Need to Trouble Gender Relations and Roles for Peace's Sake', *The Conversation*, 9 August.

Heise, L. (1998) 'Violence against Women: An Integrated Ecological Framework', *Violence against Women*, vol. 4, no. 3, pp. 262–290.

Heise, L. (2006) *Determinants of Intimate Partner Violence: Exploring Variation in Individual and Population Level Risk*, Department of Infectious Diseases Epidemiology, London School of Hygiene and Tropical Medicine.

Held, V. (2004) 'Care and Justice in the Global Context', *Ration Juris*, vol. 17, no. 2, pp. 141–155.

Held, V. (2008) 'Military Intervention and the Ethics of Care', *The Southern Journal of Philosophy*, vol. 46, pp. 1–20.

Held, V. (2010) 'Can the Ethics of Care Handle Violence?', *Ethics and Social Welfare*, vol. 4, no. 3, pp. 115–129.

Hemmings, C. (2012) 'Affective Solidarity: Feminist Reflexivity and Political Transformation', *Feminist Theory*, vol. 13, no. 2, pp. 147–161.

Henry, M. (2017) 'Problematising Military Masculinity: Intersectionality and Male Vulnerability in Feminist Critical Military Studies', *Critical Military Studies*, vol. 3, no. 2, pp. 182–199.

Henshaw, A. (2016) *When Women Rebel: Understanding Women's Participation in Armed Rebel Groups*, Routledge, London.

Herek, G. (1987) 'On Heterosexual Masculinity: Some Psychological Consequences of the Social Construction of Gender and Sexuality', in M. Kimmel (ed.), *Changing Men: New Directions in Research on Men and Masculinity*, Sage, Beverly Hills, CA.

Herman, J. (1997) *Trauma and Recovery: The Aftermath of Violence – from Domestic Abuse to Political Terror*, Basic Books, New York.

Hernes, H. (1987) *Welfare States and Women Power: Essays in State Feminism*, Norwegian University Press, Oslo.

Herzog, S. (2007) 'An Empirical Test of Feminist Theory and Research: The Effect of Heterogeneous Gender Role Attitudes on Perceptions of Intimate Partner Violence', *Feminist Criminology*, vol. 2, pp. 223–244.

Holmes, M. (2015) 'Men's Emotions, Heteromasculinity, Emotional Reflexivity and Intimate Relationships', *Men and Masculinities*, vol. 18, no. 2, pp. 176–192.

Holmes, S. and Flood, M. (2013) *Genders at Work: Exploring the Role of Workplace Equality in Preventing Men's Violence against Women*, White Ribbon Research Series, White Ribbon Foundation, Sydney.

Holter, O. (2011) 'Unravelling the Maze: Gender Equality and Men's Practices in Norway', in E. Respini, J. Hearn, B. Pease and K. Pringle (eds), *Men and Masculinities around the World: Transforming Men's Practices*, Palgrave Macmillan, New York.

Holter, O. (2014) '"What's in It for Men?" Old Question, New Data', *Men and Masculinities*, vol. 17, no. 5, pp. 515–548.

Holter, O., Svare, H. and Egeland, C. (2009) *Gender Equality and the Quality of Life*, Nordic Gender Institute, Oslo.

hooks, b. (2000) *Feminism is for Everybody: Passionate Politics*, South End Press, Cambridge, MA.

hooks, b. (2004) *The Will to Change: Men, Masculinity and Love*, Atria Books, New York.

hooks, b. (2014) *Talking Back: Thinking Feminist, Thinking Black*, Routledge, New York.

Horkheimer, M. (1947) *Eclipse of Reason*, Oxford University Press, New York.

Howell, A. (2018) 'Forget "Militarization": Race, Disability and the "Martial Politics" of the Police and of the University', *International Feminist Journal of Politics*, vol. 20, no. 2, pp. 117–136.

Howell, S. and Willis, R. (1990) *Societies at Peace*, Routledge, London.

Hoyle, C. (2008) 'Will She Be Safe? A Crucial Analysis of Risk Assessment in Domestic Violence Cases', *Children and Youth Services Review*, vol. 30, pp. 323–337.

Htun, M. and Weldon, S. (2010) 'When Do Governments Promote Women's Rights? A Framework for the Comparative Analysis of Sex Equality Policy', *Perspectives on Politics*, vol. 8, no. 1, pp. 207–216.

Htun, M. and Weldon, S. (2012) 'The Civic Origins of Progressive Policy Change: Combatting Violence against Women in Global Perspective, 1975–2005', *American Political Science Review*, vol. 106, no. 3, pp. 548–569.

Hudson, V. Caprioli, M., Ballif-Spanvill, B., McDermott, R. and Emmett, C. (2008) 'The Heart of the Matter: The Security of Women and the Security of States', *International Security*, vol. 33, no. 3, pp. 7–45.

Hultman, M. (2017) 'Exploring Industrial, Ecomodern and Ecological Masculinities', in S. MacGregor (ed.), *Routledge Handbook of Gender and Environment*, Routledge, New York.

Hun, S. (2014) 'An Evaluation of Feminist Critiques of Just War Theory', *Deportate esuli profughe (DEP)*, vol. 24, pp. 76–84.

Hunnicutt, G. (2009) 'Varieties of Patriarchy and Violence against Women: Resurrecting "Patriarchy" as a Theoretical Tool', *Violence against Women*, vol. 15, no. 5, pp. 553–573.

Hunter, S., Riggs, D. and Augoustinos, M. (2017) 'Hegemonic Masculinity versus a Caring Masculinity: Implications for Understanding Primary Caregiving Fathers', *Social and Personality Psychology Compass*, vol. 11, pp. 1–9.

Hutchings, K. (2008) 'Making Sense of Masculinity and War', *Men and Masculinities*, vol. 10, no. 4, pp. 389–404.

Hymas, L. (2013) 'Eve Ensler Connects the Dots between Violence against Women and Violence against the Planet', *Grist*, 1201 Western Avenue, Seattle, WA.

Inhorn, M. and Whittle, L. (2001) 'Feminism Meets the "New" Epidemiologies: Toward an Appraisal of Anti-Feminist Biases in Epidemiological Research on Women's Health', *Social Science and Medicine*, vol. 53, pp. 553–567.

Institute for Work and Health (2015) 'What Researchers Mean by Primary, Secondary and Tertiary Prevention', *At Work*, issue 80, Spring.

Isenberg, D. (2013) 'Intra-Masculine Bonds and Butt Cracks', *Huffington Post*, www.huffpost.com/entry/intramasculine-bonds-and-cracks_b_2313357.

Israel, A. and Sachs, C. (2013) 'A Climate for Feminist Intervention: Feminist Climate Studies and Climate Change', in M. Alston and K. Whittenbury (eds), *Research, Action and Policy: Addressing the Gendered Impacts of Climate Change*, Springer, New York.

Itzin, C. (2000) 'Gendering Domestic Violence: The Influence of Feminism on Policy and Practice', in J. Hanmer and C. Itzen (eds), *Home Truths about Domestic Violence: Feminist Influences on Policy and Practice*, Routledge, London.

Jackson, C. (1995) 'Radical Environmental Myths: A Gender Perspective', *New Left Review*, March/April.

Jefferson, T. (2002) 'Subordinating Hegemonic Masculinity', *Theoretical Criminology*, vol. 6, no. 1, pp. 63–88.

Jensen, R. (2017) *The End of Patriarchy: Radical Feminism for Men*, Spinifex, Melbourne.

Jewkes, R., Flood, M. and Lang, J. (2015a) *From Work with Men and Boys to Changes of Social Norms and Reduction of Inequalities in Gender Relations: A Conceptual Shift in Prevention of Violence against Women and Girls*, Faculty of Law, Humanities and the Arts – Papers, Faculty of Law, Humanities and the Arts, University of Wollongong.

Jewkes, R., Morrell, R., Hearn, J., Lundqvist, E., Blackbeard, D., Lindegger, M., Sikweyiya, Y. and Gottzen, L. (2015b) 'Hegemonic Masculinity: Combining Theory and Practice in Gender Interventions', *Culture, Health and Sexuality*, vol. 17, no. 2, pp. S112–S127.

Johnson, A. (1997) *The Gender Knot: Unravelling Our Patriarchal Legacy*, Temple University Press, Philadelphia, PA.

Johnson, M. (1995) 'Patriarchal Terrorism and Common Couple Violence: Two Forms of Violence against Women', *Journal of Marriage and Family*, vol. 57, no. 2, pp. 283–294.

Johnson, M. (2008) *A Typology of Domestic Violence: Intimate Terrorism, Violent Resistance and Situational Couple Violence*, Northeastern University Press, Lebanon, NH.

Johnson, M. and Leone, J. (2005) 'The Differential Effects of Intimate Terrorism and Situational Couple Violence', *Journal of Family Issues*, vol. 26, no. 3, pp. 322–349.

Johnsson-Latham, G. (2007) *A Study on Gender Equality as a Prerequisite for Sustainable Development*, Report to the Environment Council, Sweden.

Jones, A. (2013) 'Domestic and International Violence Are One and the Same', *Salon*, www.salon.com.

Jordan, A. (2018) 'Masculinizing Care? Gender, Ethics of Care and Father's Rights Groups', *Men and Masculinities*, pp. 1–22, doi: 10.1177/1097184X18776364.

Jukes, A. (1993) *Why Men Hate Women*, Free Association Books, London.

Kaldor, M. (2006) *New and Old Wars*, Polity, Bristol.

Kandiyoti, D. (1988) 'Bargaining with Patriarchy', *Gender and Society*, vol. 2, no. 3, pp. 274–290.

Kantola, J. (2004) *European Union and National Gender Equality Politics: The Case of Domestic Violence in Britain and Finland*, Second Pan-European Conference, Standing Group on EU Politics, Bologna, 24–26 June.

Kantola, J. and Dahl, H. (2005) 'Gender and the State: From Differences between to Differences Within', *International Feminist Journal of Politics*, vol. 7, no. 1, pp. 49–70.

Kantola, J. and Squires, J. (2012) 'From State Feminism to Market Feminism?', *International Political Science Review*, vol. 33, no. 4, pp. 382–400.

Kantola, J., Norocel, O. and Repo, J. (2011) 'Gendering Violence in School Shootings in Finland', *European Journal of Women's Studies*, vol. 18, no. 2, pp. 183–197.

Katz, J. (2006) *The Macho Paradox: Why Some Men Hurt Women and How All Men Can Help*, Sourcebooks, Naperville, IL.

Katz, J., Heisterkamp, A. and Fleming, M. (2011) 'The Social Justice Roots of the Mentors in Violence Prevention Model and Its Application in a High School Setting', *Violence against Women*, vol. 17, no. 6, pp. 684–702.

Kaufman, M. (1987) 'The Construction of Masculinity and the Triad of Men's Violence', in M. Kaufman (ed.), *Beyond Patriarchy: Essays by Men on Pleasure, Power and Change*, Oxford University Press, Toronto.

Kaufman, M. (2004) 'Transforming Our Interventions for Gender Equality by Involving Men and Boys: A Framework for Analysis and Action', in S. Ruxton (ed.), *Gender Equality and Men: Learning from Practice*, Oxfam, Oxford.

Keller, E. (1982) 'Feminism and Science', *Signs*, vol. 7, no. 3, pp. 589–602.

Kelly, L. (2005) *How Violence Is Constitutive of Women's Inequality and the Implications for Equalities Work*, Child and Woman Abuse Studies Unit, London Metropolitan University, for the Equality and Diversity Forum seminar, London.

Kimmel, M. (1994) 'Masculinities as Homophobia: Fear, Shame and Silence in the Construction of Gender Identity', in H. Brod and M. Kaufman (eds), *Theorizing Masculinities*, Sage, Thousand Oaks, CA.

Kimmel, M. (2002) '"Gender Symmetry" in Domestic Violence: A Substantive and Methodological Research Review', *Violence against Women*, vol. 8, pp. 1332–1363.

Kimmel, M. (2013) *Angry White Men: American Masculininity at the End of an Era*, The Nation Books, New York.

Kimmel, M. (2018) *Healing from Hate: How Young Men Get into – and out of – Violent Extremism*, University of California Press, Oakland, CA.

Kimmel, M. and Mahler, M. (2003) 'Adolescent Masculinity, Homophobia and Violence', *American Behavioral Scientist*, vol. 46, no. 10, pp. 1439–1458.

Kinsella, H. (2006) 'Gendering Grotius: Sex and Sex Difference in the Laws of War', *Political Theory*, vol. 34, no. 2, pp. 161–191.

Kivel, P. (2007) 'Social Service or Social Change?', in INCITE (eds), *The Revolution Will Not Be Funded*, Duke University Press, Durham, NC.

Klein, R. (2013) 'Language for Institutional Change', in R. Klein (ed.), *Framing Sexual and Domestic Violence through Language*, Palgrave Macmillan, New York.

Krcek, J. (2012) 'What's Wrong with Just War Theory? Examining the Gendered Bias of a Longstanding Tradition', *Inquiries Journal/Student Pulse*, vol. 4, no. 5, pp. 1–12.

Kremer, J. (2010) *Is Environmental Crime Gendered?*, master's thesis, Washington State University, Department of Sociology.

Krishnamurthy, M. (2013) 'Political Solidarity, Justice and Public Health', *Public Health Ethics*, vol. 2, pp. 129–141.

Kruger, E., Dahlberg, L., Mercy, J., Zwi, A. and Lozano, R. (2002) *World Health Report on Health and Violence*, World Health Organization, Geneva.

Kuennen, T. (2007) 'Analysing the Impact of Coercion on Domestic Violence Victims: How Much Is Too Much?', *Berkeley Journal of Gender, Law and Justice*, vol. 22, no. 1, pp. 1–30.

Kutz, C. (2000) *Complicity: Ethics and Law for a Collective Age*, Cambridge University Press, Cambridge.

Kynaston, C. (1996) 'The Everyday Exploitation of Women: Housework and the Patriarchal Mode of Production', *Women's Studies International Forum*, vol. 19, no. 3, pp. 221–237.

Latshaw, B. (2015) 'From Mopping to Mowing: Masculinity and Housework in Stay-at-Home Father Households', *Journal of Men's Studies*, vol. 23, no. 3, pp. 252–270.

Lawson, J. (2012) 'Sociological Theories of Intimate Partner Violence', *Journal of Human Behaviour in the Social Environment*, vol. 22, no. 5, pp. 572–590.

Lawson, V. (2007) 'Geographies of Care and Responsibility', *Annals of the Association of American Geographers*, vol. 97, no. 1, pp. 1–11.

Leduc, B. (2010) 'Climate Change and Gender Justice', *Climate and Development*, vol. 2, no. 4, pp. 390–392.

Lee, B. (2018) 'Environmental Violence as Collective Suicidality', *Psychology Today*, 12 September.

Lee, P. (2017) *What's Wrong with Logic Models?* LCSA: Occasional Paper 1, Local Community Services Association.

Legge, D. (2018) 'Capitalism, Imperialism and Class: Essential Foundations for a Critical Public Health', *Critical Public Health*, http://doi.org/1080/09581596.2018.1478067.

Lenton, R. (1995) 'Power versus Feminist Theories of Abuse', *Canadian Journal of Criminology*, vol. 37, no. 3, pp. 305–330.

Leonardo, Z. (2004) 'The Color of Supremacy: Beyond the Discourse of White Privilege', *Educational Philosophy and Theory*, vol. 36, no. 2, pp. 137–152.

Lerner, G. (1986) *The Creation of Patriarchy*, Oxford University Press, Oxford.

Levine-Rasky, C. (2010) 'Framing Whiteness: Working through the Tensions in Introducing Whiteness to Educators', *Race, Ethnicity and Education*, vol. 3, no. 3, pp. 271–292.

Levy, B., Sidel, V. and Patx, J. (2017) 'Climate Change and Collective Violence', *Annual Review of Public Health*, vol. 38, pp. 241–257.

Lindsay, J. (2012) 'The Gendered Trouble with Alcohol: Young People Managing Alcohol Related Violence', *International Journal of Drug Policy*, vol. 23, no. 3, pp. 236–241.

Lindvert, J. (2002) 'A World Apart: Swedish and Australian Gender Equality Policy', *NORA: Nordic Journal of Feminist and Gender Research*, vol. 10, no. 2, pp. 99–107.

Litfin, K. (1997) 'The Gendered Eye in the Sky: A Feminist Perspective on Earth Observation Studies', *Frontiers: A Journal of Women's Studies*, vol. 18, no. 2, pp. 26–47.

Livingston, M. (2018) *The Association between State of Origin and Assaults in Two Australian States*, Foundation for Alcohol Research and Education, Melbourne.

Locke, B. (2013) *The Military–Masculinity Complex: Hegemonic Masculinity and the United Nations Armed Forces 1940–1963*, Dissertations, Theses and Student Research, Department of History, Paper 65, University of Nebraska, Lincoln.

Looker, P. (1994) 'Doing It with Your Mates: Connecting Aspects of Modern Australian Masculinity', in D. Headon, J. Hooton and D. Horne (eds), *The Abundant Culture: Meaning and Significance in Everyday Australia*, Allen & Unwin, Sydney.

Lopez, H. (2011) *Militarized Masculinity in Peacekeeping Operations: An Obstacle to Gender Mainstreaming*, background paper, Department of Foreign Affairs and International Trade, Ottawa.

Lorentzen, J. (2004) *The Role of Men in Combatting Domestic Violence*, Centre for Women's Studies and Gender Research, Oslo.

Loy, J. (1992) *The Dark Side of Agon: Fratriarchies, Performative Masculinity, Sport Involvement and the Phenomena of Gang Rape*, paper presented at the Annual Meeting of the North American Society for the Sociology of Sport, Toledo, OH.

Loy, J. (1995) 'The Dark /Side of Agon: Fratriarchies, Performative Masculinities, Sport Involvement and the Phenomena of Gang Rape', in K. Beffee and A. Ruffen (eds), *International Sociology of Sport: Contemporary Issues*, Verlag Stephanie Neglsmid, Stuttgart.

Lyman, P. (1987) 'The Fraternal Bond as a Joking Relationship: A Case Study of the Role of Sexist Jokes in Male Group Bonding', in M. Kimmel (ed.), *Changing Men: New Directions in Research on Men and Masculinity*, Sage, Thousand Oaks, CA.

Lynch, K. (2010) 'Affective Equality: Love, Care and Solidarity as Productive Forces', in S. Strid and A. Jonasdottir (eds), *Proceedings from the GEXcel Theme 10 Love in Our Time: A Question for Feminism*, Orebro University, Sweden.

Lynch, K. and Baker, J. (2009) 'Conclusion', in K. Lynch, J. Baker and M. Lyons (eds), *Affective Equality: Love, Care and Injustice*, Palgrave Macmillan, London.

Lynch, K. and Walsh, J. (2009) 'Love, Care and Solidarity: What Is and Is Not Commodifiable', in K. Lynch, J. Baker and M. Lyons (eds), *Affective Equality: Love, Care and Injustice*, Palgrave Macmillan, London.

Lynch, T. (2015) *Women Who Kill Friends, Acquaintances or Strangers: A Feminist Exploratory Study*, PhD thesis, RMIT University, Melbourne.

MacGregor, S. (2006) *Beyond Mothering: Ecological Citizenship and the Politics of Care*, UBC Press, Vancouver.

MacInnes, J. (1998) *The End of Masculinity*, Open University Press, Buckingham.

MacKenzie, M. (2015) *Beyond the Band of Brothers: The US Military and the Myth That Women Can't Fight*, Cambridge, University Press, Cambridge.

Mackie, G., Moneti, F., Shakya, H. and Denny, E. (2015) *What Are Social Norms and How Are They Measured?*, University of California, San Diego, Centre on Global Justice.

Macleod, C. (2007) 'The Risk of Phallocentrism in Masculinity Studies: How a Revision of the Concept of Patriarchy May Help', *PINS*, vol. 35, pp. 4–14.

Macleod, C. and Durrheim, K. (2002) 'Foucauldian Feminism and the Implications of Governmentality', *Journal of the Theory of Social Behaviour*, vol. 32, no. 1, pp. 41–60.

MacLure, M. (2004) *Clarity Bordering on Stupidity: Where's the Quality in Systematic Review?*, paper presented to the British Educational Research Association Annual Conference, Manchester, September.

Mainardi, P. (1970) 'The Politics of Housework', in R. Morgan (ed.), *Sisterhood Is Powerful*, Vintage Books, New York.

Malone, N. (2004) *From Just War to Just Peace: Revisioning Just War Theory from a Feminist Perspective*, master's thesis, Department of Political Science, University of South Florida.

Mann, B. (2014) *Sovereign Masculinity: Gender Lessons from the War on Terror*, Oxford University Press, New York.

Marchant, H. (2005) *Radical Ecology: The Search for a Liveable World*, 2nd edn, Routledge, New York.

Marchese, E. (2008) 'No Women Allowed: Exclusion and Accountability in Men's Anti-Rape Groups', *Journal of International Women's Studies*, vol. 9, no. 2, pp. 59–76.

Marcuse, H. (1991) *One-Dimensional Man*, Routledge, London.

Marston, G. (1994) 'Invisible Boundaries', *XY: Men, Sex, Politics*, vol. 4, no. 2, pp. 12–14.

Martin, K., Vieraitis, L. and Britto, S. (2006) 'Gender Equality and Women's Absolute Status: A Test of the Feminist Models of Rape', *Violence against Women*, vol. 12, no. 4, pp. 321–339.

Martin, P. (2001) '"Mobilizing Masculinities": Women's Experiences of Men at Work', *Organization*, vol. 8, no. 4, pp. 587–618.

Masson, V., Lim, S., Budimir, M. and Podoj, J. (2016) *Disasters and Violence against Women and Girls*, Overseas Development Institute, London.

Mathews, F. (2017) 'The Dilemma of Dualism', in S. MacGregor (ed.), *Routledge Handbook of Gender and Environment*, Routledge, New York.

Matthews, C. (2016) 'Exploring the Pastiche Hegemony of Men', *Palgrave Communications*, https://doi.org/10.1057/palcomms.2016.22.

May, L. (1990) 'Collective Inaction and Shared Responsibility', *Nous*, vol. 24, no. 2, pp. 269–277.

May, L. (1992) *Sharing Responsibility*, University of Chicago Press, Chicago, IL.

May, L. and Strikwerda, R. (1994) 'Men in Groups: Collective Responsibility for Rape', *Hypatia*, vol. 9, no. 2, pp. 134–151.

Mayo, C. (2004) 'Certain Privilege: Rethinking White Agency', *Philosophy of Education*, pp. 308–316, https://ojs.education.illinois.edu/index.php/pes/article/viewArticle/1675.

McBride, J. (1995) *War, Battering and Other Sports*, Humanities Press, Atlantic Highlands, NJ.

McCaffrey, B. (2012) 'WTF Is Kyriarchy?', *The Feminist Anthropologist*, 19 July, www.reddit.com/r/Feminism/comments/wtndq/wtf_is_a_kyriarchy_the_feminist_anthropologist/.

McCarry, M. (2007) 'Masculinity Studies and Male Violence: Critique or Collusion?', *Women's Studies International Forum*, vol. 30, pp. 404–415.

McCloskey, L. (1996) 'Socioeconomic and Coercive Power within the Family', *Gender and Society*, vol. 10, no. 4, pp. 449–463.

McGregor, H. and Hopkins, A. (1991) *Working for Change: The Movement against Domestic Violence*, Allen & Unwin, Sydney.

McKee, J. (2014) *Patriarchal Ideology and Violence against Women: A Theoretical Contribution Using Longitudinal, Individual-Level Analyses*, PhD thesis, Old Dominion University, Norfolk, VA.

McLellan, B. (2012) *The Gender Equality Trap*, paper presented at the Violence against Women: An Inconvenient Reality Conference, Brisbane, Queensland, 7–9 August.

McMahon, A. (1999) *Taking Care of Men: Sexual Politics in the Public Mind*, Cambridge University Press, Cambridge.

Meier, J. (2007) *Defining Domestic Violence: Has Johnson's Typology Resolved the Gender Debate?*, paper presented at the AALS Workshop on Family Law, George Washington University.

Melbourne Research Alliance to End Violence against Women and Their Children (2018) University of Melbourne, Melbourne.

Mellor, M. (1992) 'Green Politics: Ecofeminism, Ecofeminine or Ecomasculine?', *Environmental Politics*, vol. 1, no. 2, pp. 229–251.

Mellor, M. (1996) 'The Politics of Women and Nature', *Journal of Political Ideologies*, vol. 1, no. 2, pp. 147–164.

Mellor, M. (2017) 'Ecofeminist Political Economy: A Green and Feminist Agenda', in S. MacGregor (ed.), *Routledge Handbook of Gender and Environment*, Routledge, New York.

Messerschmidt, J. (1993) *Masculinities and Crime: Critique and Reconceptualization of Theory*, Rowman & Littlefield, Lanham, MD.

Messerschmidt, J. (1998) 'Men Victimising Men: The Case of Lynching', in L. Bowker (ed.), *Masculinities and Violence*, Sage, Thousand Oaks, CA.

Messner, M. (1992) *Power at Play: Sports and the Problem of Masculinity*, Beacon Press, Boston, MA.

Messner, M. (1997) *Politics of Masculinities: Men in Movements*, Sage, Thousand Oaks, CA.

Messner, M. (2016) 'Bad Men, Good Men, Bystanders: Who Is the Rapist?', *Gender and Society*, vol. 30, no. 1, pp. 57–66.

Messner, M., Greenberg, M. and Peretz, T. (2015) *Some Men: Feminist Allies and the Movement to End Violence against Women*, Oxford University Press, Oxford.

Meyer, E. and Post, L. (2006) 'Alone at Night: A Feminist Ecological Model of Community Violence', *Feminist Criminology*, vol. 1, no. 3, pp. 207–227.

Miller, P. (2017) *Patriarchy*, Routledge, London.

Miller, S. (2010) 'Cosmopolitan Care', *Ethics and Social Welfare*, vol. 4, no. 2, pp. 145–157.

Millett, K. (1972) *Sexual Politics*, Abacus, London.

Mills, M. (1998) *Challenging Violence in Schools: Disruptive Moments in the Educational Politics of Masculinity*, PhD thesis, University of Queensland, Brisbane.

Mitchell, J. (1974) *Psychoanalysis and Feminism*, Pantheon Books, New York.

Mohanty, C. (1984) 'Under Western Eyes: Feminist Scholarship and Colonial Discourse', *Boundary 2*, vol. 12, no. 3, pp. 333–358.

Monteverde, G. (2014) 'Not All Feminist Are Equal: Anti-Capitalist Feminism and Female Complicity', *Journal of International Women Studies*, vol. 16, no. 1, pp. 62–75.

Montez de Oca, J. (2012) 'Deconstructing Men and Masculinities', *Social History Inc.*, vol. 45, no. 90, pp. 421–423.

Morgan, D. (1987) 'Masculinity and Violence', in J. Hanmer and M. Maynard (eds), *Women, Violence and Social Control*, Macmillan, London.

Morita, K. (2007) *For a Better Environmental Education: A Materialist Ecofeminist Analysis of Global Warming by a Male Japanese Ecofeminist*, Department of Social Design Studies, Tokyo.

Morrell, R. and Jewkes, R. (2011) 'Carework and Caring: A Path to Gender Equitable Practices among Men in South Africa', *International Journal for Equity in Health*, vol. 10, no. 17, pp. 1–10.

Morrell, R., Jewkes, R., Lindegger, G. and Hamlall, V. (2013) 'Hegemonic Masculinity: Reviewing the Gendered Analysis of Men's Power in South Africa', *South African Review of Sociology*, vol. 44, no. 1, pp. 3–21.

Mottram, B. and Salater, M. (2015) '"It's an Ethical, Moral and Professional Dilemma I Think": Domestic Violence Workers' Understanding of Women's Use of Violence in Relationships', *Affilia: Journal of Women and Social Work*, vol. 31, no. 2, pp. 1–15.

Murdolo, A. and Quazon, R. (2016) *Key Issues in Working with Men from Immigrant and Refugee Backgrounds in Preventing Violence against Women*, White Ribbon Research Series, Sydney.

Murphy, M. (2009) 'Can "Men" Stop Rape? Visualizing Gender in the "My Strength Is Not for Hurting" Campaign', *Men and Masculinities*, vol. 12, no. 1, pp. 113–130.

Murrie, L. (2007) 'Mateship', in M. Flood, J. Kegan, B. Pease and K. Pringle (eds), *International Encyclopedia of Men and Masculinities*, Routledge, New York.

Mykhalovskiy, E., Frohlich, K., Poland, B., Di Ruggiero, E., Rock, M. and Comer, L. (2018) 'Critical Social Science with Public Health: Agonism, Critique and Engagement', *Critical Public Health*, https://doi.org/10.180/0958196.2018.1474174.

Naranjo, C. (2018) 'The Patriarchal Mind as the Ignored Root of Interpersonal and Social Pathologies', *World Futures: The Journal of New Paradigm Research*, vol. 74, no. 3, pp. 135–157.

National Institute of Justice (2000) *Summary of Workshop Discussion: Gender Symmetry*, National Institute of Justice, Arlington, VA.

Native Youth Sexual Health Network and Women's Earth Alliance (2014) *Violence on the Land, Violence on Our Bodies: Building an Indigenous Response to Environmental Violence*, Women's Earth Alliance and Native Youth Sexual Health Network, Toronto.

Navarro, V. (2009) 'What We Mean by Social Determinants of Health', *International Journal of Health Services*, vol. 39, no. 3, pp. 423–441.

Nayak, M. and Suchland, J. (2006) 'Gender Violence and Hegemonic Projects', *International Feminist Journal of Politics*, vol. 8, no. 4, pp. 467–485.

Nelson, M. (1994) *The Stronger Women Get, the More Men Love Football: Sexism and the Culture of Sport*, Women's Press, London.

Neu, M. (2015) 'The Supreme Emergency of War: A Critique of Walzer', *Journal of International Political Theory*, vol. 10, no. 1, pp. 3–19.

Neumayer, E. and Plumper, T. (2007) 'The Gendered Nature of Natural Disasters: The Impact of Catastrophic Events on the Gender Gap in Life Expectancy, 1981–2002', *Annals of the Association of American Geographers*, vol. 97, no. 3, pp. 551–566.

New, C. (1996) 'Man Bad, Women Good? Essentialisms and Ecofeminisms', *New Left Review*, no. 216, pp. 79–93.

Nguyen, K. (2014) *Nordic Countries Worst in EU for Violence against Women – Survey*, Thomas Reuters Foundation, 5 March.

Nixon, R. (2011) *Slow Violence and the Environmentalism of the Poor*, Harvard University Press, Cambridge, MA.

Noble, C. and Moore, S. (2006) 'Advancing Women and Leadership in the Post Feminist, Post EEO era: A Discussion of the Issues', *Women in Management Review*, vol. 21, no. 7, pp. 598–603.

Nooraddini, I. (2012) *Gender Inequality and Female Victimisation*, Department of Sociology and Anthropology, University of Maryland, Baltimore.

Norgaard, K. and York, R. (2005) 'Gender Equality and State Environmentalism', *Gender and Society*, vol. 19, no. 4, pp. 506–522.

Nousiainne, K., Holli, A., Kantola, J., Saari, M. and Hart, L. (2013) 'Theorizing Gender Equality: Perspectives on Power and Legitimacy', *Social Politics*, vol. 7, no. 1, pp. 41–64.

O'Brien, K. (2017) *The Violence of Climate Change*. Georgetown University Press, Washington, DC.

O'Connor, J. (2015) 'The State and Gender Equality: From Patriarchal to Women-Friendly State?', in S. Leibfried, E. Huber, M. Lange, J. Levy and J. Stephens (eds), *The Oxford Handbook of Transformations of the State*, Oxford University Press, Oxford.

O'Neill, R.V. (2001) 'Is It Time to Bury the Ecosystem Concept?', *Ecology*, vol. 82, no. 12, pp. 3275–3284.

O'Neill, R. (2015) 'Whither Critical Masculinity Studies? Notes on Inclusive Masculinity Theory, Postfeminism and Sexual Politics', *Men and Masculinities*, vol. 18, no. 1, pp. 100–120.

O'Toole, L. and Schiffman, J. (1997) 'Preface: Conceptualizing Gender Violence', in L. O'Toole and J. Schiffman (eds), *Gender Violence: Interdisciplinary Perspectives*, New York University Press, New York.

OECD (2017) *The Pursuit of Gender Equality: An Uphill Battle*, OECD Publishing Paris.

Ogle, R. and Batton, C. (2009) 'Revisiting Patriarchy: Its Conceptualisation and Operationalisation in Criminology', *Critical Criminology*, vol. 17, pp. 159–182.

One in Three Campaign (n.d.) *One in Three Victims of Family Violence Is Male: Fact Sheet No. 3*, www.oneinthree.com.au.

Ortbals, C. and Poloni-Staudinger (2018) 'How Gender Intersects with Political Violence and Terrorism', in *Oxford Encyclopedia of Politics*, Oxford University Press, Oxford.

Ortner, S. (2014) 'Too Soon for Post-Feminism: The Ongoing Life of Patriarchy in Neoliberal America', *History and Anthropology*, vol. 25, no. 4, pp. 530–549.

Our Watch (2015) *Change the Story: A Shared Framework for the Primary Prevention of Violence against Women and Their Children in Australia*, Our Watch, VicHealth, ANROWs Our Watch, Melbourne.

Our Watch (2018) *What about Violence towards Men?*, The Line, Melbourne.

Ozaki, R. and Otis, M. (2017) 'Gender Equality, Patriarchal Cultural Norms, and Perpetration of Intimate Partner Violence: Comparison of Male University Students in Asian and European Cultural Contexts', *Violence against Women*, vol. 23, no. 9, pp. 1076–1099.

Pain, R. (2014) 'Everyday Terrorism: Connecting Domestic Violence and Global Terrorism', *Progress in Human Geography*, vol. 38, no. 4, pp. 531–550.

Pallotta-Chiarolli, M. and Pease, B. (2014) 'Recognition, Resistance and Reconstruction: An Introduction to Subjectivities and Social Justice', in M. Pallotta-Chiarolli and B. Pease (eds), *The Politics of Recognition and Social Justice: Transforming Subjectivities and New Forms of Resistance*, Routledge, New York.

Paluck, E. and Ball, L. (2010) *Social Norms Marketing Aimed at Gender-Based Violence: A Literature Review and Critical Assessment*, International Rescue Committee, Brighton.

Parashar, S. (2014) *Women and Militant Wars: The Politics of Injury*, Routledge, London.

Parkinson, D. and Zara, C. (2013) 'The Hidden Disaster: Domestic Violence in the Aftermath of Natural Disaster', *Australian Journal of Emergency Management*, vol. 28, no. 2, pp. 28–35.

Pateman, C. (1988) *The Sexual Contract*, Polity, Cambridge.

Patil, V. (2013) 'From Patriarchy to Intersectionality: A Transnational Feminist Assessment of How Far We've Really Come', *Signs*, vol. 38, no. 4, pp. 847–867.

Payson, J. (2009) 'Moral Dilemmas and Collective Responsibilities', *Essays in Philosophy*, vol. 10, no. 2, pp. 1–23.

Peach, L. (1994) 'An Alternative to Pacifism? Feminism and Just-War Theory', *Hypatia*, vol. 9, no. 2, pp. 152–172.

Pease, B. (2001) 'Moving beyond Mateship: Reconstructing Australian Men's Practices', in B. Pease and K. Pringle (eds), *A Man's World? Changing Men's Practices in a Globalized World*, Zed Books, London.

Pease, B. (2002) *Men and Gender Relations*, Tertiary Press, Melbourne.

Pease, B. (2008) 'Engaging Men in Men's Violence Prevention: Exploring the Tensions, Dilemmas and Possibilities', *Australian Domestic and Family Violence Clearinghouse*, Issues Paper 17, pp. 1–20.

Pease, B. (2009) 'From Evidence-Based Practice to Critical Knowledge in Post-Positivist Social Work', in J. Allan, L. Briskman and B. Pease (eds), *Critical Social Work: Theories and Practices for a Socially Just World*, 2nd edn, Allen & Unwin, Sydney.

Pease, B. (2010) *Undoing Privilege: Unearned Advantage in a Divided World*, Zed Books, London.

Pease, B. (2011) 'Governing Men's Violence against Women in Australia', in E. Ruspini, J. Hearn, B. Pease and K. Pringle (eds), *Men and Masculinities around the World: Transforming Men's Practices*, Palgrave Macmillan, New York.

Pease, B. (2012) 'The Politics of Gendered Emotions: Disrupting Men's Emotional Investments in Privilege', *Australian Journal of Social Issues*, vol. 47, no. 1, pp. 125–140.

Pease, B. (2014a) 'Theorising Men's Violence Prevention Policies: Limitations and Possibilities of Interventions in a Patriarchal State', in N. Henry and A. Powell (eds), *Preventing Sexual Violence: Interdisciplinary Approaches to Overcoming a Rape Culture*, Palgrave Macmillan, London.

Pease, B. (2014b) 'Hegemonic Masculinity and the Gendering of Men in Disaster Management: Implications for Social Work Education', *Advances in Social Work and Welfare Education*, vol. 16, no. 2, pp. 60–72.

Pease, B. (2014c) 'Reconstructing Masculinity or Ending Manhood? The Potential and Limitations of Transforming Masculine Subjectivities for Gender Equality', in A. Carabi and J. Armengol (eds), *Alternative Masculinities for a Changing World*, Palgrave, New York.

Pease, B. (2015) 'Disengaging Men from Patriarchy: Rethinking the Man Question in Masculinity Studies', in M. Flood (ed.), *Engaging Men in Building Gender Equality*, Cambridge Scholars Publishing, Cambridge.

Pease, B. (2016) 'Masculinism, Climate Change and "Man-Made" Disasters: Towards an Environmentalist Profeminist Response', in E. Enarson and B. Pease (eds), *Men, Masculinities and Disaster*, Routledge, New York.

Pease, B. (2017) *Men as Allies in Preventing Violence against Women: Principles and Practices for Promoting Accountability*, White Ribbon Research Series, Sydney, White Ribbon.

Pease, B. and Flood, M. (2008) 'Rethinking the Significance of Attitudes in Preventing Men's Violence against Women', *Australian Journal of Social Issues*, vol. 343, no. 4, pp. 547–560.

Pence, E. and Paymar, M. (1993) *Power and Control Tactics of Men Who Batter: The Duluth Model*, Springer, New York.

Peterson, S. (1977) 'Coercion and Rape: The State as a Male Protection Racket', in M. Vetterling-Braggin, F. Elliston and J. English (eds), *Feminism and Philosophy*, Rowan & Littlefield, Totowa, NJ.

Phillips, M. and Rumens, N. (2016) 'Introducing Contemporary Ecofeminism', in M. Philips and N. Rumens (eds), *Contemporary Perspectives on Ecofeminism*, Routledge, London.

Phillips, R. (2008) 'Feminism, Policy and Women's Safety during Australia's War on Terror', *Feminist Review*, vol. 89, pp. 55–72.

Phillips, S. (1996) 'Discourse, Identity, and Voice: Feminist Contributions to Policy Studies', in L. Dobuzinskis, M. Howlett and D. Laycock (eds), *Policy Studies in Canada: The State of the Art*, University of Toronto Press, Toronto.

Pittaway, E., Bartolomei, L. and Rees, S. (2007) 'Gendered Dimensions of the 2004 Tsunami and a Potential Social Work Response in Post-Disaster Situations', *International Social Work*, vol. 50, no. 3, pp. 307–319.

Plumwood, V. (1993) *Feminism and the Mastery of Nature*, Routledge, London.

Polk, K. (1994) *When Men Kill: Scenarios of Masculine Violence*, Cambridge University Press, Cambridge.

Pollert, A. (1996) 'Gender and Class Revisited, or, the Poverty of Patriarchy', *Sociology*, vol. 30, no. 4, pp. 639–659.

Powell, A. (2011) *Review of Bystander Approaches in Support of Preventing Violence against Women*, Victorian Health Promotion Foundation, Melbourne.

Powell, A. (2014a) 'Shifting Upstream: Bystander Action against Sexism and Discrimination against Women', in N. Henry and A. Powell (eds), *Preventing Sexual Violence: Interdisciplinary Approaches to Overcoming a Rape Culture*, Palgrave Macmillan, Buckingham.

Powell, A. (2014b) 'Bystander Approaches: Responding to and Preventing Men's Sexual Violence against Women', *ACSSA Issues No. 17*, Australian Centre for the Study of Sexual Assault, Melbourne.

Powell, A. and Henry, N. (2014) 'Framing Sexual Violence: What Does It Mean to Challenge a Rape Culture?', in N. Henry and A. Powell (eds), *Preventing Sexual Violence: Interdisciplinary Perspectives on Overcoming a Rape Culture*, Palgrave Macmillan, Buckingham.

Price, J. (2012) *Hidden Brutality in the Lives of Women*, State University of New York Press, Albany, NY.

Pringle, K., Balkmar, D. and Iovanni, L. (2010) 'Trouble in Paradise: Exploring Patterns of Research and Policy Response to Men's Violence in Denmark and Sweden', *NORA: Nordic Journal of Feminist and Gender Research*, vol. 18, no. 2, pp. 105–121.

Pringle, R. and Watson, S. (1990) 'Fathers, Brothers, Mates: The Fraternal State in Australia', in S. Watson (ed.), *Playing the State: Australian Feminist Interventions*, Allen & Unwin, Sydney.

Purkayastha, B. and Ratcliff, K. (2014) 'Routine Violence: Intersectionality at the Interstices', in M. Segal and V. Demos (eds), *Gendered Perspectives on Conflict and Violence*, Emerald Group, Bingley.

Quadara, A. and Wall, L. (2012) *What Is Effective Primary Prevention in Sexual Assault? Translating the Evidence for Action*, ACSSA Wrap, no. 11, Australian Centre for the Study of Sexual Assault, Australian Institute of Family Studies, Melbourne.

Rachlinski, J. (2000) 'The Limits of Social Norms', *Chicago-Kent Law Review*, vol. 74, no. 4, pp. 1537–1567.

Rahman, N. (2007) 'Patriarchy', in M. Flood, J. Gardiner, B. Pease and K. Pringle (eds), *International Encyclopedia of Men and Masculinities*, Routledge, London.

Ramazanoglu, C. (1989) *Feminism and the Contradictions of Oppression*, Routledge, New York.

Rankin, L. and Vickers, J. (2001) *Women's Movements and State Feminism: Integrating Diversity into State Policy*, Status of Women Canada, Ottowa.

Raphael, D. and Bryant, T. (2002) 'The Limitations of Population Health as a Model for New Public Health', *Health Promotion International*, vol. 17, no. 2, pp. 189–199.

Ratelo, K., Suffla, S., Lazarus, S. and van Niekerk, A. (2010) 'Towards the Development of a Responsive, Social Science-informed Critical Public Health Framework on Male Interpersonal Violence', *Social Change*, vol. 40, no. 4, pp. 414–438.

Reinelt, C. (1995) 'Moving onto the Terrain of the State: The Battered Women's Movement and the Politics of Engagement', in M. Ferree and P. Martin (eds), *Feminist Organizations: Harvest of the New Women's Movement*, Temple University Press, Philadelphia, PA.

Remy, J. (1990) 'Patriarchy and Fratriarchy as Forms of Androcracy', in J. Hearn and D. Morgan (eds), *Men, Masculinities and Social Theory*, Unwin Hyman, London.

Repo, J. (2006) *Gendering the Militarisation of the War on Terrorism: Discourses of Masculinities and Femininities*, master's thesis, University of Helsinki.

Repo, J. (2016) 'Gender Equality as Biopolitical Governmentality in a Neoliberal European Union', *Social Politics*, vol. 23, no. 2, pp. 307–328.

Resko, S. (2014) *Intimate Partner Violence against Women: Exploring Intersections of Race, Class and Gender*, Ohio State University, Columbus, OH.

Richard, L., Gauvin, L. and Raine, K. (2011) 'Ecological Models Revisited', *Annual Review of Public Health*, vol. 32, pp. 307–326.

Ridgeway, C. and Correll, S. (2004) 'Unpacking the Gender System: A Theoretical Perspective on Gender Beliefs and Social Relations', *Gender and Society*, vol. 18, no. 4, pp. 510–531.

Robertson, N. (1999) 'Stopping Violence Programs: Enhancing the Safety of Battered Women or Producing Better-Educated Batterers', *New Zealand Journal of Psychology*, vol. 28, no. 2, pp. 68–78.

Robertson, S., Williams, B. and Oliffe, J. (2016) 'The Case for Retaining a Focus on "Masculinities" in Men's Health Research', *International Journal of Men's Health*, vol. 15, no. 1, pp. 52–67.

Robinson, C., Bottorff, J., Pesut, B., Oliffe, J. and Tomlinson, J. (2014) 'The Male Face of Caregiving: A Scoping Review of Men Caring for a Person with Dementia', *American Journal of Men's Health*, vol. 8, no. 5, pp. 409–426.

Robinson, F. (2010) 'After Liberalism in World Politics? Towards an International Political Theory of Care', *Ethics and Social Welfare*, vol. 4, no. 2, pp. 130–144.

Robinson, F. (2015) 'Care, Gender and Global Social Justice: Rethinking Ethical Globalization', *Journal of Global Ethics*, vol. 2, no. 1, pp. 5–25.

Robinson, V. (1996) 'Heterosexuality and Masculinity: Theorising Male Power or the Wounded Male Psyche', in D. Richardson (ed.), *Theorising Heterosexuality*, Open University Press, London.

Robinson, V. (2003) 'Radical Revisionings? The Theorizing of Masculinity and (Radical) Feminist Theory', *Women's International Studies Forum*, vol. 26, no. 2, pp. 129–137.

Rodino-Colocino, M. (2018) 'Me Too, #MenToo: Countering Cruelty with Empathy', *Communication and Critical/Cultural Studies*, vol. 15, no. 1, pp. 96–100.

Rogan, A. (2015) *Risky Masculinities: Young Men, Risky Drinking, Public Violence and Hegemonic Masculinity*, PhD thesis, University of Wollongong, Wollongong.

Rogers, W. (2006) 'Feminism and Public Health Ethics', *Journal of Medical Ethics*, vol. 32, no. 6, pp. 351–354.

Rosen, L., Kaminski, R., Parmley, A., Knudson, K. and Fancher, P. (2003) 'The Effects of Peer Group Climate on Intimate Partner Violence among Married Male US Army Soldiers', *Violence against Women*, vol. 9, no. 9, pp. 1045–1071.

Rossiter, P. (2011) 'A Thorn in the Flesh That Cannot Fester: Habermas, the Duluth Model, Domestic Violence Programs', *Waikato Law Review*, vol. 19, no. 2, pp. 196–206.

Rousseau, C. (2016) 'The Dividing Power of the Wage: Housework as Social Subversion', *Altantis*, vol. 37, no. 2, pp. 238–252.

Roussel, J. and Downs, C. (2008) 'Epistemological Perspectives on Concepts of Gender and Masculinity/Masculinities', *Journal of Men's Studies*, vol. 16, no. 2, pp. 178–196.

Rowan, J. (1989) *The Horned God: Feminism and Men as Wounding and Healing*, Routlege, London.

Rowbotham, S. (1981) 'The Trouble with Patriarchy', in R. Samuel (ed.), *People's History and Socialist Theory*, Routledge & Kegan Paul, London.

Ruby, S. and Scholz, S. (2018) 'Care, Care Work and the Struggle for a Careful World from the Perspective of the Sociology of Masculinities', *Osterreichische Zeitschriftfur Soziologie*, vol. 43, no. 1, pp. 73–83.

Ruddick, S. (1989) *Maternal Thinking: Towards a Politics of Peace*, Women's Press, London.

Ruppanner, L. and Geist, C. (2018) 'How Last Night's Fight Affects the Way Couples Divide Household Work', *The Conversation*, 2 April.

Russell, R. and Jory, M. (1997) 'An Evaluation of Group Intervention Programs for Violent and Abusive Men', *Australian and New Zealand Journal of Family Therapy*, vol. 18, no. 3, pp. 125–136.

Ruxton, S. (2004) 'Introduction', in S. Ruxton (ed.), *Gender Equality and Men: Learning from Practice*, Oxfam, Oxford.

Sabo, D., Gray, P. and Moore, L. (2000) 'Domestic Violence and Televised Athletic Events', in J. McKay, M. Messner and D. Sabo (eds), *Masculinities, Gender Relations and Sport*, Sage, Thousand Oaks, CA.

Salleh, A. (1995) 'Nature, Woman, Labour, Capital: Living the Deepest Contradiction', *Capitalism Nature Socialism*, vol. 6, no. 1, pp. 21–39.

Salter, M. (2016) '"Real Men Don't Hit Women": Constructing Masculinity in the Prevention of Violence against Women', *Australian and New Zealand Journal of Criminology*, vol. 49, no. 4, pp. 463–479.

Salter, M., Carmody, M. and Presterudstuen, G. (2015) *Resolving the Prevention Paradox: The Role of Communities and Organisations in the Primary Prevention of Violence against Women*, paper presented at the Inaugural Asia-Pacific Conference on Gendered Violence and Violations, University of New South Wales, Sydney.

Sanday, P. (2007) *Fraternity Gang Rape: Sex, Brotherhood and Privilege on Campus*. New York University Press, New York.

Sandilands, C. (1999) *The Good-Natured Feminist: Ecofeminism and the Quest for Democracy*, University of Minnesota Press, Minneapolis, MN.

Sandroff, R. (1994) 'Beware of Phallic Drift', *On the Issues: The Progressive Women's Quarterly*, vol. 3, no. 2, p. 2.

Sargisson, L. (2010) 'What's Wrong with Ecofeminism?', *Environmental Politics*, vol. 10, no. 1, pp. 52–64.

Sattel, J. (1989) 'The Inexpressive Male: Tragedy or Sexual Politics?', in M. Kimmel and M. Messner (eds), *Men's Lives*, Macmillan, New York.

Sawyer, M. (2003) 'The Life and Times of Women's Policy Machinery in Australia', in S. Rai (ed.), *Mainstreaming Gender, Democratizing the State: Institutional Mechanisms for the Advancement of Women*, Manchester University Press, Manchester.

Scanlon, J. (1998) 'The Perspective of Gender: A Missing Element in Disaster Response', in E. Enarson and B. Morrow (eds), *The Gendered Terrain of Disasters: Through Women's Eyes*, Praeger, London.

Scheff, T. (2003) 'Male Emotions/Relationships and Violence: A Case Study', *Human Relations*, vol. 56, no. 6, pp. 727–749.

Scheff, T. (2006) 'Aggression, Hypermasculine Emotions and Relations: The Silence/Violence Pattern', *Journal of Sociology*, vol. 15, no. 1, pp. 24–39.

Scheffran, J., Ide, T. and Schilling, J. (2014) 'Violent Climate or Climate of Violence? Concepts and Relations with Focus on Kenya and Sudan', *The International Journal of Human Rights*, vol. 18, no. 3, pp. 369–390.

Schippers, M. (2007) 'Recovering the Feminine Other: Masculinity, Femininity and Gender Hegemony', *Theory and Society*, vol. 36, no. 1, pp. 85–102.

Schmah, K. (1998) *Ecofeminist Strategies for Change: A Case Study in Western Australia*, PhD thesis, Curtin University, Perth.

Schofield, T. (2007) 'Health Inequity and Its Social Determinants: A Sociological Commentary', *Health Sociology Review*, vol. 16, no. 2, pp. 105–114.

Schofield, T. (2015) *A Sociological Approach to Health Determinants*, Cambridge University Press, Cambridge.

Scholz, S. (1998) 'Peacemaking in Domestic Violence: From an Ethics of Care to an Ethics of Advocacy', *Journal of Social Philosophy*, vol. 29, no. 2, pp. 46–58.

Schott, R. (2008) 'Just War and the Problem of Evil', *Hypatia*, vol. 23, pp. 122–140.

Schrock, D. and Schwalbe, M. (2009) 'Men, Masculinity and Manhood Acts', *Annual Review of Sociology*, vol. 35, pp. 277–294.

Schwalbe, M. (1992) 'Male Supremacy and the Narrowing of the Moral Self', *Berkeley Journey of Sociology*, vol. 37, pp. 29–54.

Schwalbe, M. (2009) 'Denormalizing the Signs of Impending Disaster', *Common Dreams*, 18 April.

Schwalbe, M. (2014) *Manhood Acts: Gender and the Practices of Domination*, Paradigm, Boulder, CO.

Schwartz, M. and DeKeseredy, W. (1998) *Measuring the Extent of Woman Abuse in Intimate Relationships: A Critique of the Conflict Tactics Scale*, Applied Research Forum, National Electronic Network on Violence against Women, pp. 1–6.

Seager, J. (1993) *Earth Follies: Coming to Feminist Terms with the Global Environmental Crisis*, Routledge, New York.

Sedgwick, E. (1985) *Between Men: Literature and Male Homosocial Desire*, Columbia University Press, New York.

Segal, L. (1987) *Is the Future Female? Troubled Thoughts on Contemporary Feminism*, Virago, London.

Seidler, V. (2007) 'Masculinities, Bodies and Emotional Life', *Men and Masculinities*, vol. 10, no. 1, pp. 9–21.

Sela-Shayovitz, R. (2010) 'External and Internal Terror: The Effects of Terrorist Acts and Economic Changes on Intimate Femicide Rates in Israel', *Feminist Criminology*, vol. 5, no. 2, pp. 135–155.

Sety, M. (2012) 'Domestic Violence and Natural Disasters', *Australian Domestic and Family Violence Clearinghouse*, Thematic Review 3, February.

Seymour, K. (2010) *(Re)Gendering Violence: Men, Masculinities and Violence*, ANZCCC: The Australian and New Zealand Critical Criminology Conference, 2010, Institute of Critical Criminology, Sydney Law School, University of Sydney.

Seymour, K. (2012) *The Violence of Gender: Australian Policy Responses to Violence*, PhD thesis, Deakin University, Geelong.

Seymour, K. (2018a) '"Cowards" and "Scumbags": Tough Talk and Men's Violence', *International Journal for Crime, Justice and Social Democracy*, vol. 7, no. 4, pp. 132–147.

Seymour, K. (2018b) '"Stand Up, Speak Out and Act": A Critical Reading of Australia's White Ribbon Campaign', *Australian and New Zealand Journal of Criminology*, vol. 51, no. 2, pp. 293–310.

Shepherd, L. (2008) *Gender, Violence and Security: Discourse as Practice*, Zed Books, London.

Shiva, V. (2016) *Staying Alive: Women, Ecology and Development*, North Atlantic Books, Berkeley, CA.

Singh, A., Verma, R. and Barker, G. (2018) *Measuring Gender Attitudes: Using Gender-Equitable Men Scale (GEMS) in Various Socio-Cultural Settings*, Promundo, Washington, DC.

Sjoberg, L. (2006) 'Gendered Realities of the Immunity Principle: Why Gender Analysis Needs Feminism', *International Studies Quarterly*, vol. 50, no. 4, pp. 889–910.

Sjoberg, L. (2009) 'Feminist Interrogations of Terrorism/Terrorism Studies', *International Relations*, vol. 23, no. 1, pp. 69–74.

Sjoberg, L. and Gentry, C. (2008) 'Reduced to Bad Sex: Narratives of Violent Women from the Bible to the War on Terror', *International Relations*, vol. 22, no. 1, pp. 5–23.

Sjoberg, L., Cooke, G. and Neal, S. (2011) 'Introduction: Women, Gender and Terrorism', in L. Sjoberg and C. Gentry (eds), *Women, Gender and Terrorism*, University of Georgia Press, Athens, GA.

Slim, H. (2015) *Humanitarian Ethics: A Guide to Morality of Aid in War and Disaster*, Hurst & Company, London.

Sliwka, G. and Macdonald, J. (2005) *Pathways to Couple Violence: An Ecological Approach*, Men's Health Information and Resource Centre, University of Western Sydney.

Smith, A. (2013) 'Unsettling the Privilege of Self-Reflexivity', in F. Twine and B. Gardner (eds), *Geographies of Privilege*, Routledge, New York.

Smith, J. (2017) 'The Seeds of Terrorism Are Often Sown in the Home – with Domestic Violence', *The Guardian*, 11 July.

Smith, M. (1990) 'Patriarchal Ideology and Wife Beatings: A Test of a Feminist Hypothesis', *Violence and Victims*, vol. 5, no. 4, pp. 257–263.

Smith, R., Parrott, D., Swartout, K. and Tharpe, A. (2015) 'Deconstructing Hegemonic Masculinity: The Roles of Antifemininity, Subordination to Women and Sexual Dominance to Men's Perpetration of Sexual Aggression', *Psychology of Men and Masculinity*, vol. 16, no. 2, pp. 160–169.

Snider, L. (1998) 'Towards Safer Societies: Punishment, Masculinities and Violence against Women', *British Journal of Criminology*, vol. 38, no. 1, pp. 1–39.

Sokoloff, N. and Dupont, I. (2005) 'Domestic Violence at the Intersections of Race, Class and Gender', *Violence against Women*, vol. 11, no. 1, pp. 38–64.

Solnit, R. (2014) 'Call Climate Change What It Is: Violence', *The Guardian*, 7 April.

Soron, D. (2007) 'Cruel Weather: Natural Disasters and Structural Violence', *Transformations*, no. 14, www.transformationsjournal.org/wp-content/uploads/2017/01/Soron_Transformations14.pdf.

South, N. and White, R. (2013) 'The Antecedents and Emergence of a "Green" Criminology', in R. Agnew (ed.), *Annual Meeting Presidential Papers, American Society of Criminology*, http://repository.essex.ac.uk/11798/.

Squires, J. (2007) *The New Politics of Gender Equality*, Palgrave, Basingstoke.

Stanger, N. (2011) 'Moving "Eco" Back into Social-Ecological Models: A Proposal to Reorient Ecological Literacy into Human Development Models and School Systems', *Human Ecology Forum*, vol. 18, no. 2, pp. 167–173.

Stanko, E. and Hobdell, K. (1993) 'Asssault on Men: Masculinity and Male Victimisation', *British Journal of Criminology*, vol. 33, no. 3, pp. 400–415.

Stark, E. (2006) 'Commentary on Johnson's "Conflict and Control: Gender Symmetry and Asymmetry in Domestic Violence"', *Violence against Women*, vol. 12, no. 11, pp. 1019–1025.

Stark, E. (2007) *Coercive Control: How Men Entrap Women in Personal Life*, Oxford University Press, New York.

Stark, E. (2010) 'Do Violent Acts Equal Abuse? Resolving the Gender Parity/Asymmetry Dilemma', *Sex Roles*, vol. 62, pp. 201–211.

Steegh, N. (2005) 'Differentiating Types of Domestic Violence: Implications for Child Custody', *Faculty Scholarship Paper 217*, http://open.mitchell.edu/facsch/217.

Stepney, P. (2014) 'Prevention in Social Work: The Final Frontier?', *Critical and Radical Social Work*, vol. 2, no. 3, pp. 305–320.

Stewart, A., Lewis, K., Neophytou, K. and Bolton, T. (2010) *Does Combining Health Promotion and Feminist Frameworks Equal Better Health Outcomes for Women?*, paper presented at the 6th Australian Women's Health Conference, Melbourne.

Stibbe, A. (2006) 'Masculinity, Health and Ecological Destruction', *Language and Ecology Online Journal*, www.ecolonline.net/journal.html.

Stojanovic, T., McNae, H., Tett, P., Potts, T., Reis, J., Smith, H. and Dillingham, I. (2016) 'The "Social" Aspect of Social-Ecological Systems: A Critique of Analytical Frameworks and Findings from a Multisite Study of Coastal Sustainability', *Ecology and Society*, vol. 21, no. 3, pp. 1–16.

Stoltenberg, J. (1993) *The End of Manhood*, Dutton, New York.

Stoparic, B. (2006) 'Women Push for Seats at Climate Policy Table', *Women's eNews*, 6 July, http://womensenews.org/story/environment/060706/women-push-seats-at-climate-policy-table.

Storer, H., Casey, E., Carlson, J., Edleson, J. and Tolman, R. (2016) 'Primary Prevention Is? A Global Perspective on How Organizations Engaging Men in Preventing Gender-Based Violence Conceptualize and Operationalize Their Work', *Violence against Women*, vol. 22, no. 2, pp. 249–268.

Straus, M. (1990) 'Measuring Intrafamily Conflict and Violence: The Conflict (CT) Scales', in M. Straus and R. Gelles (eds), *Physical Violence in American Families*, Transaction Publishers, New Brunswick, NJ.

Subasic, E., Reynolds, K. and Turner, J. (2008) 'The Political Solidarity Model of Social Change: Dynamics of Self-Categorisation in Intergroup Power Relations', *PSPR*, vol. 12, no. 4, pp. 330–352.

Sultana, A. (2010/2011) 'Patriarchy and Women's Subordination: A Theoretical Analysis', *Arts Faculty Journal*, vol. 4, pp. 1–18.

Sundaram, V. (2013) 'Violence as Understandable, Deserveable or Unacceptable? Listening for Gender in Teenagers' Talk about Violence', *Gender and Education*, vol. 25, no. 7, pp. 889–906.

Tabachnick, J. (2009) *Engaging Bystanders in Sexual Violence Prevention*, National Sexual Violence Resource Centre, Enola, PA.

Tacey, D. (1997) *Remaking Men: Jung, Spirituality and Social Change*, Routledge, London.

Taft, A., Hegarty, K. and Flood, M. (2002) 'Are Men and Women Equally Violent to Intimate Partners?', *Australian and New Zealand Journal of Public Health*, vol. 25, no. 6, pp. 498–500.

Tallberg, T. (2003) *Networks, Organisations and Men: Concepts and Interrelations*, Swedish School of Economics and Business Administration Working Papers, Helsinki.

Tervooren, K. (2016) *Representing Women and Terrorist Violence. Faculty of Humanities*, master's thesis, Utrecht University.

Thebaud, S. (2010) 'Masculinity, Bargaining and Breadwinning: Understanding Men's Housework in the Cultural Context of Work', *Gender and Society*, vol. 24, no. 3, pp. 330–354.

Theisen, M. (2017) 'Climate Change and Violence: Insights from Political Science', *Current Climate Change Report*, vol. 4, pp. 210–221.

Thompson, C. and MacGregor, S. (2017) 'The Death of Nature: Foundations of Ecological Feminist Thought', in S. MacGregor (ed.), *Routledge Handbook of Gender and Environment*, Routledge, New York.

Thurston, W. and Vissandjee, B. (2014) 'An Ecological Model for Understanding Culture as a Determinant of Women's Health', *Critical Public Health*, vol. 15, no. 3, pp. 229–242.

Tilley, C. (1990) 'M. Foucault: Towards an Archaeology of Archaeology', in C. Tilley (ed.), *Reading Material Culture: Structuralism, Hermeneutics, Post Structuralism*, Blackwell, Oxford.

Titterington, V. (2006) 'A Retrospective Investigation of Gender Inequality and Female Homicide Victimization', *Sociological Spectrum*, vol. 26, pp. 205–236.

Tolman, R. and Edelson, J. (1995) 'Interventions for Men Who Batter: A Review of Research', in S. Smith and M. Strauss (eds), *Understanding Partner Violence: Prevalence, Causes, Consequences and Solutions*, National Council on Family Relations, Minneapolis, MN.

Tomsen, S. (2005) '"Boozers and Bouncers": Masculine Conflict, Disengagement and the Contemporary Governance of Drinking-Related Violence and Disorder', *The Australasian and New Zealand Journal of Criminology*, vol. 38, no. 3, pp. 283–297.

Tomsen, S. (2008) 'Masculinities, Crime and Criminalisation', in T. Anthony and C. Cunneer (eds), *The Critical Criminology Companion*, Hawkins, Sydney.

Tomsen, S. (2013) 'Homophobic Violence and Masculinities in Australia', in S. Magaraggia and D. Cherubini (eds), *Men against Women: The Roots of Male Violence*, UTET University, Italy.

Tomsen, S. and Crofts, T. (2012) 'Social and Cultural Meanings of Legal Responses to Homicide among Men: Masculine Honour, Sexual Advances and Accidents', *Australian and New Zealand Journal of Criminology*, vol. 45, no. 3, pp. 423–437.

Tong, R. (1997) 'Feminist Perspectives on Empathy as an Epistemic Skill and Caring as a Moral Virtue', *Journal of Medical Humanities*, vol. 18, no. 3, pp. 153–167.

Tonsing, J. and Tonsing, K. (2017) 'Understanding the Role of Patriarchal Ideology in Intimate Partner Violence among South Asian Women in Hong Kong', *International Social Work*, doi: 10.11770020872817712566.

Tonso, K. (2009) 'Violent Masculinities as Tropes for School Shooters', *American Behavioral Scientist*, vol. 52, no. 9, pp. 1266–1285.

Towns, A. and Terry, G. (2014) '"You're in That Realm of Unpredictability": Mateship, Loyalty and Men Challenging Men Who Use Domestic Violence against Women', *Violence against Women*, vol. 20, no. 8, pp. 1012–1036.

Tracy, S. (2007) 'Patriarchy and Domestic Violence: Challenging Common Misconceptions', *JETS*, September, pp. 573–594.

Treadwell, J. and Garland, J. (2011) 'Masculinity, Marginalization and Violence: A Case Study of the English Defence League', *British Journal of Criminology*, vol. 51, pp. 621–634.

Trepagnier, B. (2006) *Silent Racism: How Well-Meaning White People Perpetuate the Racist Divide*, Paradigm, Boulder, CO.

Tronto, J. (2013) *Caring Democracy: Markets, Equality and Justice*, New York University Press, New York.

True, J. (2010) *Normalising Gender in Global Governance*, paper presented at the Gender in International Governance Conference, Geneva, Switzerland, October.

True, J. (2012) *The Political Economy of Violence against Women*, Oxford University Press, Oxford.

Twine, R. (1997) *Masculinity, Nature, Ecofeminism*, www.ecofem.org/journal.

Twine, R. (2001) 'Ma(r)king Essence: Ecofeminism and Embodiment', *Ethics and Environment*, vol. 6, no. 2, pp. 31–58.

Tyler, M., Fairbrother, P., Chaplin, S., Mees, B., Phillips, R. and Toh, K. (2012) *Gender Matters: Applying a Gendered Analysis to Bushfire Research in Australia*, Working Papers in Sustainable Organisations and Work, no. 3, March, Centre for Sustainable and Organisations and Work, RMIT University, Melbourne.

Van Den Berg, W. (2015) 'Violence Is Less Likely in Homes Where Fathers Share Chores Equally', *The Conversation*, 17 June.

Vellacott, J. (1993) 'A Place for Pracifism and Transnationalism in Feminist Theory: The Early Work of the Women's International League for Peace and Freedom', *Women's History Review*, vol. 2, no. 1, pp. 23–56.

Vertuno, J. (2017) 'New Baylor Lawsuit Alleges Football Team Used Gang Rape as "Bonding" Experience', *Chicago Tribune*, 17 May.

VicHealth (2007) *Preventing Violence before It Occurs: A Framework and Background Paper to Guide the Primary Prevention of Violence against Women*, Victorian Government, Carlton, Victoria.

Vieratis, L. and Williams, M. (2002) 'Assessing the Impact of Gender Inequality on Female Homicide Victimization across US Cities: A Racially Disaggregated Analysis', *Violence against Women*, vol. 8, no. 1, pp. 35–63.

Virkki, T. (2017) 'At the Interface of National and Transnational: The Development of Finnish Policies against Domestic Violence in Terms of Gender Equality', *Social Sciences*, vol. 6, no. 1, pp. 1–18.

Vojdik, V. (2002) 'Gender Outlaw: Challenging Masculinity in Traditionally Male Institutions', *Berkeley Journal of Gender, Law and Justice*, vol. 17, no. 1, pp. 68–121.

Vojdik, V. (2014) 'Sexual Violence against Men and Women in War: A Masculinities Approach', *Nevada Law Journal*, vol. 14, pp. 923–952.

Wadham, B. (2013) 'Brotherhood: Homosociality, Totality and Military Subjectivity', *Australian Feminist Studies*, vol. 28, no. 76, pp. 212–235.

Wadham, B. (2016) 'The Dark Side of Defence: Masculinities and Violence in the Military', in M. McGarry and S. Walklage (eds), *The Palgrave Handbook of Criminology and War*, Palgrave, London.

Walby, S. (1990) *Theorising Patriarchy*, Blackwell, Oxford.

Walby, S. (2004) 'The European Union and Gender Equality: Emergent Varieties of Gender Regime', *Social Politics*, vol. 11, no. 1, pp. 4–29.

Walby, S. (2005) 'Gender Mainstreaming: Productive Tensions in Theory and Practice', *Social Politics*, vol. 12, no. 3, pp. 321–343.

Walby, S. (2011) *The Future of Feminism*, Polity, Cambridge.

Walby, S. (2012) 'Violence and Society: Introduction to an Emerging Field of Sociology', *Current Sociology*, vol. 61, no. 2, pp. 95–111.

Walby, S. and Towers, J. (2018) 'Untangling the Concept of Coercive Control: Theorising Domestic Violent Crime', *Criminology and Criminal Justice*, vol. 18, no. 1, pp. 7–28.

Walker, G. (1990) *Family Violence and the Women's Movement: The Conceptual Politics of Struggle*, University of Toronto Press, Toronto.

Wall, L. (2014) 'Gender Equality and Violence against Women: What's the Connection?', *ACSSA Research Summary*, no. 7, June.

Ward, J. (2016) 'It's Not about the Gender Binary, It's about the Gender Hierarchy: A Reply to "Letting Go of the Gender Binary"', *International Review of the Red Cross*, vol. 98, no. 1, pp. 275–298.

Warters, W. (1992) 'The Social Construction of Domestic Violence and the Implications for Treatment of Men Who Batter', *Men's Studies Review*, vol. 8, no. 2, pp. 7–16.

Watson, C. (2001) 'A Critical Response to the Keys Young Report: Ending Domestic Violence? Programs for Perpetrators', *Australian and New Zealand Journal of Family Therapy*, vol. 22, no. 2, pp. 90–95.

Watson, S. (1990) 'The State of Play: An Introduction', in S. Watson (ed.), *Playing the State: Australian Feminist Interventions*, Allen & Unwin, Sydney.

Webb, J. (1998) *Junk Male: Reflections on Australian Masculinity*, HarperCollins, Sydney.

Webb, S. (2006) *Social Work in a Risk Society*, Palgrave Macmillan, Basingstoke.

Websdale, N. (2010) *Familicidal Hearts: The Emotional Styles of 2011 Killers*, Oxford University Press, New York.

Weissman, D. (2007) 'The Personal Is Political and Economic: Rethinking Domestic Violence', *BYU Law Review*, vol. 2007, no. 2, pp. 387–450.

Welland, J. (2015) 'Liberal Warriors and the Violent Colonial Logics of "Partnering and Advising"', *International Feminist Journal of Politics*, vol. 17, no. 2, pp. 289–307.

Welsh, M. (1997) 'Violence against Women by Professional Footballers', *Journal of Sport and Social Issues*, vol. 21, no. 4, pp. 392–411.

Westendorf, J. and Searle, L. (2017) 'Sexual Exploitation and Abuse in Peace Operations: Trends, Policy Responses and Future Directions', *International Affairs*, vol. 93, no. 2, pp. 365–387.

Whaley, R. (2001) 'The Paradoxical Relationship between Gender Inequality and Rape: Toward a Refined Theory', *Gender and Society*, vol. 15, no. 4, pp. 531–555.

Whaley, R. and Messner, S. (2002) 'Gender Equality and Gender Homicides', *Homicide Studies*, vol. 6, no. 3, pp. 188–210.

Whaley, R., Messner, S. and Veysey, B. (2013) 'The Relationship between Gender Equality and Rates of Inter- and Intra-Sexual Lethal Violence: An Exploration of Functional Form', *Justice Quarterly*, vol. 30, no. 4, pp. 732–754.

White, J. and Kowalski, R. (1994) 'Deconstructing the Myth of the Nonaggressive Woman: A Feminist Analysis', *Psychology of Women Quarterly*, vol. 18, pp. 487–508.

White, R. (2005) 'Environmental Crime in Global Context: Exploring the Empirical and Global Complexities', *Current Issues in Criminal Justice*, vol. 16, no. 3, pp. 271–285.

White, R. (2016) 'The Four Ways of Eco-Global Criminology', *International Journal for Crime, Justice and Social Democracy*, vol. 6, no. 1, pp. 8–22.

White, R. and Kramer, R. (2015) 'Critical Criminology and the Struggle against Climate Change Ecocide', *Critical Criminology*, vol. 23, pp. 383–399.

Whitehead, A. (2005) 'Man to Man Violence: How Masculinity May Work as a Dynamic Risk Factor', *The Howard Journal*, vol. 44, no. 4, pp. 411–422.

Whitehead, S. (2002) *Men and Masculinities*, Polity, Cambridge.

Whitehead, S. (2007) 'Patriarchal Dividend', in M. Flood, J. Gardiner, B. Pease and K. Pringle (eds), *International Encyclopedia of Men and Masculinities*, Routledge, London.

Whitworth, S. (2004) *Men, Militarism and UN Peacekeeping: A Gendered Analysis*, Reinner, Boulder, CO.

Wiley, S., Srinivasan, R., Finke, E., Firnhaber, J. and Shilinsky, A. (2012) 'Positive Portrayals of Feminist Men Increase Men's Solidarity with Feminists and Collective Action Intentions', *Psychology of Women Quarterly*, vol. 37, no. 1, pp. 61–71.

Williamson, E. (2010) 'Living in the World of the Domestic Violence Perpetrator: Negotiating the Unreality of Coercive Control', *Violence against Women*, vol. 16, no. 12, pp. 1412–1423.

Witz, A. (1992) *Professions and Patriarchy*, Routledge, London.

Wojnicka, K. (2015) 'Men, Masculinities and Physical Violence in Contemporary Europe', *Studia Humanistyczne AGH Tom*, vol. 14, no. 2, http://dx/doi.org/10.7954/human.2015.14.2.15.

Wonders, N. and Danner, M. (2015) 'Gendering Climate Change: A Feminist Criminological Perspective', *Critical Criminology*, vol. 23, pp. 401–416.

Woody, J. (2006) 'Prevention: Making a Shadow Component a Real Goal in Social Work', *Advances in Social Work*, vol. 7, no. 2, pp. 44–61.

World Health Organization (2009) *Promoting Gender Equality to Prevent Violence against Women: Series of Briefings on Violence Prevention – The Evidence*. World Health Organization, Geneva.

Wright, H. (2014) *Masculinities, Conflict and Peacebuilding: Perspectives on Men through a Gendered Lens*, London, Saferworld: Preventing Violent Conflict, Building Safe Lives.

Wright, H. (2015) 'Ending Sexual Violence and the War System – or Militarizing Feminism', *International Feminist Journal of Politics*, vol. 17, no. 3, pp. 503–507.

Yancy, G. (ed.) (2015a) *White Self-Criticality beyond Anti-Racism: How Does It Feel to Be a White Problem?*, Lexington Books, Lanham, MD.

Yancy, G. (2015b) 'Introduction: Un-Sutured', in G. Yancy (ed.), *White Self-Criticality beyond Anti-Racism: How Does It Feel to Be a White Problem?*, Lexington Books, Lanham, MD.

Yodanis, C. (2004) 'Gender Inequality, Violence against Women and Fear: A Cross-National Test of the Feminist Theory of Violence against Women', *Journal of Interpersonal Violence*, vol. 19, no. 6, pp. 655–675.

York, M. (2011) *Gender Attitudes and Violence against Women*, LFB Publishing, El Paso, TX.

Young, I. (2003a) 'The Logic of Masculinist Protection: Reflections on the Current Security State', *Signs*, vol. 29, no. 1, pp. 1–25.

Young, I. (2003b) 'Feminist Reactions to the Contemporary Security Regime', *Hypatia*, vol. 18, no. 1, pp. 223–231.

Young, I. (2011) *Responsibility for Justice*, Oxford University Press, New York.

Zimmerer, J. (2014) 'Climate Change, Environmental Violence and Genocide', *The International Journal of Human Rights*, vol. 18, no. 3, pp. 265–280.

Zoe, R. (2013) 'Shifting Language and Meanings between Social Science and the Law: Defining Family Violence', *UNSW Law Journal*, vol. 36, no. 2, pp. 1–16.

INDEX